The French Revolution
An Economic Interpretation

FLORIN AFTALION

Translated by Martin Thom

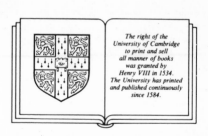

The right of the
University of Cambridge
to print and sell
all manner of books
was granted by
Henry VIII in 1534.
The University has printed
and published continuously
since 1584.

CAMBRIDGE UNIVERSITY PRESS

CAMBRIDGE

NEW YORK   PORT CHESTER   MELBOURNE   SYDNEY

EDITIONS DE LA MAISON DES SCIENCES DE L'HOMME

PARIS

Published by the Press Syndicate of the University of Cambridge
The Pitt Building, Trumpington Street, Cambridge CB2 1RP
32 West 20th Street, New York, NY 10011, USA
10 Stamford Road, Oakleigh, Melbourne 3166, Australia
and Editions de la Maison des Sciences de l'Homme
54 Boulevard Raspail, 75270 Paris Cedex 06

First published 1990

Printed in Great Britain at the University Press, Cambridge

British Library cataloguing in publication data
Aftalion, Florin
The French Revolution: an economic interpretation.
1. French Revolution, 1789–1799. Economic aspects
I. Title
944.04′1
ISBN 0 521 36241 5   hard covers
ISBN 0 521 36810 3   paperback

Library of Congress cataloguing in publication data
Aftalion, Florin.
[Economie de la Révolution française. English]
The French Revolution, an economic interpretation/Florin
Aftalion: translated by Martin Thom.
p.   cm.
Translation of L'économie de la Révolution française.
ISBN 0–521–36241–5. – ISBN 0–521–36810–3 (pbk.)
1. France – Economic conditions – 18th century. 2. France–History–
Revolution, 1789–1799. I. Title
HC275.A6613   1989
330.944′04–dc20   89–36121 CIP

ISBN 0 521 36241 5   hard covers
ISBN 0 521 36810 3   paperback
ISBN 2 7351 0304 8   hard covers (France only)
ISBN 2 7351 0305 6   paperback (France only)

To Sérine Aftalion

Contents

Contents

Figures

Chronology

1715 Death of Louis XIV.

1716 Creation of John Law's bank.

1720 Collapse of John Law's system.

1726 Fleury's ministry; stabilisation of the metallic content of the currency.

1738 Treaty of Vienna.

1748 Treaty of Aix-la-Chapelle and end of the War of the Austrian Succession.

1749 Creation of the *vingtième* by Machault.

1756 War with England.

1763 Peace with Paris brings the Seven Years' War to an end; loss of France's colonial empire.

1770 The abbé Terray appointed *Contrôleur des finances*.

1771 Maupeou exiles the Parlement of Paris.

1775 Death of Louis XV; Turgot appointed *Contrôleur des finances*.

1776 Turgot disgraced.

1777 Necker becomes *Directeur général des finances*.

1778 Alliance between France and the United States of America.

1781 Resignation of Necker.

1783 The Treaty of Versailles puts an end to the American War of Independence; Calonne becomes *Contrôleur général*.

1786 Trade Treaty with England.

1787 First Assembly of Notables (22 February); fall of Calonne and beginning of Brienne ministry (8 April); dissolution of the Notables (12 May).

1788 Suspension of the Parlements by Lamoignon (8 May); convocation of the Estates-General (8 August); Brienne disgraced, Necker returns (25 August); return of the Parlements (23 September); Second Assembly of the Notables (6 November).

1789

2 May   The deputies of the Estates-General are presented to the King.

5 May   Opening session of the Estates-General; the King's speech.

May–June   Conflict of the orders.

17 June   The Third Estate constitutes itself as the National Assembly.

20 June   The Tennis Court Oath.

23 June   Royal session; Louis XVI's programme is made public; the Third Estate refuses to disperse.

11 July   Necker is dismissed.

12–14 July   Riots in Paris; storming of the Bastille; founding of the Commune, with Bailly as Mayor, and of the National Guard, under Lafayette's command.

July   Uprisings in the countryside; uprisings in the towns; the Municipal Revolution.

4 August   Abolition of privileges.

26 August   Proclamation of the Declaration of Rights of Man and of the Citizen.

11 September   After having rejected a second Chamber, the Assembly grants the King a suspensive veto in legislative matters.

6 October   The crowd brings the King back to Paris.

2 November   Church lands are put at the disposal of the nation.

19 December   Creation of the first *assignats* (Treasury bonds).

1790

17 April   The *assignats* are turned into paper currency, enjoying compulsory circulation.

14 May   Decree stipulating how the lots of *biens nationaux* are to be sold, payment for which can be made over twelve years.

21 May   Paris is divided into forty-eight sections.

12 July   The voting of the Civil Constitution of the Clergy.

29 September   Decision to repay the exigible debt with non-interest-bearing *assignats*.

27 November   Constituent Assembly requires oath of loyalty to the Civil Constitution from all French priests.

1791

2 March   Abolition of the guild system.

20 March   The Pope condemns the Civil Constitution of the Clergy.

14 June   The Le Chapelier law prohibits 'workers' coalitions'.

21 June   Arrest of the King at Varennes.

17 July   Troops open fire in the Champ de Mars on a crowd assembled to demand the dethronement of the King.

5 August   The French nation renounces all wars fought for the purposes of conquest.

27 August   Declaration of Pilnitz.

13 September   Vote on the Constitution.

1 October   Meeting of the Legislative Assembly.

16 November   Pétion elected Mayor of Paris.

29 November   Any clergy refusing to swear the oath are declared to be suspects.

9 December   Formation of a Feuillant ministry.

1792

15 March   Formation of a Girondin ministry.

20 April   Declaration of war by the King of Hungary and of Bohemia.

8 June   The Assembly decrees the formation of a *fédérés'* camp beneath the walls of Paris.

11 June   The King uses his veto on the constitution of the camp and decrees aimed at refractory priests.

13 June   Return of the Girondin Ministers.

20 June   Failed uprising, during which the crowd invades the Tuileries.

25 July   The Brunswick Manifesto threatens Paris with destruction.

27 July   Confiscation of property belonging to *émigrés*.

10 August   The Tuileries are seized by the rioters; constitution of the insurrectionary Commune, then of the Provisional Executive Committee.

14 August   Sale of *émigré* properties.

2 September   Surrender of Verdun.

2–5 September   Massacre of prisoners.

20 September   Victory of Valmy; the Convention meets for the first time.

21 September   Abolition of the Monarchy.

25 September   Proclamation of the Republic, One and Indivisible.

19 November   The Convention promises 'fraternity and assistance' to peoples wishing to recover their liberty.

6 November   Victory of Jemappes.

27 November   Annexation of Savoy.

2 December   Renewal of the Commune of Paris; Pache becomes Mayor.

8 December   Suppression of price controls on the grain trade.

11 December   Louis XVI's trial begins.

1793

16 January   The Convention votes on the guilt of the King.

21 January   Death of the King.

1 February   Declaration of war on England and on Holland.

24 February   *Levée* of 300,000 men.

7 March   Declaration of war on Spain.

10 March   Outbreak of Vendée rebellion; establishment of the Revolutionary Tribunal; the Republic inherits the property of those who are condemned to death.

21 March   Creation of watch committees *(comités de surveillance)*.

1 April   Dumouriez goes over to the enemy.

6 April   Committee of Public Safety set up.

11 April   *Assignats* made sole legal tender.

4 May   First Law of the Maximum fixes price of grain.

31 May and 2 June   Insurrectionary uprisings culminating in the elimination of the Girondin deputies.

10 June   Decree on the division of communal lands.

24 June   Constitution of Year 1 voted by the Convention; a new Declaration of the Rights of Man.

13 July   Assassination of Marat.

17 July   All feudal dues abolished without compensation.

26 July   Decree instituting death penalty against food hoarders.

27 July   Robespierre joins the Committee of Public Safety.

23 August   *Levée en masse* decreed.

24 August   *Grand Livre de la dette publique* (national debt register) created.

29 August   Royalists hand Toulon over to the English.

4–5 September   Uprisings in the course of which the Convention is besieged; the Terror 'the order of the day'.

11 September   Establishment of the National Maximum for grain and flour.

17 September   Law on Suspects.

29 September   Establishment of the General Maximum for prices and wages.

5 October   Revolutionary calendar adopted.

9 October   Lyons capitulates and the revolt is suppressed.

10 October   Government declared revolutionary for the duration of hostilities.

22 October   Establishment of the Food Commission.

31 October   Girondins executed.

23 November   Introduction of the 'bread of equality'.

4 December   Constitution of the revolutionary government.

19 December   Recapture of Toulon.

23 December   *Vendéens* defeated at Savenay.

1794

22 February   Posting of General Maximum scales 'at the place of production'.

26 February   Seizure of suspects' property ordered (first Ventôse decrees).

3 March   'Needy patriots' are compensated by means of suspects' property (second Ventôse decrees).

14 March   The Hébertists arrested; executed 24 March.

29 March   Second law on hoarding.

30 March   Arrest of the Dantonists; executed 5 April.

11 May   *Grand Livre de la bienfaisance nationale* (national welfare register) created.

10 June   Revolutionary Tribunal reorganised; beginning of the Great Terror; all safeguards of justice are abolished.

26 June   Victory of Fleurus over the Austrians.

8 July   Entry of the French into Brussels.

23 July   Publication of a new Maximum on wages.

27 July   Fall of Robespierre.

1 August   Law of Prairial revoked.

24 August   Reorganisation of the Revolutionary Government.

18 September   The state stops paying priests' salaries.

19 November   Closure of the Jacobin Club.

8 December   Return of the Girondin deputies to the Convention.

24 December   Abolition of the Maximum.

1795

21 February   Religious freedom, and separation of Church and State.

8 March   Recall of the proscribed Girondin deputies.

1 April   Failed uprising against the Convention (12 Germinal).

7 April   Adoption of the decimal system.

20–23 May   The last insurrectionary uprisings (1–4 Prairial).

31 May   Suppression of the Revolutionary Tribunal.

21 June   Sliding scale for the depreciation of the *assignat*.

21 July   Victory of Hoche at Quiberon, against the *émigrés*.

23 September   Proclamation of the Constitution of Year III.

1 October   Annexation of Belgium.

5 October   Royalist uprising put down by Barras and Bonaparte (13 Vendémiaire).

31 October   Election of the Directory.

10 December   A forced loan voted.

1796

18 February   Destruction of *la planche aux assignats* (plate for the printing of paper money).

2 March   Bonaparte appointed General in chief of the Army of Italy.

18 March   *Mandats territoriaux* created.

10 May   Arrest of Babeuf and his fellow-conspirators; victory of Lodi.

15 May   Bonaparte enters Milan.

17 July   Suppression of the forced currency status of the *mandats territoriaux*.

1797

4 February   Return to metallic currency; an end to both *assignats* and *mandats territoriaux*.

March–April   Elections of Year V; victory of the Right.

4 September   Coup d'état of Fructidor; Germinal elections quashed.

30 September   Bankruptcy of the two-thirds.

18 October   Treaty of Campoformio.

12 November   Reorganisation of the administration of direct contributions.

1798

April   Jacobin gains in the elections.

11 May   Coup d'état; election results quashed.

19 May   Departure of the Egyptian Expedition.

24 November   Tax on doors and windows created.

1799

28 June   Forced loan from the rich.
16 October   Bonaparte arrives in Paris.
10 November   Coup d'état of 18 Brumaire.

Acknowledgements

This work owes a great deal to a number of friends, who have kindly taken an interest in it. Needless to say, the customary formula still applies, and they are responsible neither for any errors that I may have made nor for my interpretations, which they do not necessarily share.

I wish, first of all, to express my gratitude to Georges Liebert. It was he who encouraged me to write this book and who gave it a place in the 'Pluriel' series, which he edits; his generous and patient advice and his suggestions as to new directions for research have done much for my thinking on the topics touched upon in this book. I wish also to extend my warmest thanks to Geoffrey Ellis, Philippe Nemo and Patrice Poncet, a historian, a philosopher and an economist respectively, who were kind enough to subject those parts of my text which were within their various fields to critical scrutiny. René Dzagoyan, Jean-François Fayard, Claude Fischler, Daniel Grojnowski, René de Laportalière and Leonardo Liggio assisted me in various ways and I am most grateful to them. I also owe thanks to Jean Dérens and to Charles King. The former assisted me greatly in my bibliographic work at the Bibliothèque Historique de la Ville de Paris, where he is head curator; the latter arranged for the Liberty Fund, of which he is one of the directors, to organise a conference on 'The Political Economy of the French Revolution', at which I had the opportunity to compare my own perspectives with those of my colleagues, both from France and abroad.

Introduction

A few years ago, when I was teaching at New York University, I acquired the habit of browsing in a modest bookshop which has since moved but was then located a little to one side of Greenwich Village, where I was then living. 'Laissez Faire Books', as its name would lead one to expect, was wholly devoted to the sale of liberal books and journals. Its shelves contained all the classics of the genre, from Adam Smith to Friedrich von Hayek and Milton Friedman, but also science fiction authors with a libertarian outlook, such as Heinlein, and anti-psychiatrists such as Thomas Szasz, together with any number of anarcho-capitalist texts published in the obscurer corners of the United States. One day I happened to notice a reprint of a short pamphlet entitled *Fiat Money Inflation in France*.[1] Written around the turn of the last century, this pamphlet was meant to warn American politicians of the period of the dangers involved in the issue of paper money, which a number of them were proposing. The *assignats* episode of the French Revolution served as an illustration of this point. The author of the pamphlet also gave an account of the debates over the creation of the *assignats* and showed both the economic consequences (inflation and famine) and the political consequences (outbidding and the elimination of the main protagonists).

A reading of this essay convinced me that economic theory can provide a perfectly satisfactory explanation as to why the French Revolution, which was undertaken in order to put an end to 'tyranny' and to establish a just society, degenerated into looting, Terror and dictatorship. I therefore resolved to look deeper into economic interpretations of the French Revolution, but was surprised to find that the classic works had barely taken it into account at all. The depreciation of the *assignats*, the economic crisis and the famine have often been presented, even in the most reputable studies or textbooks, as contingent phenomena or as inevitable, much as harvests are dependent upon the caprices of the climate. At best, the authors of such works have sometimes pointed out that issues of paper money brought about price rises, but they have never attempted a deeper analysis of the more far-reaching causes and consequences of the proliferation of *assignats*. For the last two hundred years, the interactions between the decisions of an economic nature taken by revolutionary politicians[2] and the reactions of the social groups directly, and above all indirectly affected by these decisions would seem to have been grossly neglected.

Michelet, in his *History of the French Revolution*, totally disregards facts of an economic order and does not even mention the existence of *assignats*. Like all the great nineteenth-century historians, he concentrated almost exclusively upon politics, diplomacy and war. The only things that counted, as far as such authors were concerned, were the conflicts between the revolutionary leaders and their cliques – hence the preoccupation with the struggle between Girondins and Montagnards, and the famous debate between Dantonist and Robespierrist historians – or between orders, which, for marxists, have come to be seen as classes. By contrast, Hippolyte Taine, at odds with the idealist tendencies of his own day, assembled an impressive quantity of eye-witness accounts of living conditions in France during the Revolution, and pointed to the role played both by hunger and by the *assignats*. However, Taine's work, being opposed to the dominant ideological tendencies of the Third Republic, was largely ignored by more orthodox thinkers.

It is usual to give Jean Jaurès the credit for having been one of the first to concern himself with the economy of the Revolution. After he had published his *Socialist History of the French Revolution* (1901–4), Jaurès founded the Commission for the Economic History of the Revolution. This Commission published numerous documents concerning the economic policies of the revolutionary period. Among the first works of quantitative history, it is worth mentioning those of Pierre Caron. In 1909, Caron published tables giving the prices, month by month, at which the Treasury sold *assignats* against metal coin. These studies founded a tradition which was essentially concerned with the reconstitution of chronological series of prices (for example, of wheat), or of statistics concerning redistributions (purchase of *biens nationaux*). At the same time, a handful of authors endeavoured to reconstitute the financial history of the period, a special tribute being due to the work of Marcel Marion,[3] whom I will often have occasion to mention below. The new school of French history has also produced innumerable specialist studies which have greatly enriched our knowledge of the economic conditions of the revolutionary period.

While a considerable quantity of raw materials were being accumulated during this period, it was rare to find any attempt at undertaking a serious analysis of them. A great step forward was made when Ernest Labrousse produced evidence for the crisis which raged in 1789, and for its impact upon subsequent events. An economic factor was thereby integrated with the explanatory schemas of the Revolution. Unfortunately, however, whenever historians sought to advance economic interpretations, they made use of false, incomplete or half-understood theories. Ernest Labrousse himself,[4] after having reconstituted the price series of agricultural products in France in the eighteenth century, claimed to be able to deduce from them the evolution of incomes, cycles and crises. He therefore treated prices as 'exogenous' variables which arose (in a sense) on the outside of the economic system and then acted upon it. This way of proceeding is obviously mistaken. The general level of prices depends upon the quantity of money in circulation, whereas relative prices are an expression of the relative scarcity of goods and services. Prices are therefore only a consequence of other phenomena, and it is these latter that should be studied first. For the period with which I am concerned here, it is the superfluity of paper money which, as we shall see, accounts for the rises in the price of commodities and, indirectly, for their scarcity.

Those authors who draw their inspiration from marxism, if they are to remain true to their philosophy, ought to give a privileged place to economic analyses. It has, however, to be acknowledged that they have invariably played down the role played by the *assignats*, for it is clearly a role that accords ill with their vision of history. Albert Soboul, for example, in his *The French Revolution*,[5] devotes only two pages (out of a total of around 600) to *assignats*, to their creation and to their consequences. The latter he simply describes as 'incalculable on the social and economic plane'. Had he gone further, and shown that in fact the crisis and famine associated with the issue of paper money were at the origin of the revolutionary movements, he would have had to contradict his interpretation according to which 'the Revolution is to be explained in the last analysis by a contradiction between the relations of production and the character of the productive forces.'[6]

The economic theory of the French Revolution has made significant progress in the last few years. Numerous researchers have now abandoned the notion that an individual can have two kinds of behaviour, namely, an egocentric one when he is in the sphere of private activities, and one which is altruistic and devoted to the general interest when he places himself at the service of the state. These researchers nowadays reckon that man is a single entity in all the circumstances of his life, that he is equipped with knowledge (albeit limited), endowed with a capacity to learn, from his own mistakes in particular, and seeking always to satisfy his objectives, which are sometimes egoistic (his interests) and sometimes altruistic (his ideals). A new discipline has arisen from the works of these researchers, namely, the school of 'public choice'.[7] This discipline may be characterised in terms of its method, which consists in applying the conception of the 'rational individual', whose theoretical behaviour we have just described, to the study of social structures, such as states or political systems, which seemed until very recently to be beyond the reach of economic analysis.

One of the most striking contributions of the school of public choice has been its model of politicians and of the 'political market'. The objective ascribed to a 'rational' politician operating in a democratic system is that of obtaining the power that elective office confers. In order to be elected or re-elected, such a politician has to convince a majority of the electorate that it is in their interests to vote for him. He has therefore both to make precise promises which will have a decisive effect upon the choice of specific groups within his electorate, and to remain silent as to the costs involved in realising them (which are, generally speaking, diluted because paid for by the population as a whole) or as to possible harmful consequences (which are, generally speaking, delayed, so that they can always be laid at the door of a political adversary).

Of course, political circumstances in the period of the French Revolution were quite different from those of present-day democracy. Men with a taste for power at the highest levels of state had therefore to follow a different strategy from the one indicated above. Legitimacy did not depend upon the polls. If one hoped to become or to remain a minister, at the time of the Constituent or Legislative Assembly, or to control the decisions of the Convention, one would need the direct endorsement of the mob outside. The political system that was in operation could in fact be compared with that of direct democracy, even though it was not actually instituted as such. Those men, or groups, who managed to win recognition for themselves, in the street, in the sections or in the clubs, as representatives of the popular will, could be sure of triumphing in the Assemblies. However, the actual people, composed of *petites gens*, artisans and workers, for the most part illiterate, earned just enough to keep starvation at bay. Those who made up the people, in this sense of the word, could obviously not understand economic mechanisms as such, and therefore tended to react to the appearance of things. The *assignats* met with their favour because they enabled the tax burden to be lightened; price controls (the 'Maximum') were demanded because they seemed to be capable of checking the rising cost of basic commodities.

The system whereby power was seized in the name of the people possessed its own dynamic. Expedients such as the *assignats* or the Maximum, which seemed to solve a short-term problem, always ended up by having harmful consequences. When, however, these latter became apparent, their real cause always eluded the public's understanding, and it was anyway too late to reverse the ill-advised decisions which had given rise to them. As its problems grew more severe, public opinion clung more tightly to its demands, which became ever more radical and involved the call for new expedients. These latter, put into effect by men who in their turn had seized power in the name of the people's will, produced at best a temporary improvement in the state of things, but at the price of a graver deterioration a little later. This cycle, involving demands, a radicalisation of power and a worsening of the economic situation, was not to be broken until the fall of Robespierre on 9 Thermidor (1794).

This model of the revolutionary dynamic, which locates the origin of the Terror in decisions taken by the Constituent Assembly, claims to explain the essential (and, of course, only the essential) elements in the cascade of events between June 1789 and July 1794. Like all models, it disregards purely contingent factors occasioned by particular political actors (the flight of the King is an event of this kind, which, although of considerable importance for what followed, could easily not have happened); it leaves to one side the violence which arose from the unleashing of religious passions; it undoubtedly fails to take full account of the ideological aspects of the behaviour of the main protagonists (I will come back to this point below); finally, it does not take explicit account of the greater part of the consequences of the wars, whose origin was, however, connected, as we shall see, to economic difficulties. I shall therefore present the history of the French Revolution in terms of the major factors which dictated its course.

The term 'bourgeoisie' will appear only very rarely in what follows. Those readers who tend to associate this term with the French Revolution will no doubt be astonished by this, especially if they believe that it consisted of a conflict between social classes, whose motives for being involved were economic in nature, and which indeed saw the eventual triumph of the 'bourgeoisie'. How, in these circumstances, could I have left it out of the debate? A few words of explanation are necessary.

At the end of the *Ancien Régime*, French society consisted, juridically speaking, of three orders, which could be distinguished one from the other in terms of their specific rights. It is true to say that, immediately after it met, the Estates-General saw a confrontation between the orders represented there, from which the Third Estate emerged victorious. This victory gave rise to a nation without orders, which was juridically unified and from which legal privileges and exemptions had disappeared. However, there can be no justification for assimilating the legal categories of the *Ancien Régime* to social classes, and for confusing a political struggle with a so-called struggle for the ownership of the factors of production.

It is especially mistaken to think that 'the Revolution is to be explained in the last analysis by a contradiction between the relations of production and the character of the productive forces' or, in other words, that 'the means of production on which bourgeois power was built were first created and developed within the context of "feudal society" up until the moment at which the former mode of property had become a brake upon the advance of the "productive forces", whereupon it was necessary to "break the chains" '.[8] Alfred Cobban has given a very clear account of the errors informing this marxist interpretation of the French Revolution.[9] What he has shown is that the splits frequently emerged not so much between the former orders as across them; this was the case, for instance, with the revolt of the summer of 1789, which put peasants and landowners, a significant number of whom were 'bourgeois', on opposing sides. Indeed, investment in land was especially advantageous in a period in which merchant capital, since it entailed greater risks, did not confer the same standing upon its owner as it had once done. The conflict between town and countryside continued in other forms when, as a consequence of the inflation caused by the issue of *assignats*, the peasants caused a subsistence crisis by refusing to sell their products for paper money, which was continuously falling in value. There were basic disparities within the bourgeoisie itself in terms of wealth, status and social function. A moment's thought will persuade one of the kinds of clashes of economic interest that might arise among merchants (who might have businesses of varying size and nature), landowners, *rentiers*, financiers, officeholders, lawyers, notaries, procurators or members of the liberal professions. As if to add to the confusion occasioned by the excessively general use of terms such as 'bourgeois', 'peasant' and 'noble', one has to acknowledge that one and the same person would usually belong to several social categories at once:

> The peasant proprietor could also be a tenant farmer for part of his land, a merchant when he bought and sold produce, or a wage-earner when he worked on someone else's land. A lawyer might also be an estate manager and a merchant; he might also be a land-owner, for most persons of any social standing probably owned at least some land in town or country. In rural areas the smallholders and the rural artisanate might be quite distinct or might overlap. A noble could be a local official or a judge, an army officer, an ecclesiastic, a great landed proprietor or a working smallholder.[10]

On the other hand, a number of more recent studies have shown that, as the *Ancien Régime* was drawing to a close, the capitalist entrepreneurs, especially in new industries (such as mining or steel), together with the bankers, were often nobles, since the bourgeois preferred to invest in land in order to effect a change in his social status.[11] The great majority of Third Estate deputies in the various Assemblies were advocates, lawyers or holders of offices of one kind or another. This category of persons, which might be regarded as the equivalent, in today's terms, of civil servants, inasmuch as the activities of its members were bound up with that of the state, were far more concerned to hold public office than to be industrial entrepreneurs. One must therefore allow that the new productive forces could neither be checked by the old social order, of which they were a part, nor liberated by the representatives of the new order, which was unaware of their existence or even openly hostile to them. It is worth noting in this respect the anti-capitalist sentiments of numerous revolutionaries. The famous 'chains' invoked by the Communist Manifesto could only be broken by forces which were in reality absent from the debates of the revolutionaries.[12]

Valid though the criticisms that I have just delineated may be, a far more serious epistemological problem, to my mind, is involved in the attribution to collective entities such as the 'bourgeoisie' of faculties of willing or of acting than in errors of interpretation which may be ascribed to the choice of social categories defined in an incorrect or confused manner. Hayek has observed that human language has been formed 'in the course of millennia when man could conceive of an order only as the product of design'.[13] The concept of spontaneous order, that is to say, an order resulting from the action, but not from the intentions, of men, appeared at a relatively recent date (during the eighteenth century), and was therefore far too late to have any influence upon language. Indeed, our present-day way of expressing ourselves still involves personifying social categories, and attributing to them the will to attain particular objectives, whereas in fact the events that we observe are merely the outcome of a myriad individual decisions taken with purely personal ends in mind.

We are therefore concerned with something more serious than an imprecision in language. Scholars, historians, philosophers and sociologists have consciously adopted an archaic way of thinking which consists in attributing intentions and actions to social groups. By basing their theories quite explicitly upon the personification of social groups, these thinkers have compounded the confusion brought about by the anthropomorphicity[14] of language. I shall do my best in what follows to avoid falling into such traps. More particularly, by the term 'bourgeois' I shall mean, much as one would suppose from its etymology, citizens 'living in towns, whether royal officers, merchants, *rentiers* or various others'.[15] If I happen to attribute a specific action to a collective entity, such as the state, this will have been through negligence or for stylistic reasons, and the reader should therefore bear in mind that in such cases I really mean to speak of the action of men who act in the name of the state or in that of some other institution or social group.

Since I have rejected the use of the concept of the 'bourgeoisie' as an explanation of the French Revolution, I will by the same token refuse to attribute any 'ideology' whatsoever to this same bourgeoisie. As usually interpreted, this term, which is marxist in origin, covers the set of political, economic, religious and other ideas of the class in power, ideas which are assumed to be an expression of its class consciousness and to justify its domination. By contrast, I shall be concerned with the ideology of individuals, that is to say, with those intellectual constructs or systems of thought which are meant to give a meaning to their actions in society. Ideology, in this sense of the term, is a matter of knowledge, or rather of something that is taken for knowledge, but it also involves judgements, ethical and moral, egoistic and altruistic, which are brought to bear upon the environment. Its usefulness consists in the fact that it provides the individual with a 'world view' which readily allows him, at any time, to take decisions and, more particularly, to distinguish friends from enemies at critical moments.[16] Ideology thus constitutes, together with self-interest and ideals, one of a series of factors serving to account for human behaviour.

Almost all the deputies in the three revolutionary Assemblies were persons of some education. They shared the usual economic ideas formulated by the Enlightenment in general, by the Physiocrats and by Adam Smith. However, they did not all draw their inspiration in the same way from this set of ideas. Differences in behaviour depended upon how deeply rooted convictions were, and upon the relative weight of individual interests and ideals. More particularly, we shall see that, at crucial moments during the Revolution, important figures denied their certainties of the previous day and aligned themselves with decisions which had the advantage of immediately appeasing militant public opinion, and therefore of aiding their rise to power. We shall also see that such figures by no means sustained a systematic defence of free exchange, but that they often acted as the representatives of particular economic interests, demanding liberty for them and prohibition for their rivals.

I shall therefore advance an explanation of the French Revolution which both appeals to classical economic theory and draws upon the sorts of analysis that the new school of public choice has prompted, and which therefore takes account of the behaviour of individual actors, especially of politicians, and not of that of collective entities, such as 'the nobility' or 'the bourgeoisie'. The decisive factors will turn out to be the various issues of *assignats* and their consequences, namely, inflation, subsistence crises, interventionism and the resulting aggravation of the crisis. In order to account for such effects, I shall have to describe certain institutions or conditions peculiar to the period (the fiscal system, the monetary system, regulation of grain distribution, the place of bread in diet, and so on). This account will be both brief and somewhat oblique, and the reader will therefore not find an exhaustive discussion of the whole of the traditional economy. Conversely, I shall often stray from this domain in order to recall political events, especially those bound up with power struggles, which are an integral part of my model.

This book does not depend upon original archive research. Indeed, I have merely sought to present and to interpret facts which are already well known, and which have been culled from earlier historians' articles or books; or else, where it has been necessary to know in some detail the positions of the protagonists with whom I am concerned, I have made use of readily available editions of the texts of the period. These latter have tended to be extracts from the *Moniteur Universel*.[17] This daily has proved, in spite of its biased nature, to be an invaluable source, for it contains summaries of the debates in the different Assemblies and substantial extracts from the speeches delivered there.

I ought now to explain how this book is constructed. Chapters 3 to 8 represent the core of the work, for they constitute a narrative and interpretation of the economic history of the revolutionary period in the strict sense of the term, running from the proclamation of the National Assembly to the fall of Robespierre. Chapters 1 and 2 describe the factors which triggered the events of 1789, knowledge of which is indispensable for an understanding of subsequent events, and they therefore present an account of the fiscal crisis of the *Ancien Régime* (which, in giving rise to the meeting of the Estates-General, gave the Revolution the particular configuration which I propose to analyse here), and of the economic situation in France in 1789. Chapter 9 is devoted to the post-Thermidor Convention and to the Directory, which saw the emergence of a new form of power struggle, with crowds and public opinion playing a much reduced role. The vicissitudes of this period represent the final, catastrophic consequences of the creation of paper money. Finally, the use of econometric techniques enables me, in chapter 10, to re-examine the causes behind the depreciation of the *assignats*, a phenomenon of crucial importance for the explanatory schema advanced here. This chapter also provides me with the opportunity to discuss a number of problems indirectly linked to that of the *assignats*, namely, the distribution of wealth, respect for property rights, and the economic consequences of the French Revolution. The apppendices contain information in numerical form (the budget for 1788 is presented at the end of chapter 1) or detailed calculations whose results are used elsewhere.

1
The fiscal crisis

If we are to have some way of understanding that extraordinary sequence of events, causes and consequences which goes by the name of the French Revolution, we must begin by outlining the conditions which gave rise to it. This chapter will therefore, to begin with, be devoted to a brief description of the taxes and the manner in which they were levied under the *Ancien Régime*, and following that, will proceed with an account of the fiscal crisis which lasted throughout the eighteenth century and was only resolved with the meeting of the Estates-General. The following chapter will be concerned with the equally critical economic crisis of 1789.

The direct cause of the French Revolution was the inability of the Royal Treasury to resolve its problems. The fiscal crisis, which, from 1786, took a sharp turn for the worse, can be traced far back into the past, for the state had been living beyond its means since the beginning of the seventeenth century. Yet the day came when palliative measures, which were by then a matter of habit, and temporary expedients, which served as a method of government, no longer delivered the hoped-for results. The peculiar features of the fiscal system of the *Ancien Régime*, and the hostile reactions which it tended to provoke, also account for the impasse in which the Treasury found itself. For want of any other solution, the privileged groups, which up until then had stubbornly rejected any reform, had no choice but to agree to the Estates-General being called. As far as the representatives of the Third Estate and the liberal nobles were concerned, this Assembly would not only uncover new financial resources but would also endow France with a Constitution which would serve as an impediment to arbitrary taxation.

The taxes of the 'Ancien Régime'

Up until the Revolution of 1789, the French were subject to a system of compulsory contributions which was both complex and inequitable.

This system had arisen from the superimposition, across a long period of time, of different royal and seigneurial taxes, to which were added payments due to the Church. The present-day distinction between direct and indirect taxation is also applicable to the period with which we are concerned. Among the former, the *taille* was both the most onerous (in terms of the sums involved) and the oldest; originally it had been levied in order to finance wars and had therefore, naturally, only been imposed upon the non-combatant population, that is, the commoners, for whom it served as a kind of 'buying-out of conscription'.[1]

The *taille* was not collected in the same way throughout the kingdom. In the *pays de taille personnelle* it was assessed in terms of the whole of the means of those liable to pay. Every year the Council of State would decide, according to the needs of the moment, the total sum which would have to be raised through this tax, and they would then divide it among the *Intendants* of the kingdom. The latter would then charge the various parishes with the payment of a particular sum, this depending upon how easy collection had proved in the past. The parishes, in their turn, appointed a tax-collector whose office it was to draw up the rolls and to collect the tax. This was not an enviable task, for, though his own quota was reduced, he ran the risk of financial ruin if he failed to amass the sum that was due. Since this collector had no way of knowing what each person liable to the *taille* really earned and what they could really afford to pay, he had to go by appearances. Consequently, it was so much in the interest of those subject to this tax to affect poverty that sometimes they actually did become poor. As the *cahier de doléances* (official list of grievances) of the Third Estate in the bailliage of Nemours recorded:

> they [the peasants] did not dare to procure for themselves the number of animals necessary for good farming; they used to cultivate their fields in a poor way so as to pass as poor, which is what they eventually became; they pretended that it was too hard to pay in order to avoid having to pay too much; payments that were inevitably slow were made still slower; they took no pleasure or enjoyment in their food, housing or dress; their days passed in deprivation and sorrow.

Such a system could not help but give rise to considerable arbitrariness in the allocation of the personal *taille*, which might be further exacerbated by the likes and dislikes of the tax-collector.

This tax seemed to be more just in the *pays de taille réelle*, where it was in principle assessed on the basis of the value of commoners' goods, no matter who the owner was. However, because this value was decided upon on the basis of the declarations of those liable to taxation and in terms of ancient and often highly inaccurate cadastral surveys, extreme disparities were manifest in these areas also. The nobility's contributions, in particular, were much lower than they should have been.

Virtually the whole weight of the *taille* therefore fell on the Third Estate. Yet the commoners were affected to differing degrees by this tax, in part because of the system of collection, but also because many of them had privileges. The bourgeois could, in certain cases, benefit from situations comparable to those enjoyed by the nobles. When, for example, such men had amassed a sufficiently large fortune through trade, they sought to ennoble themselves through the purchase of titles or offices, thus winning exemption from the *taille*. The bourgeois therefore managed in many cases to avoid the *taille*, which, being the most onerous, most arbitrary and most humiliating of the taxes, fell mainly upon small farmers and labourers, people too poor to rise through the purchase of an office but rich enough to have to pay a contribution.

As time passed, a number of other direct taxes were imposed. It seemed only natural that the nobles (who were supposed to pay the *impôt du sang* or 'blood tax'), along with the clergy, should be exempt from these new forms of taxation, just as they were exempt from the *taille*. However, as the royal treasury's needs grew ever greater, attempts were made to bring the second order into line. On the eve of the revolution, it had in theory to pay the capitation tax (which dated from 1695) and the *vingtième* (which had been introduced in 1749, although a second *vingtième* had later to be added to the first). In principle, these two taxes were assessed on the basis of the real means of those liable to pay. But those with privileges successfully resisted, on the grounds that they did not wish their incomes or fortunes to be a matter of public knowledge. Consequently, both the capitation tax and the *vingtième* were ultimately levied in a wholly arbitrary manner, sometimes in proportion to the *taille* and to rent paid, with the nobility and the clergy being spared.[2] Indeed, of the three orders, it was the clergy which paid the least tax of all. The clergy actually determined the size of its own contributions, such as the 'voluntary gift' fixed at periodic intervals by its general assembly, which it was quite willing to pay.

Over and above the direct taxes paid to the Royal Treasury, the members of the Third Estate also owed contributions to the two other orders. The nobility received various seigneurial rights, including the *champart* and the quit-rent; because their nominal value had been fixed since time immemorial, their real value had dropped considerably as that of money depreciated. The same was not, however, true of the *dîme* (tithe), which was levied in kind immediately after the harvest, but whose rate, varying dramatically from one place to another, had long since ceased to represent 10 per cent of the yield. Once intended to offset church expenses the upper clergy had diverted it from its original purpose, which made it extremely unpopular.[3]

Of all the many indirect taxes, the most onerous was the famous *gabelle*, which, on the eve of the Revolution, was reckoned to yield some 58.5 million *livres* a year. It was a tax on salt, a product that was heavily used during this period because of the need to preserve numerous foodstuffs. The *gabelle* was levied at drastically different rates in different regions. Moreover, distinctions could be made between *grande gabelle* areas, where it might amount to as much as ten *sous* per pound of salt, *petite gabelle* areas, 'redeemed' areas (which had paid to be exempt from the tax at some point in the past) and areas which were wholly exempt. As was the case with all the other taxes of the period, any undermining of the status quo might lead those whose situation was a good one to revolt, if they felt that their privileges were threatened.

In order to make sure that the *gabelle* yielded a good return, the authorities had to prevent the peasants from having free access to a product which in fact they urgently needed. This is why salt was often only sold in *gabelle* stores, which were often great distances away. In order to combat the almost universal recourse to contraband salt, the authorities had, moreover, obliged the population to purchase minimum quantitites ($11\frac{3}{4}$ pounds per household per year in the *grande gabelle* areas for *sel du devoir*). Such measures obviously rendered this tax quite intolerable. Although, by the end of the *Ancien Régime*, the *gabelle* represented over 10 per cent of the total tax revenue, it was not the only tax on ordinary consumer goods. In a general sense, 'dues' were levied during the obligatory marking of products as various as hides, iron, gold and silver, or on tobacco, meats, oils, soaps, and indeed on almost every other commodity. However, the dues levied on drink, being particularly heavy, were especially hard to bear.

A number of other taxes incidentally impeded the exchange and free circulation of commodities. The *traites*, which were actually customs duties, were operative not only at the frontiers of the kingdom but also at numerous points within it (those points at which, in earlier periods, there had been frontiers too). At the *octrois*, which were situated on the edge of towns, the state or the municipalities used to levy duties on goods coming in, not only to bring their revenues up to strength but also to protect local production from foreign competition. Finally, toll-houses set up by a wide range of different authorities were to be found all over the place – 1,600 were counted in 1789 – constituting the final element in a régime which Necker described as 'a real monstrosity in the eyes of reason' but which neither he nor his predecessors had managed either to reform or to replace.

According to Necker's calculations, royal taxes represented, at the end of the *Ancien Régime*, an annual sum of 470 million *livres*, to which one should add a further hundred million raised through tithes. According to the most recent calculations, summarised at the end of this chapter, the total taxes levied did not amount to more than 390 million *livres*. Was this an excessive burden, and therefore an intolerable one, as has often been claimed? One cannot arrive at any firm conclusion on this matter, for want of knowledge regarding the weight of such taxation vis-à-vis the national product, and for want of a satisfactory definition of what constitutes excessive taxation. Conversely, it is quite plain that these taxes were unequally borne by different sections of society. This inequality had an important economic consequence, namely, that, whatever the actual needs of the Treasury, taxation could not be further increased without a radical reform. Indeed, it had become virtually impossible to make the French pay any more, either because those with privileges refused to allow any further contributions or because those without them already found it difficult to bear the existing level of taxation.

The fiscal system of the *Ancien Régime* also suffered from at least two other grave faults. The first, a relatively minor one, consisted in the fact that the actual collection of taxes that were so complex proved extremely expensive; the second, which was far graver, consisted in the system's uneconomic character. The *taille*, owing in the main to the way in which it was collected, gave the peasants every encouragement not only to deceive and to defraud but also to curb their production. Likewise, the obstacles to the free circulation of commodities served to fragment the markets and to check development and growth.

Tax-farmers and financiers

Under the *Ancien Régime*, the royal administration used to collect the direct taxes itself but subcontracted the *gabelle*, the customs dues and the *traites*. Originally, the right to collect indirect taxes on behalf of the

Royal Treasury had been leased out to several different tax-farmers. Colbert, however, sought to make the process a more concentrated one, so that, by the beginning of Louis XV's reign, there was a single, general tax-farm. This was the name given to an association of businessmen who agreed, every six years, to a (lease) contract with the monarchy.

By the terms of this contract, the government empowered the tax-farm to collect the kingdom's taxes in accord with the laws that were then in force. In return for this, the tax-farm would advance a specified amount to the Treasury, which was thus relieved of the difficulties which some of the collecting involved, and could also count upon the anticipated income. In order that they might be vested with due authority and therefore be obeyed, the employees of the Farm had won quite exceptional rights. They were entitled to bear arms, and could conduct searches and imprison those who contravened the regulations. A whole series of specialised legislations were involved in their law-suits with the tax-payers. The excess sums collected over and above the amount specified in the lease, once deductions were made for expenses, reverted for the most part to the tax-farm itself.

Tax-farming required a large initial outlay. In addition to the main farmers, who formed an association in order to negotiate a lease, a large number of *partisans, traitants* or *croupiers*, to use the terms current at the time, contributed a part of the capital and were involved in the sharing out of the profits from the tax-farm. But the role of the tax-farmers and their associates was not confined to the collection of indirect taxes. Indeed, such tax-farmers would often become the Treasury's creditors also, and would lend it the money that they had gathered, along with their personal fortunes. In the absence of banks, the tax-farmers in fact constituted the sole financial poles around which could be realised the concentration of capital which was always so desperately needed by the state.

In order to procure the liquid capital which it invariably lacked, the Treasury had recourse to various forms of credit. In the short term, it would borrow from financiers against the tax revenues guaranteed for the subsequent collection. These 'anticipations' might involve sums so large as to exceed a year's worth of revenues.

In the case of long-term loans, they were more often arranged in the form of annuities, and more especially as life annuities. Since the Royal Treasury's difficulties were so grave as to cause it every now and then to dishonour the word of the state, to suspend payment of annuities and to reduce the interest or capital that was being repaid, the money-lenders would often demand quite steep levels of recompense to set against the risks they were running. In order to conceal its working costs, the Treasury exploited the eighteenth-century taste for gambling and often proposed loans without conspicuously high interest which were associated with a number of different lotteries settled at the moment of repayment. Life annuities and lottery loans gave rise to combinations that were all the more complicated and costly (when the state honoured its word) because the hard-pressed authorities had to satisfy ever more subscribers and because its credit fell ever lower.

The general public hated tax-farmers and financiers. If they were so execrated, it was because they were associated with the collection of taxes, an activity which seemed to win them huge advantages, and because they charged the state apparently usurious rates of interest (albeit ones that could be justified in terms of the risks that they took), in a period in which feelings against loans involving interest still ran high. One can therefore readily understand how it was that tax-farmers and financiers were often the main victims of the crises afflicting the Treasury. Indeed, the ministers who persecuted them preferred to alienate a small number of generally detested individuals rather than the broad mass of tax-payers or the nobles, who were not so numerous but who were more powerful.

Another means frequently employed by the monarchy to procure ready cash was the sale of offices. These offices sometimes involved genuinely useful functions, as was the case with certain magistracies, but were just as often wholly artificial, as was the case with, for example, sellers of oysters, inspectors of fish, visiting brandy tasters, pork *langueyeurs* or butter and cheese tasters.[4] The purchase of an office appeased the vanity of those aspiring to climb higher in the social hierarchy, but it also brought financial advantages such as tax exemptions or the right to exercise certain activities protected by a monopoly. These advantages were in part counterbalanced by various more or less random duties that the authorities could impose upon officers.

After this thumbnail sketch of the Royal Treasury's main resources, it is worth enquiring how far they proved adequate to the state's expenditure. It is a little surprising for a modern reader to discover that the Treasury not only made no forecasts of its expenditure but also had a very sketchy knowledge both of its revenues and of the spending of cash after it had taken place. It was when the state found that it was lacking in resources that it had hastily to find some way of honouring its commitments, often by resorting to the most reprehensible of expedients. There was therefore no state budget under the *Ancien Régime*. It was this lacuna which, as we shall see, allowed Necker, when for the first time he drew up a balance sheet of the state's finances, to deceive the majority of his contemporaries with false figures and excessively optimistic estimates.

The origins of the Royal Treasury's difficulties

At no point in the eighteenth century did the Royal Treasury manage to disembroil itself from its difficulties. The budget was already marked by a deficit when Colbert became a minister, and he only succeeded in reducing it temporarily by means of various expedients which damaged the interests of the state's creditors. Yet the last thirty years of Louis XIV's reign, which were marked by two European wars, saw the ruin of Colbert's endeavours. State expenditure doubled between 1689 and 1697, and then again between 1701 and 1714. At the death of the Sun King, the Treasury was in a desperate predicament, and its deficit was larger, proportionally, than it was to be in 1789. The Regent contemplated draconian solutions, namely, the calling of the Estates-General and a declaration of bankruptcy. His ministers avoided this by having recourse to a number of time-honoured methods, such as repudiation of a part of the debt, the fining of financiers (at periodic intervals a court would judge them and force them to 'disgorge') and the debasement of the coinage. Since all attempts to tax privileged groups had failed because of the resistance of the nobility, it was the *rentiers* who paid for this financial purge.

Countries such as England and Holland were able, thanks to their banks, to bear deficits as large as that of France. In exchange for being granted the privilege of issuing banknotes, these institutions lent the Treasury the funds which it needed. Citing these countries as models, John Law had pointed out to the Regent what good cause there was to found a state bank in France, but, faced with stern resistance from the Council of Finances, he had to settle for the establishment of a private bank. This bank enjoyed great success in offering discounts at reasonable rates and in issuing bills exchangeable against a fixed quantity of precious metal, at a time when the actual content of the coinage was subject to ceaseless variations.

Unfortunately, John Law's ambitions knew no limit. He went on to found a *Compagnie d'Occident*, subsequently known as the *Compagnie des Indes*, which was granted a monopoly of the trade with Louisiana and with other distant territories. These ventures, which were based upon a far shakier set of principles than was the bank, employed its credit for their risky operations. Moreover, the bank, which had managed to secure for itself the privileges of issuing coin and the general receivership, ended up by amalgamating with the *Compagnie des Indes*. In the meantime, Law, who had undertaken to pay back the state debt against a government annuity of forty-five millions a year, had been appointed Controller-General. It seemed as if the Treasury's difficulties were at an end. But the system began to fall apart towards the end of 1719, when it dawned on the shareholders that, given its artificial nature, they would never lay their hands on the dividends which had been waved in front of their noses. It was around this time that, in order to replace other receipts, the issue of banknotes accelerated, totalling in the end, in October 1720, when the system collapsed, some three billions.

The state refused to accept that all those who had placed their trust in the system should be ruined, for the credit of the Royal Treasury, which, at the Regent's behest, had supported Law, was at stake. The decision was taken to honour a part of the main debt and to go ahead with a reduction in the debts, reckoned to be around 2.5 billions, which it owed the public. After the liquidation of the enterprise, the state found that it was liable for the payment of fifty-one million a year in annuities, although the King's coffers were empty. This situation, albeit a dramatic one, was not so different, all things taken into account, from the one that Law had encountered when he first came to France. The most enduring effect of his system upon the kingdom's finances was therefore not that it ruined them, but because of the deep impression this episode made upon people's minds, that it delayed until the Consulate the foundation of a Bank of France, which could have proved so useful to the effective running of the Treasury's affairs.

During the reign of Louis XV, several Controller-Generals attempted to put the kingdom's finances in good order. The classic devices to which they resorted are well known, namely, the issue of government loans and annuities followed by the reduction of these annuities, the creation of offices, lotteries, new indirect taxes, increase of the existing taxes and so on. Debasement of the coinage, that other affliction of the old financial system, was also employed, but only up until 1726, the date at which a decree definitively settled the metal content of the *écu* and the *livre*. After a relatively long period of peace, which was only broken by the War of the Polish Succession, these efforts bore fruit and the Treasury's situation improved around 1730. But new conflicts were brewing, leading to the War of the Austrian Succession and, above all, the Seven Years' War (1756–63), which once again put the Treasury to a very severe test.

Machault d'Arnouville, who was appointed Controller-General in 1745, tried to introduce a radical innovation in the field of taxation. Before his time, only exceptional taxes, such as the capitation tax or the *dixièmes*, were supposed, in principal, to be universal. Indeed, the privileged classes, as we have said, had managed to avoid them almost entirely. A new tax, the *vingtième*, was therefore intended to hit all incomes, including ecclesiastical ones, and to establish quite unprecedented procedures for checking and verification. The yield of this new tax was then supposed to go into a sinking fund for the debt, by means of which the financial situation would have been definitively improved.

The privileged classes put up a furious resistance to the new Controller-General's projects and ended up by carrying the day. Machault resigned in 1754. With him disappeared all hopes of a fundamental tax-reform, such as would have established equality with respect to taxation and would also have simplified its collection. Up until the Revolution, the clergy and the Parlements (if one excepts the brief period when they were dissolved), by now assured of their own power, were to wreck all plans for fiscal renewal.

In the aftermath of the Seven Years' War, at the end of 1769, the Treasury's situation once again became a highly dramatic one. The revenues for 1770, and even those for 1771, had already been spent. Since the state had exhausted its credit, bankruptcy appeared imminent, and was only evaded by the particularly rough and ready methods of the new Controller-General, the abbé Terray. The state proceeded, cynically and systematically, to break its word. The abbé Terray was able to take the exploitation of the state's creditors to the limit. To begin with, he enjoyed the blessing of the Parlements, although they quickly became hostile to him. Yet the monarchy, as represented by Terray and Chancellor Maupeou, emerged victorious from its struggle with the sovereign courts.

The Parlements were former law-courts whose original role had been limited to the registering of such new laws as had been decreed by the King, in order that they might be uniformly applied throughout the country and rendered compatible with the particular laws of each province. Gradually the Parlements' role had developed, and in the absence of genuinely representative institutions they had acquired the capacity to oppose laws of which they did not approve, by refusing to register them and by making 'remonstrances' to the king. The latter could decide to proceed regardless, by means of a *lit de justice*, but the procedure was always a highly unpopular one.

Public opinion therefore regarded the Parlements, which were often seen to be in open confrontation with the King, as representative bodies, and as the sole bulwarks against absolutism and despotic power. The reality was somewhat different. Those who attended the Parlements were neither appointed nor elected; being members of an aristocratic élite, they bought their offices and were not so much concerned to defend the interests of the general public but merely those of their own order. Since the venal nature of their offices shielded them from royal or ministerial pressure, they were able systematically to oppose all egalitarian fiscal reforms and, more generally, any challenge to their privileges.

Maupeou succeeded in eliminating the opposition of the Parlements, whose powers he seriously restricted, since from then on they were forbidden to present remonstrances. Once free of such constraints, the abbé Terray set out once more on the trail of reform blazed by Machault d'Arnouville, which was intended to make the *vingtième* an equitable and effective tax. Terray also aspired to re-establish a balance between income and expenditure, but his failure to win the desired economies from the King and his ministers prevented this. In 1774, upon the death of Louis XV, the abbé Terray's projects were still unrealised. Nevertheless, under his tough but effective administration, the Treasury had been saved yet again from bankruptcy and the financial situation was yet again a healthy one.

Louis XVI's missed opportunities

Upon ascending the throne, Louis XVI, after some hesitation, decided to placate popular feeling and dismiss Maupeou and Terray. Following the advice of his aunts, the new King appointed a ministry which was in fact under the influence of an old and skilful courtier, Maurepas. Turgot held the post of Controller-General, and being a close friend of the Physiocrats, he understood quite well how urgent it was to undertake thoroughgoing reforms. Since he had once been the Intendant of Limoges, he had first-hand knowledge of the problems involved in financial administration. In accordance with the economists' prescriptions, Turgot would have liked to institute a single (or virtually single) land tax, and to free agriculture, trade and industry from all statutory and fiscal checks. His proposals were very far-reaching since, through the creation of new juridical entities, the municipalities, he aspired to nothing less than the suppression of the orders, civil equality and the establishment of a representative form of government.

Only too aware of the obstacles which he faced, Turgot would have liked to introduce his reforms gradually. As far as the budget was concerned, he advised the King to make economies, set about turning the *vingtième* into a land tax and began to pay back a number of the state's debts. He therefore continued quite prudently, and with more acceptable methods, the work of financial purification begun by the abbé Terray. In addition, he went some way towards restoring free trade in grain, which had been decreed in 1764 but had remained a dead letter. The fact that he had not authorised complete freedom to export demonstrates his concern to proceed gradually, so as not to offend the prejudices and interests of the most powerful subjects of the kingdom. However, in spite of all these precautions, his measures were very ill received. The spring of 1775 followed bad harvests, and his reforms led to riots and uprisings. These episodes, which were known collectively as the 'flour war', were long held against Turgot by his enemies.

Louis XVI, in the very first years of his reign, had taken a decision which was to have momentous consequences. Under the influence of Maurepas, who was in favour of a conciliatory policy, he restored the power of the Parlements, which had been withdrawn by Chancellor Maupeou a few years before. These institutions were to act as intransigent guardians of privilege and to inhibit, up until the Revolution, every significant innovation or change in the tax system.

At the beginning of 1776, Turgot set in motion a new series of reforms. He had the King approve the suppression of the *corvée* and the abolition of the *jurandes*, which were highly powerful guilds under the *Ancien Régime*. The Parlements put up a stiff resistance to these decisions which, to be ratified, required a *lit de justice*. The Controller-General's triumph was, however, short-lived. Turgot had simply made too many enemies and it was this that brought about his downfall, not so much because of what he had already done as because of those things which, quite correctly, people suspected him of wishing to do. He was therefore dismissed in May 1776. He had done no more than touch upon the reforms which, to his mind, would have restored the royal finances, revived the country's economy and established civil equality. Louis XVI, being too weak and too indecisive, could not sustain so ambitious a project.

Necker's expedients

After an interim period of a few months, during which Clugny, as Controller-General, rid the administration of Physiocrats and hastily dismantled all that Turgot had done, the King called upon Necker. Since he had made a huge fortune from banking, Necker had not the least wish to enrich himself at the Royal Treasury's expense, but he was hungry for popular success and for social recognition. His former profession, his dealings with the cosmopolitan world of banking and his reputation as a practical man, with a distaste for all theories and all systematic approaches, seemed to make him the ideal choice for the situation. However, the American War of Independence, which was just then beginning, and which was to involve France (in 1778), occasioned new and serious financial problems.

Necker was a foreigner (from Geneva), a Protestant and a commoner. He could not therefore be invested with the title of Controller-General, and the office of Director of the Treasury was created especially for him. It was in fact he who ran the kingdom's finances, and he quickly became more popular and more influential than the real ministers. Several factors account for Necker's success. First, he refused to raise taxes, so that, for the first time ever, a French king waged a war without demanding new contributions from his subjects. Secondly, Necker enjoyed the image of a man who was both an expert and at the same time a disinterested person, a philanthropist even. Finally, he was skilled in the forming of alliances which did no damage to powerful interests and which posed no threat to influential parties.

Since the bankruptcies of Terray's period in office, which had tarnished its image, the Treasury had never quite managed to restore its full credit. Nevertheless, under these seemingly difficult conditions, Necker succeeded with his loan issues. He was not able to work miracles, but his skill was such that he managed to disguise the real financial situation and thereby to reassure the state's creditors, while at the same time offering them extremely generous conditions. To the general public, these latter were camouflaged by life annuities, which lent themselves to a whole series of different kinds of financial trickery, and by lottery operations which, as we have seen, were much appreciated by the subscribers of the period. The sums involved in the loans effected between 1776 and 1781, the year of Necker's resignation, are hard to calculate, because accounts were not kept and because the sums declared at the time of issue were usually subsequently exceeded by a considerable amount. Necker himself announced a total of some 530 million *livres*, which is probably an underestimate. According to Marcel Marion, the total number of transactions undertaken during this period must very probably have involved interest charges of forty-five million *livres* a year.

Even such ruinous loans were not sufficient to finance a Treasury which had already been in debt before the American War imposed a burden of a further 1,500 millions. Necker exacerbated the situation by spending in advance the revenues due for the years to come. These advance expenditures amounted to 150 millions by the end of 1782. In addition, a significant part of the expenses incurred during the war had still not been settled by the end of that same year.

Against this potentially disastrous combination of factors, one should offset the fact that Necker had managed to increase regular state revenues by some twenty-five to thirty million *livres* a year. This was achieved by a number of minor, but popular reforms. Thus, he took the detested General Tax Farm in hand, cutting the number of its collectors and placing the collection of certain dues under state supervision. He suppressed a few wholly useless offices, an act which, however, did not in the short term benefit the Treasury, because the officeholders had to be compensated. In addition, he succeeded in increasing the yield of the *vingtièmes* somewhat, and in imposing a number of economies upon the King's household.

Yet even when his popularity was at its height, Necker's methods did not deceive everyone. Turgot's friends, in particular, never tired of attacking and ridiculing him. He was much hated by the financiers whom he had ousted, and he could not help making a number of enemies at court. The Ministers of War and of the Navy were especially hostile towards him, because he sought to check their expenditure. Since mordant lampoons were circulating, Necker sought to defend himself by means of a grand gesture. In January 1781, he published a *Compte rendu au roi par M. Necker*, in which he laid out in detail the Treasury's expenditure and income. Public opinion was highly appreciative of the fact that for the first time ever the state of the kingdom's finances had been made known to the nation, and this reinforced Necker's image as a minister who was both skilful and honest.

Unfortunately, the figures presented in the *Compte rendu* were false. They elicited a wholly fictitious surplus of income (264 millions) over expenditure (254 millions), which was done by overestimating the former and underestimating the latter, by confusing actual with theoretical movement of funds, by omitting considerable sums outstanding on current expenses, by forgetting extraordinary expenses and by a number of other equally crude devices. When Calonne became minister, he adjusted his colleague's accounts and estimated the normal deficit for 1781 at seventy millions, a figure which, if one took account of the extraordinary expenses incurred in the course of the war, would be over 200 millions.

The majority of Necker's contemporaries did not grasp just how inaccurate a reflection of the real situation the *Compte rendu* was. As a consequence, this document was a huge success, which exasperated his enemies still further. The latter did manage, however, to drive a wedge between Necker and the Parlements by publishing a *mémoire* in which, as director of the Treasury, he proposed to curtail their powers and to amplify those of the provincial assemblies that he was proposing to create. However, one could not issue new loans without the Parlements' approval. In May 1781, therefore, Necker made a dramatic resignation.

Calonne's skill in deception

Necker's successor, Joly de Fleury, quickly discovered the true nature of the Treasury's predicament. Since it was 160 millions short for 1781 and 295 short for the following year, Fleury had recourse to massive issues of loans and reverted to the practice of selling offices (especially those for collecting taxes, which Necker had just abolished). However, he did not prove equal to the situation and resigned. His successor, d'Ormesson, an honest but inexperienced man, continued the same policy of issuing loans. Having committed the blunder of setting about the tax-farmers, who were the very people needed as lenders, he was sacked at the end of 1783.

The new Controller-General, Calonne, had a far stronger personality than that of his two predecessors. His strategy, which with hindsight has been much criticised, consisted first of all in using every expedient still open to him and then, when every way forward out of his difficulties was blocked, in proposing a plan of radical reforms. To begin with, he in his turn therefore borrowed massively, 650 millions according to his own accounting, with extremely burdensome conditions attached, especially from the *Caisse d'Escompte* (70 millions). This institution, founded by Turgot, was a private bank, which discounted bills at the maximum rate of 4 per cent, held cash deposits on behalf of private individuals, guaranteed payments and issued banknotes which were only valid within the capital. Its credit was from then on tied to that of its main debtor, the Treasury.

However, Calonne had an odd notion of how best to establish the state's credit. He claimed that, if the latter spent without restraint, people would suppose that it was free of all financial troubles and would therefore lend freely to it. He therefore treated the court very generously, was very lavish and undertook numerous public works. According to Necker,[5] in order to 'give his unpremeditated actions a systematic air', Calonne claimed that the huge scale of his expenditure should cause business to thrive, an argument that has had many advocates in subsequent years. But Calonne's policy failed and finally, in August 1786, he had no choice but to admit to the King that the Treasury was in a desperate and apparently irrecoverable situation, with an annual deficit of 101 millions, with advance payments already running at 255 millions and with all credit exhausted, the last loan that had been issued not having been covered. Increasing taxation, which was the solution usually adopted in such extreme situations, seemed impossible because it was commonly admitted, not least because of Necker's writings, that taxes were already as high as they could go. The former Director of the Treasury, still as popular as ever, had actually succeeded in giving currency to the idea that the French were the most imposed-upon people in the world. Nor did it seem feasible to accept even a partial bankruptcy, similar to the one that the abbé Terray's policies had occasioned less than twenty years before, for the number of creditors had significantly increased.

The *Précis d'un plan d'amélioration des finances*, which Calonne put before Louis XVI upon this occasion, resembled, in many respects, Turgot's proposals of years before. This was not surprising, for the new Controller of Finances had had recourse to the services of Dupont, who was a Physiocrat. The ideas of the latter had been distorted and watered down somewhat, but nevertheless the *Précis*, in its final form, advanced some basic reforms: universal taxation of land, in kind, of a twentieth to a fortieth of gross income, extension of stamp duty, lightening of the *taille* and the *gabelle*, suppression of the *corvée* in kind and of the *traites*, provincial assemblies, reimbursement of the clergy's debt, the *Caisse d'Escompte* to be turned into a national bank, etc.[6]

The Parlements would obviously never have accepted a plan which involved taxing the privileged orders in peacetime. Calonne therefore decided to proceed without their approval and present the plan to an Assembly called explicitly for the purpose of ratifying his reforms. Louis

XVI promised to support Calonne but equivocated. Finally, an Assembly of Notables, consisting of 144 members (the great majority of whom were nobles and belonged to the privileged orders), met on 22 February 1787. While it awaited the end of the Assembly's deliberations, the Treasury had to have recourse to further financial expedients, which would have discredited it still further if such a thing were possible.

This Assembly proved hostile to Calonne from the very beginning. The notables recalled that, but a few months before, he had still been making reassuring statements regarding the condition of the Treasury, whereas now he was informing them that the situation was catastrophic. It seemed to them either that the Controller-General had lied in order to obtain new resources for further bouts of lavishness, or else that he had told the truth, in which case he was responsible, thanks to his squandering, for the ruination of the kingdom's finances, which had seemed to be in a healthy state but a short time before. In either case, the notables declared that the demands of such a man ought not to be answered, and claimed that, before their own privileges were infringed, the state's expenditure ought to be put in order. Strangely enough, public opinion was in agreement with the notables, regarding them as a bulwark against arbitrary taxation.

From Brienne to the return of Necker and the calling of the Estates-General

Attacked from every quarter, Calonne was dismissed less than two months after the first session of the Assembly of Notables. Pushed forward by intrigue, Loménie de Brienne, Archbishop of Toulouse and himself a notable, was appointed head of the Royal Council of Finances, with powers still more wide-ranging than those enjoyed by the Controller-General. Louis XVI, who had no liking for Brienne, believed in his abilities. He was mistaken, however, for Brienne had in his turn to admit, after a very short passage of time, that, contrary to what he had been claiming a little while before, the Treasury's situation was desperate. The plans that he advanced therefore could not help but resemble those of Calonne. As his popularity faded, the Assembly of Notables declared that any new reform would have to be ratified by the Parlements. The convocation of this assembly had therefore been to no avail, for it was effectively declaring itself incompetent; it was disbanded at the end of May. However, the debates had been sufficiently public for the whole of the country to be aware of the gravity of the financial situation. It had now become clear that radical steps would have to be taken. Voices, including that of Lafayette, were now raised in favour of calling the Estates-General.

The new government, headed by Brienne and the Keeper of the Seal, Lamoignon, set about the preparation of fundamental reforms. Several of these reforms, more particularly those concerning free trade in grain, the emancipation of the Protestants and the conversion of the *corvée* into a pecuniary charge, were ratified. But the Parlements refused the two new taxes which were put before them, namely, the stamp duty and, most emphatically, the single land tax, to which all landowners without exception would have been subject. They declared that only the Estates-General was competent to decide upon the creation of such taxes.

Since all attempts at conciliation had failed, the King, in order to force through the ratification of the reforms, held a *lit de justice* on 6 August 1787. The Parlement of Paris declared this action null and void. A few days later, the Parlement was exiled to Troyes. The provincial Parlements refused, in their turn, to ratify the new edicts. It was now a trial of strength. However, the threat of war in Holland, for which finances were not forthcoming, forced the government to adopt a conciliatory posture. It therefore dropped the stamp duty and the land tax and proposed that the *vingtièmes* be extended up until 1792, when the Estates-General would meet. The Parlement of Paris felt able to ratify this edict and so returned to the capital on 19 September.

The conflict with the sovereign courts seemed therefore to have abated. Since Brienne had also persuaded the King to cut back sharply on his own expenditure, it seemed as though the financial situation would recover. However, the need was still felt in the short term for liquid capital, all the more urgently given the ever-present threat of war. Brienne decided to ask of the Parlements that they ratify, all at once, all the loans that had to be issued, which amounted to some 420 million *livres*.

On 19 November, the session of the Parlement of Paris took place in the presence of the King. The loans requested would undoubtedly have been ratified had the Keeper of the Seal not been stung by the harsh criticisms made by a number of the *parlementaires* in the course of the debate preceding the vote. The royal session was rudely cut short by a *lit de justice*. Clumsy handling of the situation thus meant that hostilities between the authorities and the sovereign courts began afresh. On 8 May 1788, these renewed and ever more virulent exchanges resulted in a further *lit de justice*, which deprived the Parlements of all political power whatsoever.

In spite of its struggles with the Parlements, and the unrelenting hostility of public opinion towards it, the government showed no sign of checking its reforming zeal. Unfortunately, it increasingly lacked the financial means to continue. In March 1788, Brienne published a new *Compte rendu des finances*, which sought to give cause for optimism but which indicated so large a deficit, 160 millions for that same year, that the state's creditors became still more anxious. Loans to the Treasury were still hard to obtain and the financiers were no longer prepared to make the necessary advances. In addition, the taxes were not yielding much. The reforms and the new fiscal measures had spread confusion and opposition to the government was apparent everywhere. Finally, the clergy, upon whom Brienne had been counting for a substantial contribution, voted him only a derisory voluntary gift. On 16 August 1788, having exhausted all possible means, not excluding the most paltry ones, Treasury payments were suspended. On 25 August, Brienne was dismissed. In a last attempt to conciliate public opinion, he had, but a few days before, summoned the Estates-General for 1 May 1789.

The King then recalled Necker, who stood high in the public's favour, since it believed him to be the sole man capable of tackling the financial crisis. Indeed, he succeeded, by means of new loans which only he was capable of raising, in giving the state a new lease of life, up until the time of the meeting of the Estates-General. But he was wholly unconcerned with the question which turned out to be the crucial one, namely, the procedures governing the election of the deputies, and the functions which they would fulfil once elected.

The Parlements met in September 1788, their traditional rights restored, and were greeted with popular acclaim. This final, jealous defence of their privileges was conducted with all their habitual blindness. Thus, they demanded that the Estates-General, which had last been summoned as long ago as 1614, should observe the same procedures as it had done then. Since this stipulation was wholly unacceptable, for obvious reasons, to the Third Estate, public opinion turned quite violently against them. A new Assembly of Notables declared in its turn against the doubling of the representation of the Third Estate. This decision was rejected by Necker, who, following the meeting of the Royal Council on 27 December 1788, declared that there would be a doubling of the vote, although he had not decided upon the basic question, namely, whether voting should be by head or by order. This was tantamount to placing a bomb in the chamber, and one that was to explode just as soon as the Estates-General assembled.

So it was that the fiscal history of the *Ancien Régime* led directly to the Revolution. This latter arose because the Estates-General was summoned as a last resort, when the crisis in Treasury had finally proved to be insoluble. The Assembly of the Three Orders was to meet when the administration had lost all authority, and through its vacillations had given public opinion the opportunity to mobilise around the double theme of the Constitution and the power to levy new taxes. Pending this meeting, financial problems dominated people's minds less than did the question of the representation of the Third Estate, and it was this question that occasioned the breach between the Third Estate and the Parlements.

At the end of Louis XV's reign, the abbé Terray, like other ministers before him, had resolved a grave fiscal crisis by despoiling the state's creditors quite ruthlessly. But, a quarter of a century later, his methods were no longer applicable, for the debt had grown much larger, and more crucially still, was no longer in the hands of a few financiers but rather those of a huge class of *rentiers* prepared to put up a fight in defence of their legitimate interests. As Taine wrote with respect to the loans issued during the pre-revolutionary period:

[the state] became the universal debtor; from then on, public affairs were no longer solely the King's affairs. His creditors became concerned about his expenditure; for it was their money that he was wasting; if he mismanaged things, they would be ruined. They desired to know his budget in detail, to check his books; a lender always has the right to inspect his surety. Here, then, we see the bourgeois raising their heads and beginning to look more closely at that great machine whose workings, now open to the gaze of even the lowest, had up until then been a state secret. They became political animals, and by the same token, discontented.[7]

2

The French economy at the end of the 'Ancien Régime'

In chapter 3 I shall give an account of the opening debates of the Constituent Assembly, but first I want to give the reader some idea of the structures of the French economy towards the end of the eighteenth century. Once I have described the state of agriculture, industry and trade, I shall analyse the nature of the crises occurring in this period. The authorities established by the Estates-General had in fact to cope with an especially difficult economic context. The popular movements arising in 1789, whose influence upon the course of the Revolution was to prove decisive, coincided with a major crisis. In July 1789, the price of bread rose to exceptionally high levels and unemployment was rife. Finally, I shall consider the kinds of knowledge of 'economic theory' that were becoming current towards the end of the *Ancien Régime*. We shall then be in a position to appreciate the pertinence of the decisions taken by the revolutionary Assemblies, which will be seen in the light of such consequences as could have been anticipated at the time.

Economic conditions

The previous generation of historians were particularly concerned to reconstruct the economic conditions of former times, especially those in existence at the end of the eighteenth century, which are what concern us here. They have considerably advanced our knowledge of ways of life and of working conditions in the countryside and the towns at the end of the *Ancien Régime*. However, the quantitative data that a contemporary economist likes best to employ are not available to the historian, nor are they ever likely to be. Long and very complete series of prices of agricultural products have been taken from the market price-lists of the period; we shall see below how they have been used. But other series, essential for modern quantitative analysis, were never measured with any precision in the past and can therefore only be very approximately estimated today. This is the case, for example, with the quantities produced by the various economic sectors or with demographic variables. Nevertheless, in spite of its biased and inexact nature, an overall view of the economic situation towards the end of the eighteenth century may serve to explain the social phenomena of the Revolution.

Suppose we begin by considering some relatively reliable figures. In 1789, France, the most heavily populated country in Europe, had around twenty-six million inhabitants. This large population was the consequence of a century of growth at an average rate of 0.5 per cent per year, with an acceleration towards the end of the period in question. This demographic expansion was accompanied by a rapid urban growth, with the population of the towns accounting for around 16 per cent of the total population. Paris, with 600,000 inhabitants, was by far the most important urban centre in the kingdom, with all the other towns of over 10,000 inhabitants added together not amounting to as large a number.

Agriculture accounted for approximately three-quarters of the national product. Thanks to the interplay of a number of different factors (clearances, new plantings, a drop in the number of feast days, technical advances, etc.), the productivity of the soil was increasing, but at a relatively slow pace, not very much higher than that of the growth of the population.[1] Overall, the grain surpluses in the most fertile rural areas remained very slight and hardly sufficed for the feeding of the towns and of the less productive country areas. A number of different regions were responsible for the provisioning of Paris, which dwarfed all the other towns in the kingdom, and which often posed problems for the authorities concerned.

The peasants or, more precisely, a minority of them (estimated at two million individuals), owned around 40 per cent of the land (including some 5 per cent of common land). The rest of the soil belonged to the nobility (25 per cent), to the clergy (10 per cent) and to the most well-to-do of the bourgeoisie, categories whose members did not of course cultivate their domains themselves. One should also note that in theory the peasants were never outright owners of their lands, and that they exercised only limited rights there. Being tenant farmers, they owed their lords various dues, whose real value had in fact dropped sharply with the passage of time. They could, through the payment of other, fairly modest dues, bequeath their tenancies to their heirs. Nevertheless, in spite of their relatively innocuous nature, the seigneurial rights which restricted the peasants' property rights were a source of the most bitter recrimination.

Alongside a minority of quasi-proprietors and, sometimes, rich farmers, the countryside held a large number of poor cultivators, who were generally sharecroppers (*métayers*). Finally, a significant part of the population had neither tenure nor farm nor a *métairie* and lived a miserable and precarious existence as journeymen. It would seem that demographic expansion, which increased the work-force available in the countryside, also brought about a deterioration in the course of the eighteenth century of the living conditions of a large number of these dispossessed peasants.

Two other factors further worsened the effect of demography upon the poorest section of the rural population. The first was the feudal backlash as numerous owners of fiefs sought, from around 1750, to reintroduce old rights which had fallen into disuse long before. This feudal backlash may be explained by the fact that the bourgeois, who were buying up fiefs in greater and greater numbers, were trying to maximise the return on their investments. At any rate, it indisputably had a deleterious effect on peasants' incomes.

The second factor which resulted in increasing poverty in the countryside was the curtailment of the right of free pasture on the common land, that is to say, a reduction in the area of land upon which all the inhabitants of a village could graze their livestock. The Physiocrats' influence, around the middle of the century, had led to division of the communal lands, in imitation of what had already occurred in England. The substitution of individual for collective production was supposed to increase production, with those new owners who had been given or sold previously fallow land doing their utmost to increase the yield. But the consequence of this partition and sale of the commons was that the poor peasants, if they owned a few animals, were no longer in a position to feed them. One of their meagre means of subsistence had disappeared, which made them still more destitute.

The pauperisation of a part of the country population accounts for the increase in bands of vagabonds, who readily took up the bandit's life, and for the emergence of a wretched urban proletariat, whose members were unskilled and could find no stable work. All of these rootless persons were to play a major role during the Revolution, first of all through the fear which they inspired during the summer of 1789, and second through their supplying a large part of the membership of the Paris sans-culottes.

Notwithstanding the gradual improvement shown in its productive capacities throughout the eighteenth century, French agriculture remained very backward in comparison with English agriculture. The extraordinary rises in productivity in England were the talk of Europe. In France, serious attempts were made to imitate them by establishing proprietorial rights over common land or by abolishing grazing rights, but the adoption of new techniques was still at the purely experimental stage. Unfortunately, a number of far-reaching causes prevented an agrarian revolution from taking place in France. Among these should be mentioned the fiscal burden, which weighed very heavily on the country areas and penalised any peasant who showed the slightest sign of being wealthy or simply comfortably off. The sheer quantity of regulations governing the practice of agriculture and the grain trade[2] checked all attempts at profit-making, and therefore innovation, and discouraged fresh investment. The nature of certain property rights, such as share-cropping, provided the peasants with no incitement to increase their productivity either. The inefficiency of agriculture was further exacerbated by the small size and the fragmentation of the majority of the plots.

Demographic expansion had, as we have already seen, made a work-force available. The growth in agriculture was barely capable of feeding this work-force, but this same growth, together with technological advances which had arrived from the other side of the Channel, had enabled industrial development to get going also. Its annual rate of growth during the decade prior to the Revolution very probably reached 1.9 per cent.[3] Yet in this sphere too, France lagged behind England to a considerable extent. This discrepancy can be explained by the state of agriculture (which was not yet producing significant surpluses), by corporate protectivism and interventionism, and by the lack of any sufficient concentrations of capital outside of that held by the Royal Treasury. To these strictly economic factors one should add the 'state of mind' of the most well-to-do sector of the population, which aspired to 'live nobly', that is to say, to acquire estates and to build up a rent roll, and which did not deign in general to act in an entrepreneurial manner.

France's industries were still in a rudimentary state, and over half of its production was in textiles, which remained the leading sector. Alongside the spinning and weaving of hemp, linen, and above all, wool, a cotton industry was emerging. The only other ventures of any real significance were in metalworking, glassmaking and, in particular, the construction industry. The extraction of pit-coal, which was still at a very primitive stage, was carried on in the Massif Central.

The American historian George Taylor[4] remarks that, in trade, banking and almost all industrial undertakings, capital assets were negligible, with capital being mainly invested in circulating assets. Even in the case of the textile industry, the tools (looms) were the property not of the enterprises themselves but rather of the peasants who worked in them as jobbing weavers and thereby gained an additional income during the winter months. The Van Robais cloth manufacture at Abbeville, where the number of workers employed was sometimes as high as 600, was still an exception.[5] It was only in the mining and metalworking industries that there developed forms of capitalist organisation similar to those which we are familiar with nowadays. Given these conditions, there were still as yet very few factories, and there was no real concentration of workers.

In a town like Paris, the majority of artisans and manual labourers were employed in the food, construction and textile sectors. They accounted for around half of the capital's population. There were also numerous domestic servants (16 per cent of the population), people in the King's service (8.4 per cent) and a mass of unskilled workers, layabouts and beggars (at least 25 per cent). As Jacques Godechot has observed,[6] given the high percentage of people without a specialised trade, this population, which included (according to the census of 1791) 118,784 paupers, could supply a considerable quantity of inhabitants ready and willing to take part in riots.

Under the *Ancien Régime*, those workers and artisans who had a particular trade had a place within highly organised professions. The 'sworn' trades (so called because their members had to swear an oath) had to obey a very strict discipline with respect to the conditions governing apprenticeships and access to the status of master. On the other hand, they enjoyed a monopoly, guaranteed by the public authorities, over their manufacturing and production processes. Other trades, the so-called 'regulated' ones, were subject only to the local control of the municipalities, and as a consequence were much less protected than were the sworn trades. Only a few activities, such as large-scale trade or banking (which were wholly unorganised and open to anyone), managed to escape the control of the guilds. Even nobles could practice these without loss of status.

In Louis XVI's France, the state's interference in the economy was not restricted to the regulation of trades or to the protection of production monopolies. All-powerful *Intendants*, with regional administrations at their disposal, used a firm hand in the exercise of royal authority in the provinces. It was of course their responsibility to distribute the tolls among the various parishes. But their agents also intervened in case of scarcity, and more generally to back private interests when these succeeded in presenting themselves as representatives of the public interest. The local people, having come to depend upon the *Intendants'* decisions through having been forced to accept them, seemed in case of crisis to expect subsistence from them alone. As Tocqueville notes, 'the government having thus taken the place of Providence, it is natural for each individual to call upon it to cater for his particular interests'.[7] Tocqueville, who was so astute in uncovering the origins of administrative centralisation in France, gives a perfect description of the class of civil servants who in the eighteenth century, as today, dominated those who were administered by them:

Government in France is already characterised by a violent hatred for anyone, whether noble or bourgeois, who displays some interest of their own in public affairs. The smallest independent body which shows some sign of wishing to set itself up without the government's cooperation arouses fear in it; the smallest free association, whatever its purpose may be, troubles it; it will only tolerate those which it has set up arbitrarily itself, and over which it presides. The large industrial companies are themselves a source of displeasure to it; in short, it has no intention of allowing citizens to be involved in any way whatsoever in their own affairs; it prefers sterility to competition.[8]

Crises

The French economy as a whole, as I have already observed, developed slowly throughout the eighteenth century, undergoing a more rapid growth towards the end of the period. But economic expansion, like the demographic expansion that accompanied it and to a certain extent undoubtedly gave rise to it, did not progress evenly. It suffered from irregular fluctuations which sometimes turned into extremely harsh and painful crises, resulting in dramatic scarcities and famines.

The origin of the subsistence crises was mainly climatic. Agriculture, which, as the reader will recall, accounted for around 75 per cent of the national product, still depended upon the most rudimentary technology. The caprices of temperature and rainfall played a large part in determining the size of harvests, and the peasants had no means of protecting themselves against the harshness of the seasons. Relatively slight variations in the agricultural yield had wider repercussions through the effect they had upon the provisioning of the markets, and on that of the towns

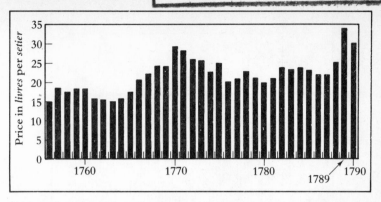

Figure 1 Annual average price of corn in France (source: E. Labrousse)

in particular. The peasants had to take away from their harvests the royal and seigneurial taxes and the tithes, to set aside sufficient grain for the next sowing, and then to store up enough to feed themselves for the coming year. It was only after these inevitable deductions had been made that, if there was a surplus, they would be able to release it upon the markets. A drop in agricultural production in the course of a bad year therefore served to bring down quite sharply the quantity of the surpluses sold and the provisioning of the towns. Thus, if we suppose, for the sake of example, that 25 per cent of the grain produced was offered for sale, a drop of only 12.5 per cent in the harvest corresponded to a fall of 50 per cent in the quantities available on the markets.

Unfortunately there are no statistics that would allow us to assess the levels of agricultural production for the period. On the other hand, we have plenty of observations regarding the prices set by the *Intendants* of the regions and numerous market price-lists (*mercuriales*). We are thus in a position to follow the fluctuations of most of the prices throughout eighteenth-century France. Figure 1, shows, for example, the development of the average annual price of corn. It is clear that there were high points in 1770 and 1789, which correspond to particularly severe crises (I shall come back to the year 1789 below). However, the variations in the average annual prices, in spite of their size, conceal the phenomenon of seasonal fluctuations, which were especially extreme in years marked by bad harvests. During these years, the price of corn might well reach, during the gap in supply between May and July, double or more the usual prices for the previous harvest.[9] Thus, one can

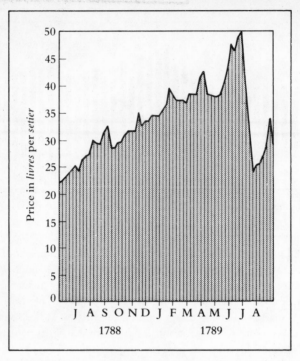

Figure 2 Monthly prices of wheat at Pontoise (source: J. Dupâquier, M. Lachiver and J. Meuvret, *Mercuriales du pays de France et du Vexin français*, Paris, 1968)

see in figure 2 that on the market of Pontoise the price of wheat had more than doubled between July 1788 and July 1789 (reaching record heights on the eleventh of that month), although it subsequently fell quite rapidly. These extremes showed the serious drop in supplies at the beginning of the summer. The small cultivators in fact tended to sell their grain in the months immediately following the harvest, either because they needed the money or because they lacked the premises for storage. If the many regulations had not rendered speculation (or 'hoarding', in the language of the period) extremely difficult, the speculators would have withdrawn the grain from consumption when prices were relatively low and when there were substantial quantities available (in the autumn), in order to put it back into circulation when prices were high and only small quantities were available (in the spring and summer). This form of speculation, which was so much decried, would have fulfilled the crucial function of constituting reserves, which would have become available when demand was stronger and people's needs were greater.

The social usefulness of the speculators was ill understood at the time, just as it often is nowadays. The very same people who would have derived the most benefit from their activities accused the hoarders of enriching themselves at the expense of the poor. In order to satisfy popular demand for regulations, the royal authorities exercised strict control over production of, and trade in, grain. Under these circumstances, crises became inevitable, especially during the gaps in supply following bad harvests. When they arose, the public authorities were asked to ensure that the hardship was equally shared, a task that they could only achieve very imperfectly.

In the France of the *Ancien Régime*, agricultural crises, brought about by the vicissitudes of the climate and perpetuated by the interference of the administration, affected not only the provisioning of the towns but the whole of the economy also. The mechanism of these general crises was a very simple one. Agricultural underproduction meant that the peasants went without a part of the monetary income with which they habitually purchased the few industrial or artisanal goods, such as clothes or tools, of which they had need. They therefore bought these goods in smaller quantities. Since at the same time, because of the high price of foodstuffs, the urban populations had also to devote a larger part of their income to food, their demand for manufactured products also contracted. The sectors of the economy which suffered the most were those which had the largest outlets, namely, textiles and metalworking. Many of the enterprises in these sectors found themselves forced to employ a smaller work-force, and often to close their doors, which aggravated the crisis still further. The resulting unemployment served to swell still more the population of idlers and cadgers in the towns.[10]

One can only appreciate just how dramatic the consequences of the rising cost of grain must have been for the life of the *petites gens*, if one grasps that, at the end of the eighteenth century, the French in popular milieux tended, outside of periods of crisis, to devote half of their income to the purchase of bread, which represented the key item in their diet. They consumed on average 1,753 calories per day,[11] the rest of their diet being made up of vegetables, fats and wine, foodstuffs which absorbed about another one-sixth of the household budget. According to George Rudé, a labourer in Paris in 1789 would earn from twenty to thirty *sous* a day, a journeyman mason forty *sous*, a joiner or a locksmith fifty *sous*. If they were fathers of two children, these poor people would have to buy around eight pounds of bread a day. When the price of a four pound loaf of bread rose suddenly eight or nine *sous* to twelve, fifteen or even twenty *sous*, most wage-earners found themselves faced with imminent disaster. It is therefore not surprising that workers were more concerned about the scarcity or abundance of bread than about higher wages ... Consequently, subsistence riots rather than strikes remained the typical and traditional form of popular protest.[12]

Such riots occurred frequently throughout the century and were in no sense peculiar to France. At the beginning of the 1780s, hunger riots had exploded in London, Geneva and Holland. It was in order to avoid popular uprisings that the royal authorities conducted their interventionist agricultural policy, one which was anyway in accord with popular wishes. They had subjected the markets to quite precise regulations, banned exports and built up stockpiles of grain, in order to compensate for poor harvests. Since the situation in Paris seemed particularly disturbing, a complex provisioning system had been set up, but it could not feed the capital effectively in the event of bad harvests.

Turgot, among others, was convinced that economic *dirigisme* was harmful and could not deliver the hoped-for results. Drawing upon his experience as *Intendant* of Limoges and upon the ideas of his friends the Physiocrats, he thought that central government was in no position to know with any degree of precision what the needs and levels of production of each region were, and therefore it could not balance out the various surpluses and shortfalls. When there were bad harvests, a number of provinces therefore went short. In such circumstances, it would have been preferable to have allowed the market mechanism free play. Then, once there was hardship, the prices would have risen higher in the most deprived regions and would naturally have attracted the relative surpluses from the other regions. The sharing out of the available resources would therefore have been more effective and more egalitarian than that achieved by regulations and by government intervention. In addition, free trade, in opening up new avenues for profit, would in the long run have boosted production and put an end to the subsistence crises. In Turgot's own words, 'liberty is the sole safeguard against dearth, the sole means of establishing and preserving, between the prices prevailing at different places and at different times, the golden mean, which is ceaselessly troubled by the inconstancy of the seasons and the unevenness of the harvests'.

Unfortunately, the moment Turgot picked to apply his ideas and to remove all restrictions from the grain trade (August 1774) was, in political terms, an inopportune one. The harvest of 1774 was clearly going to be a poor one, and the dearth which ensued was attributed to the measures taken by the new Controller-General. He had abolished the ban that had previously obliged producers to sell only at specific markets. In the spring of 1775, grain prices had not overtaken the levels reached a few years previously. Nevertheless, riots, known under the generic name of the 'flour war', prefiguring those of 1789–93, broke out at Beaumont-sur-Oise, an important staging-post for corn convoys, and then spread to several other regions. For a long time, people believed that these riots had been provoked by the court party that was hostile to Turgot. Nowadays, historians seem to reject the view that there was a plot.[13] The explanation advanced is a far simpler one, namely, that, in times of famine, the sight of grain convoys crossing a region hit by famine but destined for other markets than the local ones, was bound to give rise to anger and to pillaging, whereas the fixing of the prices of essential foodstuffs constituted the standard reaction of the populace to price rises.

Whatever the real causes of the troubles, the young Louis XVI gave in to the rioters and agreed to fix the price of bread. A little later, he also yielded to his minister's enemies. As we saw above, Louis XVI sacked Turgot and allowed interventionist measures to be adopted once again. One can gauge just how popular such regulations were by the abruptness with which the liberal policy respecting the grain trade was scrapped. The poorest people, who suffered most from the crises, were quite incapable of understanding that, in the long run, Turgot's policy would have been to their advantage. They clearly only saw the realities of the moment, namely, that the fixing of prices brought down prices and that requisitions served to provision the markets; conversely, merchants who stockpiled grain, in order to sell it elsewhere or to sell it later, were withdrawing it from immediate consumption. This same myopia, which was rooted in tradition, would also have its destructive effects during the revolutionary period.

Let us go back now to the final years of the *Ancien Régime*. While Turgot was battling it out with those who cast aspersions upon his policies, Necker published a work on legislation and on the grain trade. It was the work of a man who wished above all else to be pragmatic, who would not reject out of hand either intervention or a degree of free trade, which he thought should be limited to periods of surplus, and fundamentally believed only in his own skill at resolving problems when and where they arose. Through this attitude, he took the opposite point of view to the economists, who were accused of favouring a dogmatic adherence to systems simply because they acted according to a set of principles. His apparent moderation and his sense of realism appealed to those who lacked any real understanding of the new ideas. He had, however, to wait a few years for the opportunity to put his conceptions to the test.

In 1788, Brienne had in turn authorised a degree of liberalisation of the grain trade. But hail and rain destroyed a part of the harvest, which had otherwise promised to be a good one. Returned to power in the summer of that same year, Necker lost no time in following his own precepts. He requested an enquiry into the state of the stocks of corn, took a series of authoritarian measures designed in principle to ensure the provisioning of the markets and had an estimated forty-five million pounds of grain purchased from abroad. If Arthur Young, the English agronomist who was travelling through France during this period and whose valuable observations have been much quoted, is to be believed,[14] Necker's measures ended up by bringing about the very crisis they were meant to check. According to his testimony, the harvest of 1788 would have been a modest but by no means a catastrophic one. The spectacular interventionist measures adopted made many people fear the worst and stockpile large quantities of grain instead of releasing it on to the markets. This gave rise to a serious shortage, and the prices went higher and higher. Riots directed against the rich broke out in the spring of 1789, with participants demanding the fixing of the price of bread. In the following months, the prices of corn and bread at Paris simply went on climbing, to reach, on 14 July 1789, their highest level ever.[15]

Since the work of Taine,[16] however, historians have reckoned that climatic conditions on their own suffice to explain the shortages of the spring and summer of 1789. Emmanuel Le Roy Ladurie, in his study of climate in French history, brings out a number of specific factors, such as 'heavy rains in October and November 1787, a heat wave at the beginning of the summer of 1788, the storm and hail of 13 July 1788', which, in his view, may be held responsible for the very poor harvest of 1788.[17] As we shall see below, the dearth of 1789 played a significant part in the unfolding of events during that year. Unfortunately, we shall never know for sure if this dearth was solely due to the fickleness of the seasons or if, as seems equally plausible,[18] Necker's interventionism aggravated the consequences of a poorish harvest and thereby determined the course of the Revolution.

The popular movements of 1789 occasioned by the high price of bread were further heightened by another factor. For several years, the nascent French industries had been faced with a series of difficulties which had not been resolved. Numerous manufacturers were closing their gates. The unemployed were therefore swelling the ranks of the out-of-work population in the towns, and especially that of Paris; they would soon swell the mobs of rioters also. This crisis has often been attributed to the Anglo-French trade treaty of 1786, which to a large extent opened the frontiers of the two signatories. The immediate effect of this was that French industry, which was, relatively speaking, very little developed, had to adapt itself to competition from products, mainly textiles, manufactured on the other side of the Channel. A period of adjustment had necessarily to precede the moment when both partners in the treaty would derive mutual advantage from their exchanges. It is possible that in 1789 this initial period had not yet ended and that, on the eve of the French Revolution, the structures of the French economy were undergoing dramatic changes. This explanation, although a highly feasible one, does not seem to be wholly convincing on its own. But whatever its causes, the crisis which hit the manufacturers was real enough.

Economic thought and the Enlightenment

It seems appropriate to follow this thumbnail sketch of the French economy on the eve of the Revolution with an account of the ideas that were current during the period. I do not aspire to present an exhaustive survey of economic thought at the end of the eighteenth century. I merely wish to give the reader some notion of the kind of knowledge possessed by politicians of the period and used by them to analyse the events which they observed and to decide upon the appropriate measures to take in order to attain the objectives that they hoped to achieve. We shall see below that this kind of economic knowledge, although already relatively advanced, was not always used with much understanding. In order to win popularity, the most influential revolutionary leaders often chose to disregard it. They preferred to satisfy the most outrageous demands of public opinion, whose ignorance was only too easy to understand, and thereby run the risk of creating insoluble difficulties in the long term, rather than follow their own convictions. There were two areas in which the discrepancy between science and the arguments behind which the politicians sheltered was especially apparent, namely, the effect of issuing paper money and the question of price controls.

The eighteenth century already had a glimmering of what has subsequently come to be known as the 'quantitative theory of money'. Its originator is generally held to be Jean Bodin, a French writer who, as early as 1568, had explained the price rises of the period in terms of the influx of precious metals from the New World. His view was that the purchasing power of coin ought to be in inverse proportion to the quantity of gold and silver in existence in a given country. This idea, which had originally been a controversial one, was universally accepted a century later. The writings of David Hume, who was well known and much respected by the French *philosophes*, established its credibility once and for all.

The relation which was supposed to exist in an economy between the quantity of money in circulation and prices could certainly not escape enlightened people in the eighteenth century, inasmuch as they had lived through John Law's disastrous experiments. In the course of the century, other experiments of the same nature had served to confirm what had happened in France. The paper money issued in, for example, America, Sweden and Russia had everywhere had the same disastrous effects on prices. These episodes were of course widely known in France and were, at the appropriate moment, brought to the notice of the tribune of the Constituent Assembly. As for price controls and their economic consequences, they gave rise to numerous, lively debates in the years prior to the Revolution. These debates had, in large part, been initiated by the Physiocrats, whose historical role I shall briefly recall here.

In the 1760s, a small group of men had exercised a considerable influence upon the ideas of their time. With Quesnay, who was surgeon to the King and a favourite of Mme de Pompadour, as their leader, this group constituted the very first genuine school of economists in history. Indeed, their contemporaries had originally dubbed them the 'economists' sect', the term 'Physiocrat' appearing and becoming standard only much later.

Among the most important ideas of these economists was a theory of the formation of the 'net product' which, prior to Adam Smith's writings, served to explain how nations grew rich. Moreover, for the first time the notion of classes of individuals was invoked. This theory distinguished three different ones, namely, farmers, landowners and the more amorphous grouping of merchants, artisans and workers employed in manufactures. According to the Physiocrats, only the first of these classes creates wealth. In order to live and therefore to continue to produce, it consumes a part of what it produces and exchanges a further part for manufactured goods. Whatever then remains, that is, the 'net product', is surrendered to landowners as rent. These latter therefore receive the wealth that has been created, exchange a part of it for industrial or artisanal goods, and consume the other part.

In this scheme, the merchants, artisans and industrial workers play no part in the formation of the net product, for they simply transform labour and goods into other goods. The landowners, for their part, without participating in production either, perform a social function of absolutely fundamental importance. Having inherited rights from those who first cultivated the land, they continue in their own interests to improve it unceasingly.

Subsequent developments in economic theory have rendered the physiocratic argument outmoded, for thinkers were quick to see that the notion of production was far more fruitful than that of net product. One can see why it was developed around the middle of the eighteenth century, however, when the landowner could on his own account introduce new techniques enabling increases in agricultural production to occur, so that his economic role appeared to be the crucial one. A few years later, once the industrial revolution had begun, the crucial economic role was taken by the entrepreneur. Although already out of date by the period which concerns us, the theory of net product had had a number of interesting repercussions. It led its supporters to argue that the whole fiscal system of the *Ancien Régime*, whose complexity and character, both inegalitarian and wasteful, we have already had occasion to notice, be suppressed and replaced by a single tax. Indeed, as far as the Physiocrats were concerned, the net product went exclusively to the landowners. It therefore seemed obvious to them that they and they alone should pay taxes in proportion to their incomes. This proposal was considered absurd by many contemporaries inasmuch as agriculture was the very sector that needed to be encouraged. It nevertheless had the real merit of challenging a system of taxation that only the Revolution proved able to eliminate, and to point the way towards the type of fiscal system, at once simple and rational, that was needed.

Another physiocratic idea that was to prove influential was that of the 'natural order', a notion already present in Locke's writings. Perhaps drawing their inspiration from the then recent discoveries of physical laws, Quesnay and his disciples used this notion to imply that laws were also at work within human societies. The study, by enlightened minds, of these laws and of the natural rights of man constituted the core of the new economic science. The object of this latter was therefore defined as the search for the natural laws of society, which were obscured in some way by the interference and regulation of governments.

As far as the economists were concerned, the right to property was fundamental. If, however, one allows that a man is the owner of his own person, of his labour and of his goods, it is impossible to accept the notion that he should be prevented from selling and buying, wherever he pleases and in whatever form he pleases, the products that are at his disposal or that he requires. Regulations therefore seemed to be so many infringements of property rights, and should be abolished, along with all the other checks upon agriculture, trade and industry. According to this conception of society, governments were supposed to renounce all interference, so as to infringe upon no one's liberty, and so as to realise the natural order. Because they were convinced of the need to expel the state from the economic sphere altogether, the Physiocrats conducted an earnest campaign upon the well-known (but usually ill-understood) theme of *laissez-faire, laissez-passer*. This campaign found its justification not only in doctrinal terms, but also on account of other, far more practical considerations. The Physiocrats were much preoccupied with the quest for economic efficiency. They understood that regulation and interventionism impeded the development of production, especially because they favoured the creation of monopolies. However, as Dupont de Nemours affirmed, 'freedom of exchange . . . serves the general good, for it engenders competition; each takes pains to economise on the costs of his labour, and this economising necessarily works to the advantage of all'.

The Physiocrats were not the first to champion freedom of exchange. But it was through their writings, and through those of Adam Smith a little later, that it first received a doctrinal basis and a theoretical justification. This latter certainly made it appear very convincing. At the outbreak of the Revolution, the majority of enlightened people, who would have been familiar with the work of the *philosophes* and who would have read *The Wealth of Nations* in French translation, advocated this freedom. Their hostility to regulation was reinforced by their belief that it was just another expression of the absolutism against which they were rebelling.

Interventionists did nevertheless still exist, and they were especially prepared to defend the regulation of the grain trade. We have seen that Necker must be regarded as one of their number. In addition, the new ideas had not yet reached the general public which, in times of crisis, invariably clamoured for the implementation of the *dirigiste* policies of the *Ancien Régime*.

This was the condition of the French economy on the eve of the Revolution. Agriculture still by and large dominated the nation's production, and its productivity was only improving very slowly. A subsistence crisis was imminent, and Necker's interventionism was almost certain to exacerbate its effects. France's élites were in touch with new developments in the emergent science of economics, especially as regards the relations between money and prices, and were generally in favour of *laissez-faire*. The populace was oblivious of everything except the surface appearance of things, and therefore prone to demand regulation of the economy, price controls and the suppression of hoarding. Forearmed with this knowledge, I propose now to take up again the narrative of those events which transformed the fiscal crisis of the *Ancien Régime* into Revolution.

3

1789

A short time before Brienne fell from power, he had summoned the Estates-General, for the first of May 1789. Necker, his successor, was able, thanks to his reputation as a financial wizard, to obtain the funds required to avert the collapse of the régime. His sole ambition was to tackle outstanding problems. Yet a number of serious issues were still unresolved. How would the deputies be elected and, above all, how would they vote in the future Assembly? The Estates of the Dauphiné had accepted the doubling of the Third Estate's vote, and voting by head also. Would their example be followed?

As far as Louis XVI and Necker were concerned, the Estates-General would have to ratify the indispensable taxes which were put before them. But, for the deputies who were about to meet at Versailles, fiscal reform was neither the most fundamental nor the most urgent problem. They adopted a loftier point of view, for they regarded themselves as being above all else entrusted by their constituents with the task of 'regenerating the nation' and giving France a Constitution. Indeed, thanks to the eddies produced by the Assembly of Notables and by the preparations of the provincial Estates, public opinion had grown conscious of its own political weight, so that the deputies regarded themselves as its trustees and reckoned themselves ready to confront 'despotism'.

The ambiguities respecting the Third Estate's mode of casting its votes, and the misunderstanding between the King and the representatives of the nation over the ultimate purpose of the Estates-General, gave rise to an immediate conflict. This conflict, an account of which will be given in the present chapter, unfolded against a background of dearth, affecting the people of Paris especially severely. The existence of both an economic and a political crisis could not help but inflame the passions of all those involved. Indeed, the struggle between the *Ancien Régime* and the new Assembly could only end in the definitive triumph of one or other of the two camps.

The seizure of power by the Constituent Assembly

The Parlement of Paris, having returned in triumph to the Palais de Justice on 24 September, hurriedly decreed that the forms in operation in 1614 should still prevail in 1789. The Third Estate was furious at this humiliation. The whole of the intellectual and liberal élite, including the Lafayettes, Talleyrand, Condorcet, Sieyès, Duport and Mounier, formed its leadership, and it was these men who were to constitute the chief figures within the patriots' party. Recalled in order to resolve the dispute, the Assembly of Notables declared for voting by orders, which inflamed passions still more. War was declared between the Third Estate and the other two orders.

After the Parlement had in part revised its edict, Necker managed to persuade the Council of 27 December 1788 to accept the doubling of the Third Estate's vote. But it was still uncertain whether the voting should be by head or by order, which left each camp with some grounds for hope. After a series of further skirmishes, a royal statute settled the rules for the elections, which were to be held during March and April 1789. They unfolded in a manner which may seem surprising to us today but which very probably accounts for the peculiar, idealistic quality of the Assembly which was voted in, a body more concerned with juridical reforms than with economic matters.

Electoral procedures, being highly complex, varied from one constituency to another. Simplifying things a little, one can say that the first two orders elected their representatives directly in each bailiwick (*bailliage*) or senechalsy (*sénéchaussée*). The lesser clergy and the unfiefed nobility could also vote, which was an innovation.

The members of the Third Estate, provided that their names were inscribed on the capitation roll, met in small colleges of 100 to 200 voters, who generally chose two delegates from amongst their own ranks. Those chosen then met with delegates from the other parishes, so as to choose representatives at a higher level. Affairs might be conducted in this manner upon five different occasions, without written votes, electoral lists, candidates, parties or programmes, and often without the electors knowing precisely who it was that they were electing.

The consequence of such a system, as Augustin Cochin has made quite clear,[1] was that the majority of those elected belonged to groups of individuals all of whom knew each other, especially as they had belonged to those famous *sociétés de pensée* in which new ideas had been germinating for years. Since their training had been in the discussion and presentation of these new ideas, they could not help but be opposed to the established order. A few deputies, the most famous of whom were Cazalès, the abbé Maury and Mirabeau-Tonneau, were in favour of the *Ancien Régime*, but, since the King had not organised a party of his own, he lacked any effective or organised support among the electors.

The distinction between the three orders does not really account for the way in which the National Assembly was to react in the succeeding years, and we therefore need also to be familiar with the socioprofessional origins of the deputies. The great majority of those whom the nobility sent to Versailles were, in accordance with their own traditions, military men and landowners. More surprisingly, two-thirds of the clergy's delegation were parish priests. But it is the composition of the Third Estate's delegation which is of especial interest here. Of the 611 deputies, 45 per cent were functionaries, magistrates or holders of various offices, while 25 per cent were lawyers. There were also seventy-six merchants, forty or so landowners, a handful of doctors and professional men, but only eight industrialists and one banker.

The great majority of electors who were commoners consisted, in the country areas, of peasants and, in the towns, of artisans. Yet not a single peasant or artisan was elected. Nevertheless, the unrepresentative nature of the future Constituent Assembly did not prevent it from speaking in the name of the people. Contrary to what marxists have claimed, this Assembly did not represent the rising productive forces either, for these were all but unrepresented. Admittedly, over two-thirds of those elected were bourgeois commoners; but these bourgeois did not own the means of production of the country. Indeed, the Assembly represented the landowners, that is, the most traditional interests, and above all the royal administration and the corps which depended upon it. The men who sat in the Assembly were educated, sometimes even learned, had been receptive to currents of Enlightenment thought, but the great majority of them had had no experience of strictly economic matters.[2]

The meeting of the Estates-General was opened, with great pomp and ceremony, by the King, on 5 May. Upon this occasion, Necker made a disappointing speech, without a word about the long-awaited constitutional reforms. He simply played down the country's financial problems and made out that they might be resolved by a series of relatively modest measures. The deputies who had come to the Assembly with the intention of giving the country a Constitution found themselves having to support the bolstering-up of a fiscal system which they wished to have nothing to do with, and this was a cruel disappointment to them. Since Necker did not clarify the question of how the voting was to be done, the orders met separately to check their respective mandates. But the Third Estate, under the leadership of Mirabeau, had no intention of giving in. Having invited the privileged orders to join it, the Third Estate declared on 17 June that *it* was the National Assembly.

The first sovereign decision of this Assembly consisted in declaring 'that it voted unanimously to agree provisionally on behalf of the Nation that taxes and contributions, although illegally established and collected, should continue to be levied in the same manner as hitherto'. In theory, a decision of this sort should have had no effect upon the royal finances. In practice, however, it led tax-payers to believe that they might dodge their obligations. Furthermore, there had been frequent riots against the taxes, which were therefore collected only with some difficulty. The Assembly's attitude could not help but make the rioting worse. The refusal to pay taxes was a constant feature of the revolutionary period and it was only with the advent of the Empire that order was, in this respect, restored.

The Assembly also decreed 'that just as soon as it shall have, in agreement with His Majesty, decided upon the principles of national regeneration, it will concern itself with an examination of the public debt, placing the state's creditors from now on under the guard and the loyalty of the French Nation'. In other words, the Assembly set the country's financial problems to one side while waiting for a Constitution to be adopted, and while at the same time promising to honour the debts of the *Ancien Régime*. A declaration of this sort, which, given the gravity of the situation, would seem to have taken everyone by surprise, was actually very adroit. On the one hand, it caused the swarm of *rentiers* to rally to the support of the Revolution, in the belief that the state would honour its debts. On the other hand, it prevented the King, who was expecting the Chamber to solve the problems surrounding the country's budget, from resorting to dissolution before these same problems were solved, or in other words, before a Constitution had been promulgated.

In order to take the situation in hand, Louis XVI solemnly announced his decisions on 23 June. He accepted a number of the fiscal and financial concessions granted to the Third Estate, but he did not acknowledge as valid the decisions taken by the Assembly in the previous weeks. He declared himself to be in favour of voting by orders and let it be understood that he might well resort to extreme measures if disobeyed. The Third Estate, continuing to employ its tactic of passive resistance, refused to allow the executive arm the financial means it so urgently required, and treated the royal session as null and void. In the days that followed, members of the other orders came to swell its ranks. The King, very probably surprised by the resistance that he was encountering, ended up by yielding and by inviting those deputies of the nobility and of the clergy who were still recalcitrant to join with the Third Estate.

The King's submission to the Assembly may well have been no more than a delaying tactic. For, in secret, he was making preparations to go on to the offensive. Troops were massing between Paris and Versailles. On 11 July, Necker, who was still extremely popular, in spite of his speech of 5 May, was dismissed, and his place was taken by a minister with reactionary views. The first response to this seemingly violent gesture came from the streets.

The new organisation of government

As we have already seen, a severe economic crisis was raging in the spring of 1789. The price of bread was climbing steadily and unemployment was rife. Because the authorities had lost control of the situation, people felt able to act with impunity, and this sense of general licence, together with the dearth, unleashed riots, usually of a violent nature, throughout France. As early as April, the Faubourg Saint-Antoine, goaded by hunger and the fear that wages might fall, had revolted; law and order had been re-established, but only at the cost of many lives. Riots erupted in the provinces (Taine reckoned that there were around three hundred),[3] and the grain convoys were pillaged. In July, however, when mutinous troops sided with the rioting populace, the situation in the capital worsened appreciably. Fear of an aristocratic plot caused feelings to run high. The King therefore took his last decisions in an atmosphere of extreme insecurity and violence. The rioters in Paris responded by rising up and, in their search for arms, attacked the Hôtel des Invalides and, on 14 July, the Bastille. Two days after these momentous events, which had a profound effect upon public opinion, so symbolic did the capture of the ancient prison seem, Louis XVI appeared before the Assembly as a defeated person, ordered his troops to disperse and recalled Necker. During this period, the first émigrés, fearing both for their property and for their lives, crossed the frontier.

Paris was also the scene of a number of other important events. On 13 July, the electors of the Third Estate, meeting at the Hôtel de Ville, decided to form a National Guard, to be commanded by Lafayette, and set up a Commune, with Bailly as Mayor. The municipal revolution quickly spread to the provinces. Almost everywhere in France, the royal administration's somewhat disjointed authority was replaced by that of independent bodies which, in an attempt to maintain law and order, ascribed all existing powers to themselves.

Although violence was thereby avoided in the majority of towns, it did not spare the countryside. Some have argued that it was provoked by fear of bandits, by resentment of the notables and of the old ruling classes, by the awakening of the most barbarous of instincts in a time of great uncertainty or, quite simply, by the wish to destroy the evidence of feudal forms of servitude, and indeed of every kind of financial obligation. By burning the châteaux and the abbeys, the peasants destroyed the deeds recording their subjection to what remained of the feudal régime. Yet they also attacked ordinary bourgeois (for example, Jews in Alsace), to whom they owed money. Alongside this revolt against lords and creditors, the peasants also conducted a campaign against the Treasury, refusing to pay tithes, overturning customs barriers and looting the salt stores.

The Assembly was alarmed by the disorder, the attacks upon property, the threat of anarchy and the powerlessness of the law to intervene. The plan conceived to bring an end to the unrest, and to appease those involved, was a grandiose one. Those responsible for this plan included illustrious personages such as the Duc d'Aiguillon and the Duc de Noailles, who were two of the wealthiest men in France. Their scheme involved clearing the ground by legally granting the peasants a part of those reforms that they had just granted themselves. However, the collective intoxication of the night of 4 August meant that the concessions and surrenders went much further than had been anticipated. The situation became a little calmer in the course of the following days, as the reforms stipulated were about to be turned into decrees; after a number of intense debates, the Assembly revoked a number of the decisions which it had taken. Nevertheless, on 11 August, it voted for the wholesale destruction of the 'feudal system'.

Since the feudal system had long since ceased to exist, the deputies were hard pressed to define just what it was that they wished to abolish. There had been a time, long before, when the *seigneurs* had held a coherent set of rights. Some of these rights concerned ownership of land, whereas others involved personal servitudes or monopolies, and still others had been purely honorific. In the course of time, the original owners of these rights had sold, surrendered, rented out and sometimes abandoned them. At the end of the eighteenth century, most of them were no longer linked to each other and had fallen into disuse. Gradually, commoners who had made their fortunes in business had purchased or leased these rights and tried to extract as much profit from them as possible. The deputies, who, as we have seen, whether nobles or bourgeois, often owned land themselves, wished to abolish feudal rights but were loath to touch private property, so long as it was legitimate. For this reason, personal servitudes, for example, were abolished, but many other rights were preserved or declared redeemable.

However, the decrees of 11 August did not only abolish a series of dues of feudal origin. Their importance also consisted in the fact that they established the juridical unity of the nation. Justice became free of charge, penalties were made the same for all, public posts were made open to 'talents', guilds and the guild-masterships were suppressed and equality before taxation was declared. On 26 August, the Assembly announced, in the Declaration of Rights of Man and the Citizen, the principles which were to inform its actions. Property was declared to be 'inviolable and sacred'.

One of those decisions taken on 11 August, namely, the abolition without compensation of the ecclesiastical tithe (with the somewhat illusory proviso that it would continue to be collected, on a provisional basis, the state anyway assuming responsibility for church expenses) turned out to have momentous consequences. This compulsory levy was very inequitable and had occasioned a great deal of discontent. However, its suppression was very much to the advantage of the often quite wealthy landowners, who had bought their lands at a price which reflected the drain upon their resources that the tithe represented. Its preservation, with the proviso that it be adjusted somewhat, would therefore not have constituted an injustice and could have provided the state with resources which it urgently needed and which, in one way or another, it had to appropriate. But the majority of the Assembly, in spite of the pleading of Dupont de Nemours and the opposition of Sieyès, wanted to abolish this extremely unpopular tax.

I would further add, in order to give a complete view of the Assembly's activity in the economic sphere during the frenetic month of August 1789, that on 29 August it confirmed domestic free trade in grain and flour, while at the same time maintaining an embargo on their exportation.

Since there was no Constitution, the far-reaching reforms decided upon by the Assembly in the course of the summer posed an absolutely fundamental problem. Did they have to be approved by Louis XVI in order to be effective? This question gave rise to a debate upon the organisation of the various powers. The left wing of the Patriots' party, opposed to all limitations upon the legislative power, whether it was wielded by an upper Chamber or by a royal veto, prevailed. However, in the very short term, a compromise enabled the monarch to wield a suspensive veto, provided that he approved the August decrees.

Louis XVI, possibly in the hope of deriving some advantage from the Assembly's internal divisions, again resorted to force and had some troops draw near to the capital. Once again, rioting caused him to back down. In spite of hopes of a good harvest, dearth continued well into the autumn, either because the millers, on account of the drought, were unable to grind the corn, or more probably because anarchy still held sway in the provinces. There was serious unrest. During the famous insurrection of 6 October, the Paris mob, once again driven by hunger,[4] made its way to Versailles, where it invaded the palace and forced the royal family to follow it to Paris. In spite of this humiliation, the King and his ministers were still, in theory, the holders of the executive power. In fact, the Assembly had already to some degree seized hold of it, but without entrusting it to any representative organ. It was effectively distributed amongst all of its members and belonged to the majorities that were no sooner formed than dissolved, as one vote succeeded another.

But the Assembly was not free to dispose of the power which it had begun to conquer. Like the King, it too had become a prisoner of the mob, and more particularly, of its most extreme and most violent elements. Henceforth, this mob was to exert constant physical pressure upon the deputies. It was present at the Chamber's sessions, and never hesitated to make the most clamorous interruptions, hailing deputies, threatening with death those who were unlucky enough to offend it, intimidating those who were unsure which way to vote, sending deputation after deputation to express its demands, making and unmaking representatives in the clubs and the sections and, above all else, levelling the constant threat of new riots at the Assembly.

Financial problems

In the short space of five months, the political régime in France had been wholly overturned. The Assembly had brought down the social, judicial and administrative systems of the *Ancien Régime*. It had laid the foundations, albeit very shaky ones, of a constitutional monarchy. A considerable amount of work had been done, but the crucial problem, that of the state's finances, which was the ostensible reason for the Assembly's meeting in the first place, was wholly unresolved. It could even be said to be exacerbated, for the taxes which, while a fiscal reform was awaited, should, according to the decree of 17 June, still have been paid, were barely being collected at all. Only the taxation of the former privileged groups procured the Treasury some resources. But the Assembly, concerned to ensure its own popularity, would not let such funds be spent and decreed that they be used to lower the contributions of those formerly eligible for the *taille*.

As well as having very meagre incomings, the Treasury had to cope with constantly rising levels of expenditure. It was, for example, funding the charity workshops which had been opened so as to provide work for those workers who had been laid off by the economic crisis. At Paris, in order to restore calm to the popular districts, it subsidised bread, which was an extremely costly operation. However, since the Assembly had decided to allow it no more financial resources until it had given the Nation a Constitution, how could the executive power survive?

During the month of August, Necker launched two loans, which were not adequately subscribed. This failure dealt his popularity a severe blow. The Treasury resorted to the most pathetic expedients. The King, the Queen and their ministers made the symbolic gesture of handing their tableware over to the Mint. Each day, the Assembly also received more modest gifts, from every part of the country. Yet it still failed to attack the root of the problem. This may have been because it failed to appreciate just how urgent the situation was, and therefore continued to adopt essentially passive tactics, or because events unfolded in so complex a manner that it did not know what measures to take. It was on 19 September that the idea first arose of having the state free itself of its debt by printing paper money guaranteed by future tax revenue. On that same day, Gouy d'Arsy, a wealthy planter from Santo Domingo, proposed the levying of a 'patriotic tax'. This was effectively a tax on capital, whose condition had therefore to be calculated. The resulting income, assessed at 400 million *livres*, could therefore only be gathered very slowly. Gouy d'Arsy's plan was that, while awaiting the collection of such sums, the Treasury should settle with its creditors by means of *mandats nationaux*, that is, bills acknowledging a debt, which paid interest and which would be annulled once the patriotic tax had been collected. This solution, which clearly prefigures the *assignats*, actually involved restructuring the national debt so as to oblige the creditors to accept one debt in place of another. It was not adopted.

On 24 September, Necker yet again rose to inform the Assembly of the gravity of the financial situation. He proposed that the state cut back drastically on its own expenditure, and since ordinary loans no longer seemed practicable, he demanded the launching of a compulsory loan. Those citizens earning over 400 *livres* a year would have to contribute a quarter of their incomes, this matter to be settled simply by the declaration of each person involved, with repayment occurring when financial circumstances permitted it.

Necker's request gave rise to a very serious debate. Since it brought to light the desperate plight of the Treasury, would not the best solution rather be not to repay the state's creditors and declare it bankrupt? Of course, on 17 June, as we have seen, these creditors had been placed 'under the guard and the loyalty of the French nation'. But the Assembly nursed intense prejudices against financiers and capitalists, that is, those who would have suffered most from a declaration of bankruptcy. Here is how one deputy wrote of this matter to his constituents:

They are trying to stab us in the back, and to intimidate us through these considerations regarding the impending ruin of the state. However, since this bankruptcy would only affect the big capitalists of Paris and of the large towns, whose excessive rates of interest are ruining the state, I can see no great harm in it.[5]

Another deputy mounted the Tribune 'to upbraid this class known as capitalists . . . a deadlier scourge even than the aristocracy', and his speech met with the approval of several other orators, who were also ready to renege upon the commitments of the newly created Assembly.

It is also possible that a number of the Constituents considered that the state's financial ruin was a thing to be encouraged, since it would guarantee the Assembly's continued existence and would increase its power. Dupont, the deputy for Nemours, was one of a tiny number who were actually concerned to find genuine solutions to the financial problems. As we shall have occasion to see, he made a whole series of different proposals, but was only very rarely heeded.

Thus, either by carelessness or by design, the Assembly threatened to bankrupt the state. It was Mirabeau who prevented this from happening. In one of his most famous speeches, he begged it to approve Necker's plan, which, in his view, had the advantage of harming only a minority of the population, namely, the rich:

Two centuries of depredations and brigandage have dug out a chasm in which the kingdom is about to be engulfed. We must fill in this terrifying chasm. Well, gentlemen! Here is a list of all the landowners of France. Choose the richest of them, so as to sacrifice the smallest number of citizens. But choose you must! For should not a small number perish in order that the mass of people be saved? Let us set to work! These two million notables have the wherewithall to make good the deficit.

Swayed by the eloquence of so great an orator, the Assembly believed that by alienating but a small minority of its citizens it might still save the state. It was seduced by the idea of sacrificing the 'rich' – for did wealth not always have a somewhat suspect origin? – and it therefore allowed Necker to proceed with his plan. The right to property was thus flouted, a matter of weeks after it had been declared inviolable and sacred.

But Mirabeau's intervention had not been without political motives. The tribune of the people took good care not to undertake a thorough-going defence of Necker's proposal, arguing that it was necessary to act quickly, that there was no time to debate its substance and that anyway no other solution had been advanced. He therefore left Necker himself, as minister, with sole responsibility for an operation which could well fail or prove unpopular.

Dupont, however, was quite outspoken, and pointed out the weaknesses of Necker's plan. He reminded his audience that France's net annual income was 1,500 millions, a half of which went on the payment of already existing taxes. The remainder, some 750 millions, seemed too small a sum to supply the levy of seventy-five millions that the minister had proposed. Indeed, the forced loan was to prove of very little help to the Treasury, since its yield, no more than thirty-two millions in all, was not wholly collected before 1792. But Dupont did more than just criticise Necker's scheme; he also advanced a solution of his own. He demonstrated that, if the state took responsibility for church expenses, for the clergy's debt and for its charitable works, while at the same time collecting the ecclesiastical revenues in its stead, the tithe included, it would have an annual surplus of some forty-eight millions. This sum, which was sufficient to guarantee the servicing of the loan, would make it possible to heal the financial situation of the state. This plan was not immediately adopted, possibly because the Assembly was determined to abolish tithes, as the decrees of 11 August had stipulated. Yet it was to be revived, in more or less the same form, by Talleyrand, on 10 October.

A few days after Dupont's intervention, Mirabeau gave a speech whose full significance would only become apparent later, in August 1790, when the debate on the *assignats* took place (upon which occasion he defended them). In the meantime, the Assembly was discussing an article of the Constitution which stipulated that 'no tax, in kind or in money, can be levied; no loan whether manifest or disguised can be raised without the express consent of the representatives of the nation'. Everyone seemed in agreement regarding this point. Need one add, however, that this express consent ought also to apply to paper money? Mirabeau answered that it should indeed, considering the fact that the issue of paper money was at the same time a loan and a tax:

I would agree with those who describe such an issue as a theft or a loan at sword-point but I would also allow that, in exceptionally critical circumstances, a nation may be forced to have recourse to bills of state (one should banish from the language the infamous term 'paper money'), and that there would be no grave inconvenience if these bills had a free and ready representation, and if their repayment were acknowledged and certain within a defined period of time. Yet who would dare to deny that, in such circumstances, the nation alone would have the right to issue bills of state, since this is paper which one is not free to refuse? Under any other circumstances, all paper money is an offence to good faith and to the nation's liberty; in its circulation, it is a kind of plague.

From Mirabeau's ambitions to Dupont's wisdom

In the course of the debates in the Constituent Assembly regarding financial questions, we find a considerable number of orators presenting the most fantastic of schemes. In its early stages, the Assembly even went so far as to examine still more wayward projects formulated by private citizens. Subsequently, it ceased to take them into account, but disorder and lack of foresight still reigned supreme. Given such conditions, even the most important decisions were often taken in a purely improvised manner, simply because an orator's passion had managed to sway the deputies. Only a handful of men showed any steadfastness or intelligence in the prosecution of their projects. But the sheer diversity of theoretical positions, and the clash of rival ambitions, led inevitably to confrontations. Those whose views were later proven correct tended not to prevail. Indeed, it was their rivals who usually won the day, at least when they managed to represent the popular will or, in other terms, to advance measures which provided the largest measure of satisfaction for the militant element in public opinion.

Necker regularly appealed to the Chamber for new resources. His skill in the past had lain in presenting the state's finances, when he had been in control of them, in a favourable light, and in ensuring that his loans were covered. Now that he was in an unfamiliar and difficult situation, he lacked the imagination needed to win over an Assembly that was less and less prepared to come to his aid, since it saw him as the representative of the disgraced executive arm. Furthermore, he found Mirabeau blocking his path, and Mirabeau was at this period one of the most prestigious and most influential figures in the whole of the Assembly, and furthermore a man who, since he coveted Necker's place, opposed his projects and did his utmost to discredit him.

Until shortly before his death, on 2 April 1791, Mirabeau was to play a prominent role in all financial matters. However, the opinions which he expressed and the decisions which he inspired were often ambiguous and contradictory. It seems that the scheme he pursued, in all sincerity, on behalf of the nation, was the establishment of a constitutional monarchy in which the King would really have held the executive power. In order to put this scheme into effect, Mirabeau showed no hesitation in employing intrigue and he may well have been involved in machinations of an underhand nature.[6] Since personally he was in great need of funds, he ended up by reconciling his ideals and his self-interest, and so accepted the task of being secret adviser to the Court, which did not listen much to him, but which rewarded him handsomely.

It may be that certain of the positions that Mirabeau was driven to adopt were inspired by political calculation and by a wish for power, with economic motives being no more than a pretext. This is perhaps true of the obstacles he placed in Necker's path. It may also be true of the stance Mirabeau adopted in 1790, when, in spite of his previous condemnations of paper money, he was the most passionate advocate of *assignats*. Yet Mirabeau was possessed of theoretical knowledge which could have made him one of the most competent and far-sighted financial experts in the Assembly. There were many occasions in which he chose to make no use of such knowledge, preferring rather to use his remarkable talents as an orator to defend, and thereby to ensure the triumph of, false and demagogic ideas.

It was therefore Dupont who was to play the part of the expert who was competent and far-sighted but who was little heeded, because he never opted for the most facile approach. This variously gifted child prodigy had become one of the most influential of the Physiocrats. He had been one of Turgot's collaborators, and had continued to serve the royal administration after Turgot himself had retired. Elected as a deputy of the Third Estate for the bailiwick of Nemours, his approach when in the Assembly was always to give expression to an economist's point of view, his sincerity in this being such that he never sought either political advantage or personal glory.[7]

While cultivating those close to Quesnay, Dupont had made the acquaintance of the Marquis de Mirabeau, one of the most renowned of all the Physiocrats. This scientist and writer, who had a proud, authoritarian and whimsical personality, demanded of his immediate circle that they admire him and share all of his ideas. He had therefore had his elder son, Honoré Gabriel, study, under the supervision of Dupont, the science practised by his friends the economists. Unfortunately, the ambitions that he had nourished with respect to the future tribune of the people were not in the intellectual domain alone. Disappointed, so it is said, by his repellent physical appearance and, as time went on, by his unpolished manners, he bullied and maltreated him during his lifetime, even being prepared to send him to prison.

When the young Mirabeau was languishing in the dungeon of Vincennes, after a scandalous escapade, it was Dupont, who was bound to him by the closest ties of friendship, who intervened in order to persuade the Marquis to set his son at liberty. Under these circumstances, instead of showing gratitude towards his former teacher, Mirabeau displayed a great want of tact. Some time after he had regained his liberty, he tried to oust Dupont from his position as secretary of the Assembly of Notables by presenting as his own two reports that Dupont, their real author, had given him to read during his period of imprisonment. Because of this episode, during the period when Mirabeau and Dupont were both deputies in the National Assembly, their former friendship had been replaced by indifference, or even animosity.[8]

The nationalisation of church property

While the Assembly was taken up with the laborious business of drafting the articles of the future Constitution, the state's financial problems remained wholly unresolved. Necker regularly appeared before the deputies to remind them of these problems, but the solutions he proposed were nothing but temporary expedients. Finally, a solution generally held to be definitive was found. On 10 October, Talleyrand proposed that the state, in order to provide itself with the means to tackle its creditors, should appropriate the enormous wealth represented by the possessions of the Church. This notion had been current for some time. Dupont, for example, as I have already observed, had presented a project whereby the state would be allowed to use the surplus of the clergy's financial resources as surety for a loan, but the deputies baulked at the thought of undermining property rights. How could they unleash so massive an attack less than three months after they had declared that property was 'inviolable and sacred'?

It was the Bishop of Autun, Talleyrand himself, who managed to formulate arguments allowing a majority of the Assembly's members to waive their scruples. The subtle proof by means of which he justified the placing of church property 'at the disposal of the nation' rested upon the claim that its property had been entrusted to the clergy in the first place only so that it could carry out functions such as charity, assistance to the poor or education. All that one therefore had to do, to ensure that the donors' original intentions were respected, was to have the nation assume responsibility for the livelihood of those who had placed their lives in the service of religion, and to take on the obligations entailed by tenure of the property:

I am sure in my own mind that the clergy is not a proprietor such as other proprietors are, since the goods which it owns, and which it cannot dispose of, have been given not for the interests of persons but for the performance of [religious] functions.

It is clear that the Nation, holding a very extensive sway over all the bodies which exist within it, although it may not have the right to destroy the whole body of the clergy, because this body is essential for the conduct of religious services, is certainly within its rights in destroying particular aggregations of this body, if it judges them to be harmful or merely of no use, and this right with respect to their existence necessarily entails a far-reaching right over the disposal of their property.

What is no less sure is that the Nation, through the very fact that it is the guardian of the will of its founders, can and must abolish those benefices which no longer have any function; that, by a logical sequence of principles, it has the right to vest in the relevant ministers, and to divert to the profit of the public interest, the yield from property of this nature which is at present vacant, and to dispose in a similar fashion of any such properties as become vacant subsequently.

Talleyrand's proposal was the object of a heated discussion. Thouret spoke in its defence and then advanced a further justification of it. This jurist argued that those bodies which were 'moral or fictive persons' could not possess or exercise the same property rights as 'real persons or individuals'. According to Thouret, 'individuals exist independently of the law and prior to it', whereas bodies exist only by virtue of the law. Consequently, these 'bodies have no real rights through their nature' and are 'merely a fiction, an abstract conception of the law, which can create them as it pleases and which, after it created them, can modify them at will'. The Assembly therefore simply had to decree that the clergy would be 'incapable in perpetuity of having the ownership of any real estate or premises' and their properties could be placed 'at the Nation's disposal'.

Of those orators who rallied to the defence of church property, the speech which caused the most stir was undoubtedly that delivered by the abbé Maury. He accused the 'greedy speculators of the Stock Exchange', the 'wealthy money merchants',[9] of having speculated on the 'ruin of the clergy' while waiting 'for the sale of the church lands to bring about an equalisation in the value of all public effects and thus to increase of a sudden their fortunes by one-quarter'. The abbé Maury then appended to this diatribe, which in no sense invalidated Talleyrand's and Thouret's arguments, a warning to all property owners:

our possessions serve to guarantee yours. Today it is we who are under attack; but do not deceive yourselves, if we are stripped bare, your turn will come soon . . . the people will take advantage of the ensuing chaos to demand that they too have a share of the spoils, which, no matter how ancient a title of ownership there is, will not be proof against invasion. It will exercise over you all those rights which you exercise over us; it will say that it is the Nation, and that one cannot prescribe against it.

It was Mirabeau who rounded off the discussion. He advanced one last argument in favour of the project, an argument which reflected his own particular conception of democracy:

let me say, to all those prepared to contest it, that there is no legislative act that a Nation may not revoke; that it can change, when it so pleases, its laws, its constitution, its organisation and its mechanism; the same might which has created can destroy, and everything which is simply the effect of a general will must cease the moment that this will has changed.

Since no barrier whatsoever, be it natural law or constitutional rule, should therefore, in Mirabeau's opinion, be allowed to prevail against a legislative majority, the representative system becomes what Hayek has called an 'unlimited democracy',[10] and what Benjamin Constant had criticised under the name of 'unlimited sovereignty'.[11] Elected representatives, invested with all powers, might thus employ them either to impose the will of a majority, or indeed a minority, upon the remainder

of the population – which was the form of tyranny experienced at the
time of the French Revolution – or to bestow advantages upon groups
with particular interests, even if it were to harm the rest of society, as is
commonplace nowadays.

Finally, on 2 November, the Assembly voted by 586 votes to 346
(with forty abstentions) to accept Talleyrand's proposal (as amended by
Mirabeau) that all church property should be placed at the disposal of
the nation, it being '[the latter's] responsibility to meet church expenses
in a fitting manner, to furnish a livelihood for the Church's ministers and
to provide for the relief of the poor'. But the Assembly refused to
shoulder the responsibility for the clergy's debts (thereby selling the
latter's creditors short), and above all stuck to the principle, as voted on
11 August, that the tithe should be abolished. Those opposed to the
project had tried to draw the Assembly's attention to the consequences a
failure to respect the principle of a right to property might have. Their
defeat was not occasioned by the weakness of their juridical arguments
but rather by the failure of the Assembly to find any other solution to its
problems.

If the gravity of the Treasury's situation was to be assuaged, it was still
necessary to realise the value of the land which the state had confiscated,
which amounted to some two billion *livres*. Since the Treasury's debtors
could not be paid in land, this delay meant that the country's financial
problems were as pressing as ever.

On 14 November, a little after this crucial debate, Necker again
appeared before the Assembly, this time to request funds to the value of
170 million *livres*. He argued that, to find this amount, the *Caisse
d'Escompte* should be turned into a National Bank. In exchange for the
privilege of issuing 240 million *livres*' worth of paper money, the bank
would lend 170 million *livres* to the Treasury at a reduced rate of 4 per
cent, in addition to the 70 million already owed the *Caisse* by the state.
Assuming that taxes would be collected in good time (a highly improbable
hypothesis in itself), and therefore that the Treasury would not slide
still deeper into debt, this total of 240 millions could have been repaid, or
so Necker claimed, as the patriotic contributions came in and as the sale
of church property proceeded.

Mirabeau, as was only to be expected, opposed Necker's proposal. He
explained that the project was not a viable one, for a National Bank was
supposed to be able to pay for the bills that had been issued, and it lacked
the necessary coin. He also claimed that the *Caisse d'Escompte*, because it
had not paid its creditors on time, was discredited. He waxed indignant

at the idea of the state allowing special privileges and guarantees to a private institution and exclaimed, with his habitual stridency: 'Let us dare, sirs, let us dare to feel at last that our nation may raise itself up so high that it may, in the management of its credit, do without pointless intermediaries.'

Dupont was quick to respond to Mirabeau. He spoke in defence of the *Caisse d'Escompte*, which had been set up by his mentor and friend, Turgot, and he demonstrated that its paper money had suffered less depreciation than that of the state. Lavoisier, who represented the shareholders, made it plain that the financial situation was in perfectly good order. Yet, notwithstanding all this support, Necker's project was defeated. According to Dupont, the banks ought to lend to the state at market rates and receive neither privileges nor monopolies from it. According to the other view, however, the state would not have to subject its finance to the good graces of private institutions and could create its own monetary tokens as and when it needed them. The events of the following years were to prove the state only too quick to abuse its financial freedom and, when hard-pressed, to forget the most basic common sense.

Towards the end of 1789, a year that had seen so many episodes that were to prove of crucial significance for the eventual course of the Revolution, the Assembly took steps which made the issue of paper money ever more inevitable. As the financial crisis was still wholly unresolved, as Necker raised the topic again and again, and as his own Committee of Finance was predicting that, if ninety millions were not forthcoming before the end of the year, there was no point in talking of a Constitution, the Assembly as a whole had at last come to appreciate how urgent it was to take steps. A commission that had met for this purpose presented a plan which was inspired to some extent by Necker's proposals and which argued for the issue of debt acknowledgements pledged upon the yield of the future sales of church property.

Dupont, together with Talleyrand, who, alone of all those on the Committee of Finance, shared his views regarding the danger of paper money, advanced an alternative plan, which argued that the Treasury should settle with some of its creditors through the immediate sale of *biens nationaux* (national property) to the value of 100 millions. They therefore accepted that the state could dispose as it wished of church property and not only of the surplus of the revenues that the clergy received. But they still wanted the Assembly to assume responsibility for the Church's debt and to continue to collect the tithes in its place.

Once the alternative plan had been rejected, the Assembly decreed, on 19 and 21 December 1789, that an 'emergency Treasury' (*Caisse de l'Extraordinaire*) especially created for the purpose should issue 400 million *livres'* worth of *assignats* in denominations of 1,000 *livres*, bearing an interest rate of 5 per cent; 170 millions' worth of these *assignats* were then supposed to be delivered up to the *Caisse d'Escompte* as reimbursement for the advances it had made in the past and for the 80 millions it had still to advance, the remainder serving to repay the most pressing creditors.

This operation could be seen as a loan which, instead of being freely subscribed to by the public, was to be imposed upon the state's creditors. In modern terms, it could be described as a compulsory restructuring of the public debt. To lend credence to the notion that the *assignats* were secured by recently nationalised property and to reassure creditors, who saw that they were being offered a new paper money in place of an old one, it was declared that they would be received in advance as payment for lands put up for sale. This was in fact a fiction, for the exchange value of each *assignat* in terms of land was not fixed (nor, indeed, could it be). Once the *biens nationaux* were put up for auction, their paper value would grow as the *assignats* depreciated. The purchasing power of these latter was therefore in no way guaranteed.

The Assembly had therefore finally found a solution, or at least the semblance of one, to the problem which had led to its convocation and which had merely been exacerbated by the decisions it had taken during the first eight months of its existence. If, indeed, the state's finances were in so parlous a state, it was because the taxes of the *Ancien Régime* had been abolished before there had been the chance to set up a new fiscal system. So preoccupied was the Assembly with the struggle to assert its own power against that of the King and his ministers that it would seem to have shown only too little concern with such matters. Some deputies even believed that the executive's financial predicament merely increased its dependence upon themselves, and therefore did not desire any improvement in the situation. This may have been why the solution of declaring the state bankrupt, which would have established a *tabula rasa*, was not adopted.

Bankruptcy may seem a harsh and cynical measure, but one must allow that a state can only satisfy those of its citizens from whom it has borrowed by taking money from other citizens, who are generally taxpayers. At any rate, property rights can no longer be respected when the state is in debt, since, in order to repay, and therefore to respect the rights of, its creditors, it is obliged to use force in order to levy resources. In 1789, the state could not resort to taxation, the way of raising money under compulsion that was then widely accepted. It had therefore to choose its victims in some other way. All solutions involving the overt despoliation of a category of citizens were rejected, for the deputies did not wish to attract the hostility of any particular element among their constituents. The only viable victims were therefore the rich, insofar as they were few in number, a factor which considerably reduced their electoral, and hence their political, weight. They would, of course, have to pay heavily. Yet, notwithstanding what the demagogues claimed, their fortunes could not suffice to satisfy the state's needs. It was therefore the whole of the population that was to be heavily taxed by the *assignats* and by the inflation which they unleashed, albeit in an indirect, and therefore politically acceptable, manner. Thus, not only did the Revolution despoil a large number of the citizens who had wished for it, but it also provoked a crisis from which all Frenchmen suffered.

4

The 'assignats'

The Constituent Assembly had taken three crucial decisions in 1789. No sooner was it established than it *de facto* relinquished the right to collect the taxes of the *Ancien Régime*, while at the same time it announced that it would honour all past debts. At the end of the year, the *assignats* – in their first form, as state bonds – would, it was hoped, open up new opportunities for borrowing. The Treasury's financial difficulties were thus exacerbated, for the first of these decisions further reduced the state's already inadequate fiscal revenues, the second maintained in existence the heavy burden of the royal debt, whereas the third could only yield fairly limited resources.

In this situation, there was only a limited number of possible choices. The Treasury could, for example, levy the necessary taxes. Since the Revolution had been made precisely in order to oppose taxation, this possibility was never even entertained. The Treasury could, on the other hand, postpone settling up with its creditors until the advent of better days, but such a decision would certainly cause grave displeasure to the latter, and furthermore could not be regarded as a lasting solution while the country's finances were in disarray. Thirdly and lastly, it could persevere with the time-honoured method of borrowing heavily and settling old debts with what the new ones yielded, but public opinion was concerned that there be some change in policy. Not wishing to entertain any of these solutions, the Assembly was forced to find a new one, which would have to be 'politically acceptable', that is to say, a solution that would seem to require sacrifices of no one (save, perhaps, of the rich).

Continuing financial difficulties

The Constituent Assembly was quick to grasp that the December decrees would not free the state from its embarrassments. Gradually, the idea of a purely fiduciary form of finance gained ground. The merchants of Paris were the first to canvas the idea. They were obliged to accept notes proffered by their clients which had been issued by the *Caisse d'Escompte* (to the value of approximately 150 millions). The compulsory circulation of such notes was restricted to the capital, so the merchants were unable to use them to settle accounts with their suppliers from the provinces, who would not accept such a currency. They therefore wished for the compulsory circulation to be extended to the whole of France, which would have meant the creation of a genuinely national paper money.

In addition, the *Caisse d'Escompte* was subjected to fierce criticism, the argument being that the state ought not to make use of a private intermediary for issues which, it was said, it could very readily effect itself. So it was that a number of deputies formed the notion of a paper money that would be issued by the state itself, with a compulsory circulation throughout the national territory. This conception, which was most resolutely defended by the Jacobin Club, still had to overcome strong prejudices.

At the beginning of 1790, several arguments in favour of paper money became current. A deputy's speech of 26 January gives us a sense of them:

Now ... that we have a permanent and independent body, which alone has the right to pass laws, we are assured that the paper money which it might create would be contained within just limits ... that a legislator undertaking commitments in the name of the nation would honour his commitments towards the nation ... that the security that would be mortgaged there would not be used for any other purpose ... that the depredation of public funds would not take place, that the total sum of paper money shall be faithfully used for the public good, for the relief of the people, and that we shall have no fear of the so-much-dreaded disadvantages of an excessive quantity of such money and of its loss of credit.[1]

Necker was still among those opposed to the issue of paper money. On 6 March, he presented a statement to the Assembly, in which he again described, in somewhat alarming terms, the financial situation. The first two months of the year had seen the deficit climb, Necker claimed, to fifty-eight millions, and the emergency requirements for 1790 amounted to some 294 millions overall. He set out, as was his wont, a series of partial measures, involving loans, stringent economies, delays in spending and advance use of revenues etc. The Assembly, being determined to opt for thoroughgoing measures, wanted no part in these methods, which in their view were a hangover from the *Ancien Régime*. What could it do in such circumstances?

In the name of the Committee of Finance, Montesquiou, one of the first noble deputies to align himself with the Third Estate, and a man with something of a reputation as a financial expert, challenged Necker's figures. He put forward a quite different set of calculations, which he had obtained by anticipating that the normal payment of taxes would be resumed, and which were therefore wholly illusory. Montesquiou argued that one should jettison the principles of the old finance and steer 'by measures of a higher order above all the embarrassments . . . '.

These measures 'of a higher order' consisted in issuing a new form of paper money. By now a majority of the Assembly was close to acknowledging that it was necessary to resort to emergency measures. But numerous deputies, mindful of John Law's system, feared the uncontrollable effects of the unlimited circulation of paper money. In order to overcome their resistance, it was explained to them that the issue of the notes would anticipate the future revenues realised by the sale of public lands (hence the name of *assignats*) and would as a consequence have real sureties. One then had to convince them that the sales that had been announced would occur on the dates specified.

Numerous deputies were reassured by the proposal made by Bailly, Mayor of Paris, in the name of his municipality, that an arrangement be made by means of which, or so it was claimed, the *biens nationaux* serving as surety for the *assignats* would be disposed of. The town of Paris was to receive from the state properties valued at 200 millions, to be sold at auction. In the short term, its side of the agreement would involve handing over 150 millions of bonds to the state, which would exchange them for paper money at the *Caisse d'Escompte*.

On 17 March, on the basis of Bailly's proposals, the Assembly decided to transfer 400 millions' worth of *biens nationaux*, which were then to be sold at various different municipalities. There was no longer any question of receiving municipal bonds in exchange, but the operation helped to reassure the Constituents that the auctions would be successful. Thus, the fear, which some still felt, that paper money might be issued before the corresponding sales had been effected, was dispelled, and a path was cleared for the policies which Assembly was to pursue in the course of the following months.

The first debate on the 'assignats'

It was on 9 April that Anson, who was believed to be an expert and a practitioner, and who was therefore someone esteemed by the Assembly, proposed, in the name of the Committee of Finance, that the *assignats* created by the decrees of 19 and 21 December 1789 should from then on have 'value as currency throughout the kingdom' and 'should be treated as hard cash [*espèces sonnantes*] by all recipients both public and private'. An official declaration of this kind was necessary for, since John Law's bankruptcy, only 'hard cash' (that is, metal coins) had been allowed in circulation. Thus, the Assembly, by an act of will, was attributing to the paper money whose fabrication it had undertaken, but that people were reluctant to accept, the characteristics of gold or of silver.

Anson's project also specified that the *assignats* should bear an interest rate that had been reduced to 4.5 per cent (it stood in the end at 3 per cent), that they would serve first of all for the withdrawal from circulation of the notes of the *Caisse d'Escompte*, which were posing such problems for the merchants of Paris, and that they would be publicly destroyed as and when they were received in payment for *biens nationaux*.

The debates on this proposal lasted up until 17 April. The supporters of the measures proposed by the Committee of Finance adopted and elaborated upon the arguments which Anson had advanced. In their view, three major arguments could be marshalled to justify the transformation of the *assignats* into means of payment:

(1) The paper money should rescue the state from its financial embarrassment, by giving it the means to provide for its immediate needs. It was in fact necessary to repay the loans advanced by the *Caisse d'Escompte* and to cover the current deficit, while at the same time relinquishing any prepayments. This was of course the main reason why the Assembly wished to issue *assignats*. According to some relatively recent estimates, the monthly average tax revenue in 1790 bordered upon fifteen millions as against around fifty-five millions in outgoings (see, in figure 3, p. 72, the monthly comparison of returns and expenditure for the years 1790 and 1791).[2] The state therefore lacked forty millions a month to balance its budget, and the *assignats* represented virtually the sole available means to achieve this. In reality, however, it was at best a temporary measure, for, unless substantial economies were made and unless the collection of taxes was accelerated (and no steps to this effect were in fact taken), the projected issue of 400 millions would be used up in a little less than a year. However, since the sheer size of the deficit was not admitted, the deputies could not understand just how urgent the Committee of Finance's request was.

(2) 'The *assignats* should make up for the scarcity of cash' and 'revive

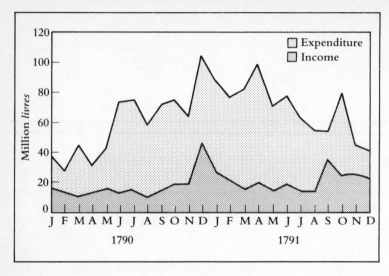

Figure 3 Monthly state expenditure and income for the years 1790 and 1791 (source: F. Braesch)

trade and manufactures, by reviving a circulation which has languished because of the lack of means to sustain it'. It was certainly true that the substitution of a national paper money that was accepted everywhere for the notes of the *Caisse d'Escompte*, which only had compulsory circulation in Paris, would resolve the problems affecting the capital's trade with the provinces. But orators such as Pétion also claimed that the bringing into circulation of the *assignats* would also relaunch the economy which, as we have seen, was stagnating.[3]

(3) The proposed operation should serve to bind all citizens to the public good, for 'each would wish to see an acceleration in the sale of public and church lands and property'. This argument, which was anyway somewhat obscure, actually hid another, more significant one, namely, that the purchasers of *biens nationaux* would have no interest in seeing the reactionaries triumph, for they would confiscate these newly acquired properties. In order to defend their own interests, these purchasers would therefore become defenders of the Revolution. The *assignats* would, it was thought, serve to promote the sale of *biens nationaux*.

The supporters of *assignats* added to these three major justifications a number of other subsidiary ones, whose purpose was to reassure particular categories of waverers. Those mindful of John Law's system, who feared a loss of confidence in paper money, were informed that the latter would have a 'special mortgage mortgaged upon particular properties'. This made it different from Law's paper money based on non-existent gold mines. This was of course a completely specious argument, for the value of a currency is only genuinely guaranteed if its holder is assured that he can exchange it against a quantity of goods that is known and specified in advance. So it was that, in the period of the gold standard, francs and other coinages could be converted at any moment into a specific weight of precious metal. However, in the case of *assignats*, it was indeed specified that they would be accepted as payment for demesne lands, but since the exchange rate was not fixed in advance (and could not be either), it would deteriorate as the paper money proliferated and as its value fell.

Those who feared that too much money might enter into circulation were again reassured that the slow rate at which the *assignats* were fabricated, together with their periodic destruction, which would be undertaken as and when sales were effected, would forestall any 'glut'. As things turned out, it was the sale of the public lands which was slow, whereas the fabrication of *assignats* proceeded apace.

The Assembly contained a number of orators who reckoned that the Committee of Finance's proposal was inadequate, among them Martineau, a future Montagnard. He wanted the issue to be of 800 million *livres* and he wished the paper money to carry no interest, for it would, he said, 'excite greed, do nothing to promote confidence and give rise to speculation', and would cost the state eighteen millions a year. To convince his colleagues, since they were not reassured by the territorial security bestowed upon the *assignats* and persisted in their fear that they would depreciate in the future, he informed them that 'paper money, in times of despotism, is dangerous; it fosters corruption. But, in a nation which has been responsible for constituting itself, and which itself supervises the issue of banknotes, which determines the proportions and uses, this danger no longer exists.' One can thus see the reappearance, on the Left of the Assembly, of an idea which had already been advanced at the time of the discussion on the National Bank, towards the end of 1789, which implied that the representatives of the people, because they were supposed to work for the good of the people, could not help but behave wisely, whereas private persons, impelled by their egoism, acted against the general interest. Anson, in a bid to wring consent from the Assembly, had likewise employed a Rousseauan argument towards the end of his speech. 'Everything suggests,' he declared, 'that the circulation of *assignats* is the best of all operations; indeed, it is the freest, because it is founded upon the general will.'

Those who spoke out against the Committee of Finance's proposal were generally on the Right of the Assembly, among them, the abbé Maury and Cazalès, both of whom were remarkable orators, and Boisgelin, Archbishop of Aix. All three, who were subsequently to be émigrés, had placed their talents at the service of Church and King. Their speeches, being discredited in advance, could not therefore hope to convince. They were suspected in fact of camouflaging with spurious arguments their wish to check the sale of church property. Nevertheless, their reasoning was sound, and their formulations prophetic. They explained that the *assignats* were necessarily going to depreciate, thus occasioning a rise in price of basic commodities, the ruin of the state's creditors and the impoverishment of the workers. Indeed, since the money that would finally be used to pay the taxes would be totally depreciated, it would even bring about the downfall of the Treasury. As far as these spokesmen of the Right were concerned, the issue of *assignats* was contrary to property rights and opposed to the real interests of the state, and therefore essentially immoral. In addition, Cazalès used the debate as an opportunity to demand that the power of the monarchy be re-established, since it alone, in his view, would be capable of restoring order and confidence:

Credit depends upon the foundations of government, upon the liquidation of debt and upon the collection of taxes. So long as the people is armed from one end of the kingdom to the other, so long as you have not granted the executive all of the powers that it requires, you will never be able to guarantee the collection of taxes. If you do not hasten to re-establish the authority of the King, no authority will manage to force the provinces to pay . . .

I propose to put a weighty truth before you: disorder will continue for so long as the King is not an integral part of the legislature; for what confidence can one have in an Assembly which has no limits outside of itself and whose decrees as a consequence are mere resolutions, which may be changed today by the same authority that formulated them yesterday? . . . How can one place much hope in the success of a paper currency which will not be protected, as was that of the *Caisse d'Escompte*, by the interests of the bankers?

For his part, Dupont de Nemours, who a few months later was to become one of the most passionate opponents of paper money, adopted a more nuanced position with respect to this first issue. He began by pointing out that the state could not create value simply by printing paper; and then went on to advocate the creation of *assignats* without compulsory circulation but with a guaranteed repayment in metal coin. Fundamentally, he was still defending the position that it was crucial to tackle the state's financial difficulties by means of what today we would term a 'restructuring' of the debt. He was no more heeded than the abbé Maury or Cazalès had been, and the Assembly adopted Anson's proposal, with a few minor modifications, on 17 April.

It is of some interest to note how, on the margins of the strictly economic debate, an exchange of views concerning the limits of the Constitution took place. For Cazalès, *assignats* were immoral because, he believed, they would bring about the ruin of those who had placed their trust in the state; as we have seen, he wished the Assembly, by placing limits upon the power which it granted itself, to forbid itself the right to effect arbitrary spoliations and to reawaken the confidence that the people ought to have in it. Pétion, who was later to be the Girondin Mayor of Paris, replied that, if the safety of the people required it, paper money could not be immoral! He too entertained a totalitarian conception of power, such as was to culminate in the dictatorship of the Committee of Public Safety (and, as far as Pétion himself was concerned, in death under particularly terrible circumstances). According to him, the deputies, who spoke in the name of the people, embodied its will, were acquainted with its interests and ought to hold all the powers in order to act in its best interests. Anyone on the outside (the King) or on the inside of the Assembly (the Right) who was opposed to the will of the majority could only be an enemy of the people.

Another momentous decision was taken by the Assembly in April, this time concerning the tithe. It was decreed that the latter was to be abolished once and for all, and the Assembly thus relinquished an annual income of over 100 million *livres* at a time when the state was beset by severe financial difficulties. The clergy's debts were upon this same occasion defined as 'national', the greater share of church property being entrusted to the various provincial administrations, with the state assuming responsibility for church expenses and for the livelihood of ministers.

A little later, on 14 May, the Assembly implemented the decree previously decided upon regarding the sale of 400 millions' worth of public lands. Because the deputies feared that the sale might not go well, and because it was their declared purpose to help the less well-to-do classes, the buyers were able to take advantage of extremely favourable terms. After an initial payment which ranged, depending upon the nature of the property involved, from twelve to thirty per cent of the auction price, periods of twelve years, coupled with an interest rate of five per cent, were permitted for the settlement of the balance.

The second issue of 'assignats'

While the Assembly was debating the advisability or otherwise of issuing *assignats*, Necker was still keeping it informed of his financial difficulties. On 17 April, he had received an advance of twenty millions, followed by another of the same amount on 11 May. Each time the deputies protested and complained that they had been warned too late of the Treasury's real needs. In the end, however, they complied with his demands. In the space of six months, the Assembly voted him advances totalling 215 million *livres*, of which a significant part derived from new monetary issues. It is thus clear that, from the moment they were invented, the *assignats* were earmarked for current expenditure.

No matter how optimistic Necker, as usual, seemed, and no matter how confidently he foresaw an end to his difficulties, no one was convinced any more. It was becoming plain just how massive the Treasury's needs really were. The idea was put forward of making a sale of *biens nationaux* far larger in scale than had been decided upon in April. On 9 July, the Assembly, taking into consideration 'that the alienation of the public lands is the best means of extinguishing a large part of the public debt, of assisting agriculture and industry and of bringing about the enlargement of the national wealth through the division of these *biens nationaux* into private properties', decreed that, aside from the forests and properties whose enjoyment was reserved for the King, all national domains could be alienated. Thus, a surety was prepared for any future issues of paper money, a thing already contemplated by a number of deputies.

In order to understand the exact state of the kingdom's finances, and in order to take the appropriate decisions in response, the Assembly had asked the Committee of Finance for a report on this topic. It was Montesquiou who presented it, on 27 August 1790. According to him, the state's total debt amounted to 4,241 million *livres* of which 2,339 millions was for the invested debt (that is to say, consisting of life annuities or perpetual annuities, whose capital would never be reimbursed) and 1,902 for the debt that was redeemable (and therefore reimbursable) in the more or less long term. The corresponding interest charges would have been 167.7 and 89.8 millions per year respectively.

Taking amortisation into account, the Treasury would thus have to disburse annually 281 million *livres* in charges on loans, to which would have to be added the other public expenses of a total of 360 millions per year (including, for instance, church expenses and ecclesiastical pensions, which were now the responsibility of the state), in short, a total of 641 million *livres*.

Montesquiou observed that, under the *Ancien Régime*, contributions (including the tithes) never amounted to more than 630 millions. Even if one were to take into consideration the fact that, under the new régime, those who had formerly held privileges would be taxed for some thirty-two millions, the charges which would be imposed on the larger part of the nation seemed much too heavy. How could they be reduced? Speaking on behalf of the Committee of Finance, Montesquiou advocated the sale of church property, which would liquidate the 1,902 millions of the redeemable debt and thereby reduce interest payments by some 89.5 millions per year. He envisaged two ways of realising the value of church property, and called upon the Assembly to choose between them. It could accept, as payment for church property, either all debts indiscriminately binding upon the state (which debts, for technical reasons, would have been previously changed into a single instrument, named *quittances de finances*) or *assignats* with compulsory currency bearing no interest, and which would be previously issued for precisely this purpose. Montesquiou was quite clearly more favourably disposed towards the second solution.

Necker then drafted a report warning the Assembly of the dangers attendant upon any further issues of *assignats*. On 27 August, before anyone could have read this report, Mirabeau mounted the tribune. In a very long speech, he went back on his earlier position and urged the deputies to approve the measures which Montesquoiu had proposed. He went on to dismiss all objections and to assert that the April issue of *assignats* had not given rise to the catastrophes that had been predicted (which was in fact untrue, for, as Necker pointed out in his report, the paper money had already, in the space of a few months, lost from 5 to 6 per cent of its value with respect to the coinage). Next, with a blend of appeals to patriotic motives and to economic considerations, he presented an interminable series of sophisms which succeeded, regrettably, in taking in a large part of his audience. For, as the deputy Bergasse-Laziroule observed, 'abstract truths not being within the scope of all men, orators can easily gain a hold upon them, corrupt or mystify them as they will'.

Mirabeau began by defending the notion, which had frequently been advanced during the debate in April, that the efficient operation of the economy required the circulation of a certain quantity of money. Now, he observed, if the present quantity of coin was inadequate, the new issue of *assignats* would instill 'movement in business' and 'revive industry'. Mirabeau rejected the idea that there was any risk of an excess of coin, for 'the overflow ... would naturally reverse itself in the payment of the debt contracted through the acquisition of the *biens nationaux*.' He then claimed that, 'wherever a holder of *assignats* is to be found', the Assembly would be able to count upon a defender of the measures it had taken – whereas it was actually more probable that such a holder would try to get rid of a form of money which did not inspire confidence, instead of striving to reinforce it.

Finally, he claimed that, for church property to be easily sold, one had to bring it within the reach of the 'less well-to-do' citizens by making easily available the means that had been designed for its purchase, namely, the *assignats*. This argument, which played upon the egalitarianism of the Left of the Assembly, was certainly the most flawed of all those advanced by Mirabeau. The tribune of the people pretended to be unaware that in order to acquire public lands it was not enough for an individual to have banknotes come into his possession, for he had also to be in a position to use them for such a purchase rather than for bread or for other basic commodities. Any purchase in fact presupposes the possession of real resources; the monetary tokens used at the moment of exchange are only a particular form of such possession and can always be obtained by surrender of some reserve assets. Mirabeau's reasoning had therefore involved a confusion between wealth, which is measured in monetary units, and the monetary tokens employed at the moment at which transactions are sealed, which was precisely the point that Dupont was to make in his intervention of 25 September. 'It is not coin itself,' he remarked, 'that you need, it serves merely as an instrument and as a balance. One buys only with accumulated capital; it is therefore such capital that should be used in the sale of *biens nationaux*.'

Mirabeau's speech was greeted with loud applause and continued to have an effect upon the Assembly throughout the very lively debate which followed. It ended with the reading of Necker's report, which, as had been expected, was against a massive issue of *assignats*. But the minister had by now lost the last vestiges of his former popularity, and faced with a choice between his recommendations and those of Mirabeau (who still coveted his place), the Assembly's decision was a foregone conclusion.

Yet those opposed to *assignats* did not lay down their arms so easily. They lacked neither arguments nor the will to defend them. Thus, speaking before the Society of 1789, a club founded to check the growing influence of the Jacobins, Lavoisier demonstrated that the real value of the church property available for the reimbursement of the debt was barely in excess of 1,050 millions.[4] Quoting David Hume, he went on to predict that an issue of 2,000 million *assignats*, doubling the quantity of money in circulation, would bring about an 'increase in the value of all things', and that, with French manufactures then no longer being able 'to compete with foreign workshops', national trade would be 'altogether ruined' and metal coin would flee abroad.

Lavoisier was not the only one to think that Montesquiou had massively exaggerated the amount of the redeemable debt, probably so as to convince the Assembly of the need to carry through the measures proposed. If one dismisses the notion that the issue of the *assignats* was a manoeuvre designed to line the pockets of a few speculators (although certain deputies were quite prepared, as we shall see, to entertain it), it becomes plain that they were designed to finance the Treasury's current expenditure. By means of them, Mirabeau, Montesquiou and the Left of the Assembly sought to avoid any return to harsh fiscal policies, which would of course have been very unpopular.

Another voice from outside the Assembly that was raised in opposition to the issue of *assignats* was that of Condorcet, who noted with irony that there was a contradiction involved in claiming both that the *assignats* would be rapidly withdrawn from circulation (which could never occur, given the twelve-year delays in payment granted to the prospective purchasers of *biens nationaux*), and that they would serve to relaunch agriculture, industry and trade, which would clearly require a certain length of time.

But the most important debates took place within the Assembly itself, where the confrontation between advocates and opponents of the *assignats* was to last up until 29 September. The rule was that each speaker holding forth on a particular subject should speak from the tribune once and once only. Since the agenda was a very crowded one, the discussion entitled 'the liquidation of the public debt' alternated with a number of others and as a consequence dragged on for a long time. During the first days of September, it took only second place in the debates on finance, the star figures in both camps holding back until later.

Those in favour of *assignats* reiterated the arguments which had already been aired in April. They claimed that the *assignats* would compensate for the scarcity of coin and revive trade and industry (a loss of confidence was impossible, for they would benefit from a special mortgage), and that they would bind all citizens to the Revolution. Montesquiou and Mirabeau had recalled these arguments and refined them also. Their new argument consisted in linking the issue of the *assignats* to the rapidity of sale of the *biens nationaux*, which was itself necessary if the burden of taxation was to be lightened.

A number of different speakers added further variations to the repertoire of arguments established by the supporters of paper money. The abbé Gouttes advocated *assignats* in smaller denominations, in order to 'help the people to make small purchases'. Rewbell seconded him, explaining that, if the *assignats* issued in April had not held their value, it was because they could not be used to satisfy routine, everyday needs. Then Anson, elaborating upon this last point, advocated interest-free *assignats*; in this way, he said, they would circulate more freely, and being more useful, they would be more highly valued. We of course know, as people already knew at the time, that the reverse is true. The increment of liquidity conferred upon a financial instrument by the circulation of small denominations and by the absence of interest merely serves to accelerate depreciation. Let me add one further sophism, taken from the editorial of the *Moniteur Universel* for 17 September 1790, which also reiterated a number of the above-mentioned speakers' claims: 'This new currency, being more widespread, will cause the rate of interest to bend; someone who today places his money at 7, 8 or 10 per cent will find no more borrowers than if he placed it at 4 or 5 per cent.' A few years later, the interest rates would be from 7, 8 and 10 per cent ... per month![5]

Pétion was not concerned with financial logic, no matter how unsound. Lacking sufficiently persuasive arguments of his own, he undertook to discredit his adversaries, whom he accused of acting out of self-interest rather than from conviction:

Do you know who has something to fear from the *assignats*? The bankers and the speculators. What would then become of speculations? Do you know who has something to fear from the *assignats*? A Minister of Finance. Why? Because once the state's creditors are paid off, the minister would no longer have a hold over them.

Those opposed to *assignats* saw that the inflation of prices would undoubtedly provide them with their main argument, which would also be considerably strengthened by the depreciation observable since April. It is worth noting, among the footnotes of history, the fact that Brillat-Savarin, the future author of *La Physiologie du goût*, at the time a deputy of the Third Estate, was one of the first to employ this argument. Then came the turn of Boislandry, a merchant from Versailles, whose astuteness and command of financial theory enabled him to dismiss the allegations of his adversaries. He used the monetary histories of several other countries as the basis for a number of lucid predictions about the inevitable consequences of the proposed issue of *assignats*:

In America, during the last war, Congress put a considerable quantity of paper money into circulation. This paper money, after having fought a vain battle against public distrust, was annihilated, so to speak, by itself, in the hands of the property-owners, to the extent that 100 dollars of paper money are now barely worth five dollars in coin. The Danes, the Swedes and the Russians also have paper currency. In all these nations, it has ... paralysed money; everywhere it has impeded trade and industry ... Paper money in Sweden, even though it was mortgaged against royal properties, was so debased, during a certain period of time, that a ducat in coin was worth ten ducats in paper money; yet it was a paper money based on land values, similar in all respects to the one you are advocating.

But the debate did not really come to life until a few days later, when Barnave, one of the leaders of the Left, went on the offensive and denounced the publication of a pamphlet aimed against the *assignats*, which he described as 'inflammatory'. Dupont immediately acknowledged that he was the author of the pamphlet in question and managed to read the Assembly his *Effets des assignats sur le prix du pain, par un ami du peuple,*[6] so that they might appreciate its virtues. Explaining that 'the *assignats* are good for the rich, who have many debts to pay' but bad for the people, who have to pay more for bread, he won a vote of thanks from the *partie droite* while the *partie gauche*, in some embarrassment, asked that Barnave's accusations be disregarded and the agenda followed.

Talleyrand spoke on 18 September. His speech, a model of clarity and pithiness, and a genuine display of economic theory, still impresses us today. He demonstrated that *assignats* were not needed for the selling of public lands; that they would have the effect of making basic commodities dearer, and since the latter were rising in price at a faster rate than were salaries, they would 'impoverish every kind of labourer, and consequently damage manufactures and the prosperity of the country areas'; that the state would suffer a loss, since taxes would be paid in devalued *assignats*; and, finally, that, in its foreign exchanges, France would have to pay for what it imported in gold, but would be paid in devalued paper money for its exports.

Since the Assembly wanted to know what the various provincial towns felt about the advisability of issuing *assignats*, a somewhat sterile debate was conducted in the course of the next few days. It seems as if, in reality, the hostility towards the *assignats* was general. As Marcel Marion has observed, merchants and industrialists were not the only ones to express their repugnance for paper money. Indeed, numerous administrative bodies and private individuals, who were either consulted or spontaneously made their opinions known, were in unanimous agreement on virtually every point. Yet the supporters of the *assignats* managed to produce contradictory petitions, accused their adversaries of being unpatriotic and thus sowed confusion.

The popular press, as one would expect, supported the Left of the Assembly, and accused those who were opposed to the project of wishing to restore the *Ancien Régime*. It was in very much this spirit that Loustalot wrote in his *Les Révolutions de Paris*, the best-selling newspaper of the day:

The aristocrats' party blushes when one mentions the *assignats*, whereas the patriots see it as the sole means of saving the state. The bankers, the money-changers and, in general, all the speculators of Paris are doing their utmost to resist this issue. From this we conclude that this operation must indeed be highly advantageous to the people, since so many who are its natural enemies are sparing no effort or difficulty to oppose it.

The debate became serious again on 25 September, when Dupont mounted the tribune. He spoke dispassionately and with great rigour. According to him, his adversaries' arguments could be summarised as follows: 'We have exigible debts and we must settle them; we have public lands to sell, and we must get rid of them at the highest possible price.' But, Dupont observed, by issuing *assignats* the nation was not really paying its debts: 'In forcing your creditors to exchange an interest-bearing proof of debt for another which bears no interest, you will have borrowed, as M. Mirabeau has said, at sword-point.' He then went on to explain that the issue of the *assignats* was in no way capable of facilitating the sale of public lands, that one does not buy with currency, which is merely an instrument for the settlement of a transaction, but with accumulated capital. Finally, he demonstrated that, in exchanging a paper money which did not bear interest for one that did, taxes would not in reality be reduced. This apparent saving of 100 millions of interest meant in reality that, interest no longer being paid, a financial burden which had been borne by everyone now fell on the shoulders of the state's creditors only. It was they who, being the losing party in the affair, would pay the 'tax' which the *assignats* seemed to be eliminating.

Numerous other speakers had already claimed, before Dupont, that paper money would cause prices to rise. Dupont began by presenting a theoretical justification of this point before launching into an account of the more complex financial developments. More particularly, he explained the mechanisms which enabled shrewd speculators to use devalued *assignats* to buy *biens nationaux* for next to nothing. Events were to prove him right, as huge fortunes were amassed by these same means. He also announced that, in the last analysis, the Assembly would be asked for much more than the issue of 1,900 billions that was necessary for the settlement of the exigible debt. In this case too, Dupont was to be proved right.

Dupont's line of reasoning was very probably far too complex for the great majority of Constituents to understand. The previous speaker to mount the tribune, Custine, had doubtless been much more to their liking, for he had left them in no doubt as to who their adversaries were: 'Should this Assembly, which has destroyed aristocracy in all its forms, show mercy towards these capitalists, these cosmopolitans, who know of no fatherland but the one where wealth can be accumulated?' Dupont, however, warned his colleagues against simplistic arguments and facile rhetoric: 'Bad logicians have committed more crimes involuntarily than bad men have by design.'

Mirabeau was better placed than anyone to understand the meaning of the words of his former tutor. He was also very probably anxious about the effect that such words might, in spite of everything, have. The rule was, as I have already pointed out, that each speaker should only comment once upon a given subject. However, so strong a hold did the deputy from Aix-en-Provence have over the Assembly that he managed to mount the tribune a second time. He spoke at great length, probably for several hours, with all his habitual flair and lyricism. His speech was littered with unfounded assertions ('it has to be allowed that an *assignat* or an equivalent portion of *biens nationaux* are one and the same thing'), threats ('I number among the enemies of the state, I regard as entertaining criminal intentions towards the nation, anyone who seeks to shake this sacred base of all our projects for [national] regeneration [the *assignats*]'), and jokes ('you are told that the existing *assignats* are already hampering circulation. Perhaps those who actually own *assignats* will be so good as to tell us wherein precisely their embarrassment lies'). These facile rhetorical tricks were often greeted with rapturous applause. When Mirabeau returned to his seat, it was plain that he had won the day.

Bergasse-Laziroule, a little-known deputy of the Third Estate from Foix, took Mirabeau's place at the tribune. He too put forward the by now familiar arguments of those who were opposed to paper money, which, though sound enough, were not likely to win round an Assembly whose preference was for lyrical flights. *Assignats* would, he maintained, drive coin abroad, produce inflation of prices, and would despoil the state's creditors, etc. Bergasse-Laziroule showed great perspicacity for his time in emphasising the destructive consequences the inevitable depreciation of paper money would have upon trade, industry and agriculture. But the real interest of his speech lay in the fact that he was prepared to doubt the honesty of the supporters of *assignats*:

The *assignats* were not dreamed up in order to settle the exigible debt or to sell the *biens nationaux*. On the contrary, the exigible debt was an ingenious invention whose purpose was to justify the introduction of the *assignats*, a project already under consideration. All the money changers of the capital had been set to work; a huge quantity of public financial assets had been appropriated, bought on credit at a loss of 20 or 30 per cent, and it had been found advantageous and convenient to be reimbursed for it at par by the public Treasury. This is the patriotism they have been trying to drum into us; this is the secret of paper money.

As coincidence would have it, a deputy who was no relation but who was also called Bergasse, and who represented the seneschalsy of Lyons, had levelled a similar set of accusations in April. There is of course little likelihood of our ever knowing whether these allegations were or were not well founded, yet, be this as it may, they were in fact phrased in the same calumnious tone as the supporters of the *assignats* had themselves adopted. The latter often warded off arguments drawn from law and economic theory with personal attacks which cast doubt upon the sincerity and disinterestedness of their adversaries.

The crucial debate upon the liquidation of the public debt could not be concluded until one of the great orators of the Right had made his intervention. It was the abbé Maury who responded to Mirabeau's speech. The arguments he advanced were cogent, but the Assembly turned a deaf ear to them, its suspicion being that any attack upon *assignats* was simply a cover for a defence of church property. His style, however, was suited to an audience that was more responsive to a hectoring tone than to reasoning. Waving two of John Law's banknotes above his head, he exclaimed: 'Here it is, this fatal paper, soaked in the tears and the blood of our fathers; I have seen great piles of it. Consider these notes as so many beacons on reefs, if you would avoid shipwreck.'

The abbé Maury was wasting his breath, for after a number of minor incidents, the Constituent Assembly voted, on 29 September, by 508 votes to 423, as follows:

The National Assembly decrees that the state's non-invested debt, together with that of the former clergy, shall be paid off, according to a sequence to be specified, in *assignat* currency without interest. No more than 1,200 million *assignats*, including the 400 million already decreed, will be in circulation. Those *assignats* which revert to the Emergency Treasury will be burnt. No new fabrication [of these notes] will be permitted without a decree of the legislative body, on condition that they not exceed the value of the *biens nationaux*, and that there be no more than 1,200 millions in circulation.

Two months after it had been decided, by virtue of this decree, to issue a considerable quantity of paper money, on 27 November, the Assembly proceeded to impose the 'civil oath' upon practising clergy. Thus, in the course of 1790, a year which historians generally regard as the happiest or quietest year of the Revolution, two decisions were taken which, by occasioning famine and by stirring up religious passions, were to have a decisive influence upon subsequent events.

A few years later, while drafting his own account of the Revolution, Necker explained why the Constituent Assembly had had recourse, against his own recommendations, to paper money. Whatever the ex-minister's own errors had been, his point of view is worthy of our consideration:

When all resources were exhausted, the Assembly created its paper money, which became famous under the title of *assignats*, and which, by further extending the facility for spending without receiving, made the running of finances so easy and so convenient. The government was then still less disposed to put pressure upon the tax-payers and to demand sacrifices of them; it was then that the executive's consideration and strength were no longer put to any difficult test; and so it was that the establishment of a fictitious currency, through its freeing of the administration from the imperious yoke of reality, enabled the legislators to abandon themselves with more confidence to their abstractions; and the need for money, so crude an embarrassment, never again served to distract them from their lofty thoughts.[7]

5

The finances of the Constituent Assembly

By making church property available to the nation, and by deciding to issue 1,200 million *livres* of *assignats*, the Constituent Assembly seemed to have provided itself with the means to settle the state's debts and thereby to improve public finances. Yet a fundamental problem had still to be resolved. Since the assembly had at the very first abolished the fiscal system of the *Ancien Régime*, it had to create a new one from the fragments. This task was to occupy it for a good part of the year prior to the adoption of a Constitution and the election of a new chamber. During this period, it had also to complete the decrees of August 1789 and thus finish the liberalisation of the country's economy, as well as its juridical unification. Finally, its almost total substitution of itself for the executive meant that it was responsible for dealing with the already disastrous consequences of its first monetary decisions.

The new fiscal system

The *cahiers de doléances* of 1789 were unanimous in identifying the collection of taxes as the tyranny most responsible for the people's sufferings. In many cases, its abuses were interpreted in the same fashion, namely, that the ministers, being free to do with the collected taxes as they wished, spent them in a wholly arbitrary manner, taking no account of the fact that the money came from the tax-payers. In order to fuel their extravagance, they invented a virtually infinite series of irritating and vexatious new taxes which weighed heavily upon the peasantry.

No matter which of the three orders they belonged to, many members of the Constituent Assembly were agreed that there was a highly simple ideal to be followed in this matter, namely, the establishment of equality before the tax-collector, so that each person contri-

buted to the common charges in proportion to his income. As Marcel
Marion has observed:

the replacement of the old taxes, which had been inequitable, assessed unjustly
and levied with a degree of harshness, with moderate contributions, which were
free of all arbitrariness, equitably distributed across the whole of the nation and
among all inhabitants without exception, was certainly one of the greatest
benefits that the country was entitled to expect.

However, it was less easy to put this ideal into practice than one might at
first have supposed. This was because, first of all, their illusions regarding
the benefits of the Constitution and the true nature of man were such as
to lead numerous deputies astray. Since citizens were presumed from
now on to be devoting themselves naturally to the public good, many of
the projects put before the Assembly were wanting in even the
elementary measures of constraint and control which are required for a
fiscal system to work efficiently. A deputy by the name of Vernier, for
example, mounted the tribune in order to explain that 'under the *Ancien
Régime* . . . the French showed no scruple in hiding their property from
the property tax . . . But today, tax will be regarded as a sacred debt, the
hiding of one's property as theft from the state, and the denunciation of
others as a virtue.' Secondly, the creation of the Emergency Treasury
and of the *assignats* had endowed the Treasury with massive financial
resources. So long as the latter were diverted from their original object,
the repayment of the redeemable debt, it therefore became possible to
prevaricate without having to ask the country to make such sacrifices as
would be necessary for the balancing of the state's budget. Finally, given
the heterogeneity of the old taxes, the proliferation of privileges and
exemptions and the unpopularity of the various officials and collectors,
an entirely new organisation of fiscal administration was necessary. The
old structures had been wholly rejected by public opinion, and it would
therefore have been mistaken to count upon a clear and just tax being
established in the short term.

The Assembly only began to be genuinely concerned with fiscal
reform on 18 August 1790. On that day, La Rochefoucauld at long last
presented his report, in the name of the Committee of Taxation. Once
they had been discussed, amended and modified, the propositions
contained in this report were turned into decrees during the last months
of 1790, becoming operative, or so it was hoped, in the fiscal year of
1791. This haste was to prove just as irksome as the long months of delay
that had preceded it.

The cornerstone of the Constituent Assembly's new fiscal policy was the land tax (*contribution foncière*, or simply *foncière*). Since the greater part of the country's income derived from the land, it seemed only natural that the latter should be taxed most heavily. However, contrary to the Physiocrats' wishes, it was not to take the whole weight of it. Indeed, the Assembly anticipated creating, in addition, a tax on personal property, a *patente* (tax paid by merchants and professional men) and a series of indirect taxes.

The land tax had the peculiar – indeed, for a late twentieth-century observer, the bizarre – feature of being an assessed tax. Each year, the legislative authorities were supposed to fix a total levy and then allocate it in proportion to the revenues of all the landed properties of the nation. Thus, in theory, this tax corresponded perfectly to the principles of justice so dear to the Assembly. In practice, however, it was quite otherwise. Indeed, the real incomes of the French were not known, since the taxes of the *Ancien Régime* had been assessed in relation to incomes which were fictitious and bore no relation to reality. Besides, no cadastral survey existed either. How, in such circumstances, could one decide who was supposed to pay what?

It was left to the municipalities to answer this question. Both Turgot's project and that of Dupont had reserved a special place for local assemblies in the administration of the country, and the Constituent Assembly, adopting this same decentralised conception, did likewise. A law of 14 December 1789 decided what their function and mode of election was to be. More particularly, this law set up the Councils General of the communes, which were elected by direct suffrage by all active citizens, and which were invested with extensive powers.[1] The departments, on the other hand, which were created a little later, were to be governed by Councils elected by indirect suffrage and were likewise granted serious responsibilities. Between the communes and the departments were the districts and the cantons, whose functions were much more limited.

The task of establishing the basis of the land tax was therefore left to the municipalities. Had they been given the time, they might in theory have succeeded in determining how the taxation of land should have been assessed. But it was wholly unrealistic to demand of them, especially in the case of the village municipalities (whose members were often virtually illiterate), that they carry out the extremely complex calculations that were required for the assessment of revenues from the land, by following rules which were only given their definitive formulation after several months of vacillation.

Notwithstanding the claims made by La Rochefoucauld in his report, resistance to such taxation did not cease just because the abuses had done. The fact that the taxes were now assessed and collected by those elected by the nation did not prevent extortion or injustice on the one hand or fraud and ill-will on the other. The country municipalities were in no hurry to concern themselves with public matters, preferring instead to work in the fields. When they did agree to carry out their civic duties, they often subordinated the general interest to their own private concerns. As a consequence, tax registers were drawn up only very belatedly. According to Marcel Marion, on 19 May 1792, only 27,920 communes out of a total of around 40,000 had completed their work. At the end of June 1792, the Doubs department was the only one to have finished its registers, whereas twenty or so others had not even begun theirs. Another consequence was that the registers did not correspond to real incomes, which were, of course, very much underestimated. How could it have been otherwise, since one had depended upon the good faith of those whose interest lay in deceiving the state? The members of the municipalities seemed much keener to win the favour of those they administered by allowing them to defraud rather than to cooperate with the tax-collection system; they therefore drew up the registers on a purely arbitrary basis, generally by scaling down the incomes of tax-payers, and sometimes by scaling them up and allowing countless deceptions to go undetected or unchallenged.

As the land tax was an assessed tax, it would not have mattered so much if all the incomes that were registered had been scaled down in the same proportions. But this was not how it turned out, for fraud and dissimulation were not evenly distributed. The victims of the system were those tax-payers who, either by choice or by force of circumstance, were the most frank in their declarations. The arbitrary taxation of the *Ancien Régime* was thus succeeded by another, equally arbitrary system. The project of an equitable fiscal system was stillborn.

For the year 1791, the Assembly reckoned that the tax on land would bring in at least 300 millions (once the appropriate amount had been deducted for the costs of collecting, with a number of associated contributions included), that is, around half the funds anticipated. Other taxes and duties were necessarily expected to supply the remainder of the takings. At very short notice (the law of 13 January 1791), the Assembly had to decide upon the principle respecting a second kind of contribution, which would affect incomes not derived from the land. Since these other incomes were no better known than were those based upon land, one had to calculate this so-called 'moveable' contribution (*contribution mobilière*) on a purely arbitrary basis. The Assembly considered by turns the possibility of accepting the tax-payers' own declarations and that of adopting lump sum payments, with differing amounts to be paid by the various professions. In the end, a complicated formula was arrived at, which involved the application of several different criteria at once. It took into account not only rents but also the number of servants and beasts of burden owned by each active citizen, that is, each person paying a basic tax to the value of three days' labour. Rents were supposed to be estimated where tax-payers were tenants or else they were ascribed to the owners of their lodgings. Then, by means of a table which took into account amount of rent paid and family circumstances, a hypothetical income was arrived at, which was taxed at one *sou* per *livre* (5 per cent).

The establishment of registers for 'moveables' seemed an even more time-consuming and irksome task than the drafting of those for land had been, and the means of assessment even more arbitrary. The censuses and the corresponding calculations, which were also the responsibility of the municipalities, turned out to be extraordinarily complex and were quite beyond either the competence or the commitment to the public good of the local administrations. Those hit the hardest by the resulting injustices were in fact civil servants, and in particular priests, whose salaries had for a while now been paid by the state. Since their salaries were common knowledge, they could not make false declarations and were therefore virtually the only citizens whose actual incomes were taxed.

Further difficulties arose when it had to be decided what share of the tax burden was to be borne by each of the eighty-three departments. For want of a better criterion, it was decided to base the assessment upon the taxes that had been paid under the *Ancien Régime*. The Assembly was thus obliged to draw its inspiration from the system whose abuses and iniquities it had itself criticised, and against which it had made the Revolution. It also added a further injustice to the previously existing ones, which arose out of the apportionment of the taxes paid by the former regions in terms of the departments. For the latter found themselves having to share out their quotas among the districts of which they were composed. They applied a range of different criteria which, once again, could not help but be arbitrary, thus causing still more discontent and strengthening numerous taxpayers in their resolve to defraud and to deceive.

Even before it had become evident just how fierce resistance to taxation was, it was apparent that the state's expenses could not be met by the 300 millions of the land tax and the 60 millions collected annually for 'moveables'. The members of the Constituent Assembly therefore racked their brains in an attempt to dredge up new resources. They reckoned that the abolition, through the law of 2 March 1791, of guild-masterships provided them with an opportunity. Thus, they demanded of all those wishing to devote themselves to a business, a trade or a profession that, in return for the liberty regained to some degree by the abolition of the guild system, they pay a particular tax. This was how the *patente* arose, the sum to be paid being calculated on the basis of the rents paid for premises. In spite of the 10 per cent on this tax which the Communes deducted, and notwithstanding the elementary nature of the calculations involved, its yield was just as disappointing as that of all the others.

Given the ill-will of the tax-payers and the carelessness of local government, it rapidly became clear that the new fiscal system was not going to work satisfactorily, at any rate not in the short term. Nevertheless, the Assembly decided, at the beginning of 1791, to abolish the collection of the majority of the indirect taxes, customs dues, bills and city tolls, which were, admittedly, extremely unpopular, but which had the advantage, as far as the state was concerned, of yielding excellent returns. All that remained of the *Ancien Régime* was the register of title deeds and the stamp duty.

The question of foreign protectionism and that of taxation were inseparably connected. For customs dues represented an important source of funds for the state, and were therefore the subject of lively debates. One of the few industrialists in the Assembly, Goudard, a silk manufacturer from Lyons, made a proposal which, since it advocated 'protecting' French goods, was wholly opposed to the laissez-faire spirit of Physiocratic doctrine. His proposal was rejected, but the text that was finally adopted (on 2 March 1791), although far more moderate in tone than his own had been, still stipulated the imposition of entry and exit dues upon the majority of commodities, and total export or import bans upon a number of them. This decree clearly illustrates the fact that the members of the Constituent Assembly were quite prepared to disregard the economists' teachings when political interests (those of the actual producers, who were in a position to put pressure on them) were involved. They abandoned the notion of introducing complete free trade, just as they had shelved the principle of a stable currency.

It is worth mentioning here, although it has no direct bearing upon fiscal problems, that the year 1791 also saw the passing of two series of laws which were to have a considerable impact upon the whole economic life of the nineteenth century. On 14 June, following agitation among the carpenters of Paris, the Le Chapelier law, which banned all workers' associations, was passed, an enactment which was wholly consonant with those theories that judged all monopolies to be contrary to the general interest. Furthermore, at the end of the year, after the state had renounced any right to intervene in industry and had eliminated any manufactures enjoying special privileges, letters patent, in imitation of the English system, were created.

Evaluation of the new fiscal system

The Constituent Assembly's illusions were very quickly dashed. The French were no readier to accept taxes required of them by their legitimate representatives than they had been to tolerate those of the *Ancien Régime*. As demands and protests arose on all sides, the Assembly agreed to 'bend' the rules which it had just laid down. At the same time, defrauding of the tax-collection system, together with delays in payment, caused it to make its controls more stringent. But these partial and timid attempts at reform did little to improve the very inefficient collection of taxes, as we shall see below. However, the Assembly was less concerned with ensuring the practical success of its work than with justifying it in the eyes of the public.

In an *Adresse aux Français* (of 24 June 1791), the Assembly sought to prove that the charges it was levying were lower than those of the *Ancien Régime*. The accounts it presented on this occasion were unfortunately far from convincing. They gave totals of around 691 millions for the old fiscal takings and 587 millions for the new ones (sixty of which went to the departments, and twenty-six of which paid for the collection costs). Closer inspection would suggest, however, that the former were exaggerated and the latter underestimated. Moreover, even if, for the sake of argument, a normal collection was achieved, the new takings would not have been enough to cover the state's expenditure. Which meant that they would have to have been supplemented by further, direct charges or by loans whose burdensome effects upon tax-payers would be felt much later.

In their commentary upon these figures, the members of the Constituent Assembly observed that thirty-six millions' worth of new charges would be paid by the former privileged classes, which would by the same token lighten the burden of the ordinary citizens. If there were tax reductions in the new system, this was attributed by them to substantial economies in the costs of collection (eighty millions, or so it was asserted) and they further claimed that, under the new régime, the French, being subject to fewer abuses, would benefit from the time and money which they had in the past expended upon litigation (amounting, it was asserted, to another seventy-eight millions).

Since the new fiscal system never really worked, it is impossible for us to judge whether it was more or less onerous than the old system. It is, however, worth noting that the proportion of indirect taxes was reduced, if only because of the abolition of the salt tax, whereas the burden of taxes affecting landed property increased. If French peasants had made regular and appropriate payments of land tax, they would very probably have paid more tax after the Revolution than before.

However, as I have already observed, the real situation was quite different. The fiscal system established by the Constituent Assembly was too complex and was put into operation both too late (the collections for the years 1789 and 1790 were supposed already to have taken place when the new system was installed) and too suddenly to generate the level of takings necessary to balance the state's budget and to prevent the piling up of huge deficits. Since there was no knowledge of what incomes really were, and since there were no cadastral surveys available, the Constituent Assembly had recourse, in its estimation of the contributions that were appropriate in each case, to criteria as arbitrary as those employed under the *Ancien Régime*. In order not to alienate public opinion, it made do with lax and inadequate controls. All of these errors in combination meant that the anticipated level of takings was never reached.

According to Braesch's studies,[2] the total amount of money collected through taxes in 1791, the first year in which the new system was supposed to be fully operative, came to 249 million *livres*. Taking into account the above-mentioned delays in the compilation of the registers, only money collected from the end of that year can have been meaningful for the new system's takings. Thus, the last four months of 1791 each produced on average 26.5 million *livres*, equivalent to 318 millions per year, a figure appreciably lower than the expected 587 millions. Conversely, the state's expenses not only turned out to be higher than its income, but also far exceeded the sums anticipated. Indeed, they amounted to 822.7 millions in 1791.

Some historians[3] hold that the deficits of 1790 and 1791 could be attributed to emergency expenditure incurred through the liquidation of old debts, while others disagree. Braesch, who belongs to the second camp, has shown that, during the two years in question, fiscal receipts were much lower than the ordinary budgetary forecasts. The deficit or default for fiscal returns, if calculated against the forecasts, was 58.6 per cent in 1790 and 57.2 per cent in 1791. So significant a shortfall goes to show that recourse to *assignats* was prompted not so much by unusually high levels of expenditure as by poor forecasts based upon illusions, inaccurate calculations (as mentioned above) and, above all, by the clear reluctance of a majority of the Assembly to exert the requisite degree of fiscal pressure.

Since the Assembly wished to make the burdens it imposed upon tax-payers seem as light as possible, it had made the departments and the municipalities responsible for a set of expenses for which, in reality, it should have assumed responsibility itself. Those towns whose incomes had been greatly reduced, especially after the abolition of the city tolls, had to tackle the economic crisis with their own resources. They had to fund policies which involved, as often as not, purchasing grain in order to distribute it to the poor or to sell it cheap to the bakers, and to set up, at great expense, charity workshops to keep the unemployed busy. As Guillaume-François Laennec's testimony for the town of Nantes suggests,[4] such policies merely served to exacerbate local difficulties:

We have seen vagabond outsiders in this town, who, as winter approaches, are drawn from the depths of the countryside by the lure of these opportune public works, disdain to return there when the good weather returns, obstruct all the avenues of industry by their riotous behaviour, seek out opportunities at crossroads to offer their shameless services to the unwary passer-by, threaten those who choose not to employ them, and vie with our own people for the little work that trade, in spite of the general inactivity, offers.

The municipalities managed to extricate themselves from the difficulties occasioned by their overspending and by the flood of needy persons coming into their towns from the surrounding areas only by cashing in on the sale of *biens nationaux*, and where possible by obtaining subsidies from central government.

The Constituent Assembly had therefore failed in its purpose. The *Ancien Régime* had never managed to run its finances effectively and had been forced to live by a series of expedients; when these ran out, it was overthrown. The new regime, however, proved to be even more spendthrift, ran up an unprecedentedly huge deficit, and in order to reduce it, resorted to the very worst of subterfuges, the sole one still open to it and one which even the King's ministers had not dared to try, namely, the printing of money.

The 'assignats' and the monetary crisis

It is possible that, as early as August 1790, certain deputies sympathetic to the issuing of *assignats* saw paper money as being not so much a means of paying back the state's creditors, which is how they actually presented it to the world, as a source of funds for covering the budgetary deficit. As far as they were concerned, the liquidation of the national debt would simply have been a device for winning the approval of the Assembly, since it did not seem opportune to court popular disfavour by recognising officially just how grave the state's financial difficulties were. Less than a year later, it was becoming clear that the state could survive only by having systematic recourse to the lifeline of the *assignats*. A new paper issue of 600 millions was voted in on 19 June 1791, this time with some haste and with a great deal less publicity than during the debates of the previous year.

When this proposal was put to the vote, the funds realised by the earlier issues, amounting to some 1,200 millions, had already been virtually spent. The Emergency Treasury had advanced the Treasury around 771 millions, there were still some fifty millions in reserve and less than 400 millions had been employed to settle a small part of the national debt. At this time, since 200 millions' worth of *assignats* had been taken in payment for *biens nationaux* and then burnt, the amount of paper money in circulation bordered upon a billion *livres*.

The consequence of so extraordinary an increase in the quantity of monetary tokens in circulation, as might have been (and indeed was) anticipated, was of course a fall in the value of the *assignats*. During the summer of 1790, they lost 20 per cent of their value against the coinage (in one year, the loss had been 10 per cent), in other words, eighty *livres* in coin could be exchanged for a hundred-*livre* note (see figure 4, p. 96, which gives the rate of depreciation of the *assignats* against the coinage).[5] This was not so startling. We shall see below, however, what effects even a moderate degree of inflation was to have upon the economic circuits. I want at this point to turn to another phenomenon, one which was a characteristic feature of 1791.

The reader will recall that, during the major debates of April, August and September 1790, one of the points of disagreement between speakers concerned the question of issuing *assignats* for low denominations. In the

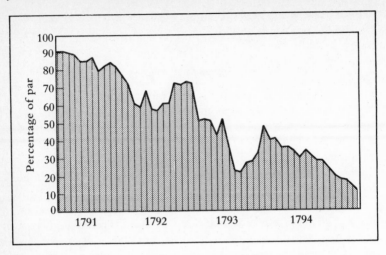

Figure 4 Value of *assignats* (source: P. Caron)

end, it had been decided that the smallest denomination should be fifty *livres*. This decision was to have consequences which were both very serious and so unexpected that not even those opposed to the issue of *assignats* had predicted them.

Under the *Ancien Régime*, there existed two categories of money, accounting monies and payment monies. The first, consisting of the *livre* (*tournois*), and its subdivisions, the *sou* and the *denier*,[6] was used to define the current prices of commodities and the terms of contracts (leases, debts etc.) The second had an actual, physical existence. These monies were gold, silver or copper coins with a range of different names (*louis, écu, liard*), and they were used for transactions. The sovereign was responsible for deciding the relation between accounting monies and real monies, and since 1726 this relation had remained stable, with a gold *louis*, for example, being worth twenty-four *livres*, and a silver *écu*, six *livres*. This system was turned upside down by the appearance of the *assignats*.

Since the value of the *assignats* was quoted in *livres*, which were a unit of accounting money, their purchasing power was, in theory at least, fixed. However, their proliferation could not help but bring down their purchasing power, since an increasing quantity of paper money was needed to pay for a fixed quantity of goods and services. But there was no good reason why the purchasing power of coins, whose quantity varied hardly at all, should do likewise. The *assignats* were therefore bound to depreciate vis-à-vis the coins. It is easy enough to see what the consequences would be. A debtor could, for example, pay off his debt of 300 *livres* by giving his creditor twelve *louis* and two *écus*, or on the other hand, by giving him three *assignats* of 100 *livres*. As the paper money depreciated, the second means was invariably chosen. Coins quickly went out of circulation, since it was in no one's interest to use them to effect payments. Gresham's law, which holds that bad money drives out good, was perfectly illustrated by this case.

The lack of low-value *assignats* did much to complicate the situation. Fifty *livres*, which was the smallest denomination, represented a considerable sum of money, since, at the start of the Revolution, a worker tended to earn from two to three *livres* a day. Under these conditions, it became a real problem to know how to make small payments, such as ordinary people had to make for their day-to-day purchases, for the coins habitually used for this purpose had gone out of circulation and no paper money had taken their place. Actual purchases therefore became rarer. More seriously still, employers lacked the coin to pay their employees' wages. In the ordinary course of things, they should have been able to exchange *assignats* for low-value coin. But these exchanges, given the depreciation of the *assignats*, could not be effected on a par. Employers could therefore only pay wages in coin that was overvalued with respect to paper money. The price of labour therefore rose and offers of employment fell. This resulted in rises in the level of unemployment, which was already disturbingly high.

Given a situation of this kind, the services of money-changers were very much in demand, and at the same time criticised. Throughout the land, these persons suffered assaults which were not always purely verbal. However, the Assembly understood their role to be of value, and requested the municipalities to provide them with some protection. 'Special protection' was also accorded the 'patriotic banks', institutions which had sprung up almost everywhere in response to the monetary crisis. They tended to function as genuine fractional reserve banks. They served the public by issuing low-denomination notes known as *billets de confiance*, as a counterpart to which they held in reserve a quantity of *assignats*, to cover a part of the value of the issue, and invested the remainder. They were obliged by law to deposit at the registry office of the municipalities a guarantee in *assignats*, but no quota was imposed. There could therefore be no control over the relations between the *assignats* placed in deposit and serving as a surety, and notes issued. Since the manner in which patriotic banks invested their assets was not known, and since forgeries were proliferating (made all the easier by the fact that sixty-three different kinds of paper money were circulating at this period in Paris), the public accused them both of hoarding and of untimely issues which gave rise to inflation. Curiously enough, historians have been unanimous in reiterating these accusations, and it is only very recently that their basis in fact has been questioned. It now seems that the majority of the patriotic banks (with the possible exception of the main Parisian ones) were soundly managed and that the issues of their notes were not excessive. It was only when, in February 1792, the tax-collectors refused to accept the *billets de confiance* (probably for fear of accepting counterfeits) that a crisis developed and confidence in *billets de confiance* was temporarily lost. Although the *caisses* could re-establish confidence by redeeming their notes on demand, a bitter debate in the Legislative Assembly (28 March 1792) regarding measures to be taken to control the *caisses* resulted in a panic. Many *caisses* then ran into difficulties: in particular, the Paris *Maison de Secours* had to be assisted by the city to the tune of three million *livres*. Econometric studies would also seem to suggest that the issues of *billets de confiance* were in no way excessive.[7] For a long time, these banks, because they described themselves as patriotic, benefited from the support and sympathy of public opinion. On the other hand, the money-changers, who were performing a genuine economic service, being regrettably little understood by the public, were stigmatised.

On 6 May 1791, the Assembly responded to the monetary crisis by ordering the printing of 100 millions' worth of *assignats*, in five-*livre* denominations. These came into circulation in July. This act involved an implicit acknowledgement that the *assignats* were not intended solely for the purchase of *biens nationaux*, but that they were to be used as real money. Be this as it may, the facilities for the printing of these new paper notes were still inadequate and their denominations still too high to resolve the difficulties of the day. Once it had grasped that this was so, the Assembly also made a bid to boost the circulation of small coins. In order to procure the necessary copper, it proposed the melting down of church bells, but this plan ran up against a large number of technical problems. The Assembly therefore decided to buy copper on the open market too. The resulting increase in demand for this metal boosted its price, so that the actual value of the individual coins outstripped their face value as currency. Private individuals thus found it worth their while to melt down coins in order to sell the metal back to the Treasury.

Since the authorities found no solution to the monetary crisis, its effects compounded those of inflation. The provisioning of the towns actually deteriorated more and more, for the peasants were now bringing very few commodities to market, so as to spend immediately the proceeds from what they had sold without having to hoard bills which were, as they realised, depreciating. Since the harvest of 1790 was a good one, the subsistence crisis occasioned by this sort of behaviour was delayed and only became exacerbated during the winter of 1791–2. But the economic crisis was worsening. Those peasants who were selling less cereal were, by the same token, buying fewer manufactured goods. Moreover, the monetary crisis, as I have emphasised, brought about a rise in the cost of manpower. For these two reasons, the demand for labour and the wages of the urban workers both fell. These workers were the first victims of the *assignats*, although these latter had been created in the people's name.

The sale of the 'biens nationaux'

While the *assignats* were diverted from their original purpose, their creation seemed nevertheless to be justified by the highly successful sale of the *biens nationaux*. The final bids for the lots put up for auction were often far higher than the official estimates. The difference was often almost as much as 70 per cent, as Marcel Marion has demonstrated for a sample of seventeen departments, for sales effected before the end of 1791. In addition, the craze would seem to have been a general one. It spread throughout France, including the departments of the West and the Vendée (which, on the other hand, was so devoted to its 'good priests'), and affected all layers of the population, up to and including the royal family. Several factors account for the success of these sales. There had been relatively few opportunities for spending the cash sums released by the abolition of tithes and of feudal dues, and the non-payment of taxes. Business was in general slow, industry, as we have seen, was stagnating, and the state was issuing no more loans. Conversely, the possibility of making payments that were spread over a twelve-year period and the depreciation of the *assignats* meant that the purchasing of *biens nationaux* seemed a highly profitable operation.

Such transactions were indeed highly profitable for the purchasers and very deleterious for the state, which was actually selling off the nation's wealth. The monumental error committed by the Constituent Assembly, and by subsequent governments, consisted in creating a paper money which was accepted as being on a par in payment for *biens nationaux*, and above all in bringing about an accelerated depreciation which no one had expected. It may be worth placing special emphasis upon this latter point, since historians seem not to have noticed it. The fact that bids were on average 70 per cent higher than the official estimates can readily be explained if one assumes that the purchasers calculated their offers in the knowledge that they would pay 20 per cent of the price in cash, and the balance after twelve years at 5 per cent interest; that, at the time of sale, the *assignat* had already lost 20 per cent of its value (taking the situation as it was around the middle of 1791), and above all that one could reckon that it would continue to depreciate at a rate of 10 per cent per year (the calculation by which one arrived at this result is given in Appendix IV).

If the average rate of depreciation of the *assignats* had continued to be only 10 per cent per year, the Treasury would in the end have sold the *biens nationaux* at their estimated value in real terms. The bidders, spurred on by the competition and taking into account the anticipated erosion of the currency, made offers that on average corresponded to the genuine value of the properties. Indeed, it was because inflation subsequently exceeded all their expectations that they ended up by paying their annual instalments with a currency that had lost almost all its value (by the end of 1795, the *assignat* had been devalued by more than 99 per cent). Calculations made *a posteriori* show that the purchasers of 1791 or 1792 ended up, in terms of real money, paying between a quarter and a half of the value of their original bids, while those who bought properties in subsequent years probably paid even less.

On 20 September 1791, the Assembly, which had arisen out of the Estates-General, disbanded in order to give way to the Legislative Assembly, which had just been elected. Its task had been to give France a Constitution and to replace the old fiscal regime with a new one. It therefore seemed to have honoured its commitments, but unfortunately the decisions which it had taken during its twenty-eight months of activity were only just beginning to take their toll. It bequeathed to its successors a difficult economic situation which the inexperienced men of the new Chamber were to prove incapable of mastering.

The majority of members of the Constituent Assembly had demonstrated time and time again that their main concern was to respond to the wishes of their constituents. Indeed, they went still further, for they tended to do their utmost to take decisions which might win the approbation of the mob. Whereas, as we shall see, it was not re-electable, it could in theory have raised itself above immediate, electoral contingencies. This was something it did not do at all, favouring instead options which offered immediate satisfaction to the militant element in public opinion, even if in the long term they turned out to be disastrous.

In conclusion, the Constituent Assembly's main error was therefore perhaps not so much the issuing of 1,200 million *livres'* worth of *assignats* as the creation of conditions which made the new issues inevitable. The fatal error it committed, as regards the régime it sought to establish, consisted in making it extremely difficult to collect *Ancien Régime* taxes, which should have been collected up until the time when a new fiscal system was installed, and subsequently in failing to take precautions to ensure the income that was needed. By depriving the state of the necessary means for the balancing of its budget, the Constituent Assembly exacerbated the deficits which had brought about the collapse of the *Ancien Régime* and forced the new régime to live by expedients also.

The loss in value of the credit which the state held vis-à-vis the purchasers of the *biens nationaux* was not of course the sole regrettable consequence of the issue of *assignats*. The advocates of the new paper money had argued that it would give new vigour to business, yet it had the opposite effect and helped to disturb the basic economic mechanisms. This manifested itself in two different ways. On the one hand, the depreciation of the paper money vis-à-vis the competing coinage gave rise to a monetary crisis that was unique of its kind. On the other hand, the peasants' loss of confidence in the *assignats* led them to bring fewer basic commodities to market. Conditions were thus ripe for a subsistence crisis, which assumed ominous proportions during the winter of 1791–2, and was to prove wholly disastrous a year later.

6

The rising cost of living, anarchy and war

The flight of the King, as well as throwing France and Europe into confusion, had the paradoxical consequence of reviving for a time the fortunes of the moderates, who favoured a property-based constitutional monarchy. The Constitutional Assembly, by endorsing (on 15 and 16 July 1791) the idea that the King had been abducted, absolved Louis XVI of all blame. The republican demonstration, held a short time later on the Champ de Mars, was ruthlessly suppressed. One might have supposed that the Revolution had ended.

The Feuillants, who had just broken with the Jacobins, formed the moderate wing of the Legislative Assembly, which met first on 1 October 1791, and they seemed to be numerically dominant. Out of a total of 650 members elected, 264 had joined the new club, with only 136 aligning themselves with the Jacobin club. But the Constituent Assembly had left a truly explosive situation. The country's financial and administrative condition had never been so chaotic; the ill-timed issues of *assignats* were beginning to have their destructive effects and anarchy and civil disobedience were rife.

Once Robespierre had moved that the members of the Constituent Assembly could not be re-elected, new men succeeded them, but they were necessarily inexperienced in government and wholly unprepared to tackle the kind of situation which they had been bequeathed. Many of them were advocates and lawyers and were therefore completely uninterested in economic problems, which were so grave in the period just then beginning. They took no steps to take the situation in hand. Indeed, failing to grasp the deeper origin of the events which were troubling the country, they invariably ascribed them to the intrigues of the counter-revolutionaries. Their struggle, like that of all patriots, whether genuine or supposed, was therefore directed against the real or imaginary plots of the émigrés, refractory priests and foreign powers. Absolutely nothing was done to remedy the monetary and financial situation. Finally, the bid for power of the followers of Brissot, who managed to wrest control of the ministry from their rivals, the Feuillants, led the Assembly to declare war on Austria, on 20 April 1792. Subsequently, the rising cost of living, the shortage of basic supplies and the first of France's military setbacks reinforced the power of the Jacobins, who enjoyed the support of the Commune of Paris, of the clubs affiliated to them and of the people of the sections. However, before coming to the events of the summer of 1792, which saw the triumph of the Jacobin cause, we should consider the financial and economic history of the Legislative Assembly.

Anarchy and fiscal crisis

By September 1791, not only had the taxes of that year not been paid in full: even their allocation to the various districts and communes was proving to be a lengthy process. In the months that followed, actual collection was also disturbingly slow. On 1 December 1792, for example, the takings from the land tax for 1791 were only around thirty-four millions (against an anticipated total of 300 millions), and the yield of the tax on 'moveables' was tiny. Seven months later, the takings from the three direct taxes for the year 1791 were still no more than 104 millions. On 1 October 1792, they barely amounted to 152 millions.

Since the taxes already voted in had not provided sufficient resources to meet the Treasury's needs, the Legislative Assembly set out to create new ones. It examined a number of different projects. The majority of such projects were rejected, for the Assembly was still reluctant to unleash an attack upon property rights or to renege upon a promise made by the state. In order not to undermine the latter's already compromised standing still further, the deputies, notwithstanding the antipathy which they felt towards the owners of financial assets, whom they equated with speculators, decided not to tax unearned incomes; indeed, when issued they had been exempted from any levies. A tax upon doors and windows was also proposed, and then rejected; it was to meet with more success some years later. For the time being, no new resource could be tapped.

The Legislative Assembly, like the popular press, held the 'counter-revolutionaries' responsible for the low tax returns. More especially, refractory priests were accused of using their preaching to persuade their flocks to resist taxation. They had, it was said, declared in their sermons that the putting of one's name on the new registers was an offence against

God, and the actual payment of taxes led to eternal damnation. Clavière, the Minister of Finances, wrote a pamphlet with the revealing title of *Conjuration contre les finances* (Conspiracy against finance), in which he denounced 'the intrigues of the priests, who fan the flame of fanaticism in districts where the spirit of the Enlightenment has not penetrated, and where the authorities are not strong enough to curb the seditious'.

Ascribing a refusal to pay taxes to plots seemed at once logical and in accord with the spirit of the times. Yet, but a short time before, the claim had been made (and Clavière was still making the claim) that the French, once they were delivered from tyranny, would no longer oppose taxation. If, nevertheless, in this, the 'third year of liberty', they were still doing so, it could only be because they were being goaded on and led astray by the aristocrats and other henchmen of the *Ancien Régime*.

An objective examination of the facts allows one to refute allegations of this sort. There were of course refractory priests, who did preach civil disobedience. But their influence upon fiscal matters would seem to have been minimal. We know, for example, that the Doubs, one of those departments in which refractory priests had the most influence, was also the first to complete its tax registers and to proceed with the collection of taxes. Likewise, in November 1792, the district of Le Faouet in Morbihan, which was also devoted to its priests, was the only one to have paid all of its taxes for 1791. Conversely, Paris, a city that considered itself to be in the vanguard of the Revolution, where patriotism was most ardently preached, had by this same date paid only a quarter of what it owed in taxes.

Since there would seem to be no correlation between the presence of refractory priests and the non-collection of taxes, it is clear that the latter phenomenon had other causes. These causes are obvious to us today, as they might have been to any impartial observer of the period. Very briefly, the municipal authorities, whose responsibility it was to run an overcomplicated fiscal system, lacked the necessary competence or enthusiasm, and the majority of citizens, being free of sufficiently dissuasive sanctions and checks, were quite prepared to evade their civic duties.

The situation was still much as it had been in 1790 and 1791. The Legislative Assembly was therefore once again obliged to rely upon the same expedients as before. The Committee of Finance estimated that the returns for 1792 would amount to around 530 billions. It was, however, clear that the collection of taxes would continue to be ineffective and that this sum would never be reached. The Assembly should have grasped that it was not in receipt of the anticipated income and adjusted its expenditure accordingly. It did not do this, indeed quite the reverse, since it continually increased its levels of expenditure, which had initially been calculated at 774 billions. The state's extravagance may be accounted for by three different factors, namely, the subsistence crisis, preparations for war, and the depreciation of paper money.

Food shortages grew worse throughout the country. The departments and municipalities had to face up to grave difficulties in provisioning. The state, being frequently begged for help, granted subsidies, imported grain at great expense or accorded generous aid to the needy. The town of Paris was especially favoured in this respect, as provincial deputies noted. The army proved very costly to run also. As preparations for war continued, new needs emerged, such as construction of fortifications, purchasing of equipment, and more funds for soldiers' pay. To provide for the latter, *assignats* had to be used, though even more devalued abroad than in France itself, in order to buy the necessary coin, which was the only thing the troops would accept. In addition, the continuous but irregular fall in value of the paper money made it impossible to make budgetary forecasts; the Treasury did no more than acknowledge that it was having to spend larger and larger sums of *assignats*, and those that it encashed had a lower and lower real value.

The few cuts in expenditure accepted by the Assembly were too limited to have any real impact upon the budget. A decree abolishing the allowances of refractory priests came into force in some areas, in spite of the King's veto. Another austerity measure consisted in scaling down ministers' salaries. These were the sole, utterly derisory economies put into effect during the winter of 1792. It would have been wiser to suspend debt repayments immediately, but after a prolonged debate, the Assembly rejected a measure which, in its view, was too reminiscent of the practices of the *Ancien Régime*. Pressure of events was later to cause it to revoke this decision.

The deputies thus seemed to be unaware of the true gravity of the fiscal situation. Their speeches were imbued with a naive optimism and, if their claims were to be believed, the payment of taxes would soon return to normal levels and considerable sums would be made available for the reorganisation of the administration. Even a man like Condorcet, who was so competent and habitually so lucid in economic matters, felt able to adopt a reassuring tone in his *Discours sur les finances* of 12 March: 'One should really not exaggerate; if the tax returns, if, indeed, the state of the registers in March, April and May is anything to go by, 1793 should definitely produce a sum equal to the sum assessed, and credit will very soon be on a sound footing once more.'

Further issues of 'assignats'

Unable to ensure that a normal collection of taxes took place, forced to meet ever more expenditures, and loath to make substantial economies, the Assembly, if it was to honour its obligations, had no option but to resort to the Emergency Treasury and to paper money. Since it was becoming increasingly difficult to deny that the *assignats* were depreciating, having lost 40 per cent of their value against the coinage by the beginning of 1792, a number of deputies looked into the possibility of staving off their collapse. Several speakers asked that the quantity of notes in circulation be cut down. But these glimmerings of clear thinking had no real effect. In these circumstances, as in others, the majority of deputies continued to invoke plots to account for the depreciation of the paper money. Clavière, who may be taken as a typical representative of this majority position, but who also passed for a financial expert, asserted that, in theory, the *assignat* ought not to depreciate, since it had a surety in land. Consequently, the attested drop in its value could only be due, as far as he was concerned, to foreign intrigue. The Minister of Public Contributions declared: 'Since neither France nor its Revolution are short of enemies, it is not hard to imagine how hired bankers might be doing their utmost to wreck our finances, and to disrupt our commercial affairs, from both without and within, by effecting an artificial lowering of the exchange rate.' He concluded by observing that 'our first financial operation will therefore involve a war against the Coalition of the Princes'.[1]

The Legislative Assembly, which, by contrast with the Constituent Assembly, had no firm adversary of paper money in its ranks, seemed to be satisfied by these flimsy explanations and no longer hesitated before voting in new issues. So it was that, in December 1791, it ordered the printing of 300 million additional *assignats*, bringing the total printed to date to 2,100 millions (a part of which was not yet in circulation) as against some 355 million destroyed. In April 1792, it decided upon a further issue of 300 millions and raised the ceiling of authorised circulation to 1,600 millions. This ceiling was to be raised again in July to two billions, when a new issue of 300 millions was introduced. In the meantime, to compensate for the shortage of low-denomination notes, the Assembly had denominations of fifty, twenty-five, fifteen and ten *sous* printed.

Outside of the Chamber, there were a number of economists who, having no stake in the political struggle, could see quite clearly what effect the *assignats* were having. Thus, Louis Boislandry, a former deputy, who had opposed the issuing of paper money when in the Constituent Assembly, presented his *Considérations sur le discrédit des assignats* (Considerations on the discredit of the *assignats*) to the Legislative Assembly in February 1792. He proposed a double price system, one being reckoned in coin, the other in *assignats*, and he also argued that the date at which the latter were to be withdrawn from circulation should be announced in advance. This proposal would have brought the crisis occasioned by the inflation of paper money to a halt and it would also have enabled the state to realise the true value of the *biens nationaux* it had sold, but it was not heeded.

As it was putting the new *assignats* into circulation, the Legislative Assembly also introduced a number of measures designed to check the issuing of *billets de confiance*. But these measures never came into effect, and abuses and fraud continued. The behaviour of the *Maison de Secours de Paris* was characteristic in this respect. This organisation, avowedly a patriotic one, had extremely onerous liabilities, since the huge quantities of paper money that it had issued exceeded by several millions the number of *assignats* it had invested. A further, aggravating circumstance was that its surpluses had been used to purchase wines, furniture and jewellery, and therefore constituted, in the idiom of the day, 'hoarding'. Under the Convention, it claimed the right, by invoking the name of the 'people', to have its liabilities wiped clean by the Treasury. Finally, one had to wait until the summer of 1793 for the *billets de confiance* to disappear for good.

It is worth noting that the Legislative Assembly advanced a wholly new justification for the new issues. The *assignat*, which had been invented as a way of paying off the state's debts, had become by force of circumstance the main resource of the budget and was used by the Treasury in all of its routine business. During the debates of 1790, no one had admitted that this was the case, but it began now to be openly acknowledged. Those addressing the Assembly from the tribune even went so far as to claim that the *assignats* had actually been designed for this purpose. On 15 May 1792, the new situation was officially sanctioned, with a decree restricting the liquidation of the debt to repayments of claims lower than 10,000 *livres* and for a paltry sum of six millions per month.

The official position from now on was that the *assignats* were to serve as the Treasury's principal resource. However, the proliferation of money, well beyond the anticipated amount, posed the problem of adjusting issues to the value of the surety. When the first debates on this question were held, the members of the Constituent Assembly had tied paper money of a nominal value of 1.2 billions to land whose estimated value was around two billion *livres*. However, with the latest issue of *assignats*, in July, the quantity of authorised paper money in circulation had exceeded the value originally ascribed to the *biens nationaux* (the paper money had, admittedly, lost almost half of its value by this time, but the deputies refused to take this fact into consideration). It therefore seemed necessary to increase the value of the surety. A new source of real estate, the properties belonging to the émigrés, was just then becoming available to the Assembly, and it showed no hesitation in seizing it. The émigrés, by their irresponsible and provocative actions, had become a target for the attacks of patriots and revolutionaries. Their patrimonies, which had been under sequestration since February 1792, were confiscated on 27 July. They were thus added at a very opportune moment to the public properties that were to be sold, and therefore served as an additional surety for the *assignats*.

Shortly afterwards, on 25 August 1792, the Assembly took a decision which amounted in practice to the abolition of feudal rights. The Constituent Assembly had preserved these rights by making it possible to buy them back again. From now on, the holders became proprietors, save where the owners of the former rights could produce the original contract (in general, irrecoverable) proving their right to the property in question. However, a number of public properties that had already been sold had feudal rights attached to them. The purchasers of such properties thus found themselves despoiled. The state itself was also, through this decision, renouncing its title to certain of the public lands that it had confiscated, and was thereby depriving itself of the resources that their eventual sale might release, even though it was in desperate need of them.

The rising cost of living

It was with the approach of autumn, just at the time that the Legislative Assembly was taking charge, that the *assignat* began to depreciate at an unprecedentedly fast rate against the coinage. Up until that time it had held its own fairly well, since, when the third issue was effected, in June 1791, it still stood at around 85 per cent of its face value. From October onwards, its descent, although intermittent, gathered speed, with dramatic consequences for *rentiers*, creditors of all sorts, low-wage earners and, indeed, for the state itself. The crisis occasioned by the inflation of paper money may be explained as follows.

The advent of the *assignat* had meant that two currencies existed at one and the same time. One of them, being a metal coinage in stable quantities, maintained its purchasing power. The other, being a fiduciary currency, proliferated to such a degree that it lost its value against goods exchanged in the context of the economy as a whole. It was in every individual's interest to pay for his purchases in *livres-assignats*. This approach being the only rational one, everybody, simply by adopting it, was hoarding metal and spending paper. The main consequence of this behaviour was a general rise in prices. In fact, it was not at all in the sellers' interests to accept *assignats*. In order to defend themselves against what the buyers were doing, the sellers, knowing full well that they would always settle up with paper money, simply raised the prices on display. They thereby received in *assignats* the same purchasing power as they would have received in coin if the latter had been tendered in payment. But they only released on to the market as many goods as were necessary to generate the sums of money which they themselves required for their own purchases. There was therefore a drop in the supply of all basic commodities, and this factor served in turn to raise prices.

Basic provisions therefore became more and more expensive, both because they were scarce and because of the depreciation of the currency. The demand for artisanal or manufactured products fell, because peasants were buying less and because a large part of everyone's weekly budget had to be spent on food. Those producing luxury goods were not affected by the fall in the purchasing power of ordinary people, but they were, on the other hand, losing a good number of their clients, either because they had emigrated or because they had gone into hiding. The crisis was therefore a general one, and the economy was stagnating. As a consequence, the demand for manpower was much reduced, and wages were stagnating as regards their nominal value and falling as regards their real value. The living conditions of workers, wage-earners and artisans were therefore bound to deteriorate. The conditions of *rentiers*, and of creditors in general, were generally not much better, since those indebted to them were tending to free themselves from their obligations through payments in depreciated *assignats*.

The hardship undergone during the winter of 1791–2 may be explained by phenomena similar to those described above.[2] Later on, under the impact of new factors, paramount among them the war and the regulation of the economy, the crisis was to become still more serious. The virtually uninterrupted rise in prices and the increasing shortage of basic commodities resulted in widespread rioting, in the course of which crowds of desperately poor people would make ever more radical demands. These crowds found, in the Assembly, the clubs and the press, spokesmen who claimed to embody the will of the people and to act in its name. The 'sugar crisis', which broke out at the beginning of 1792, was a very telling example of this.

During the month of January, the price of sugar in Paris rose suddenly, from around twenty-two to twenty-five *sous* a pound to one *écu* (sixty *sous*). Two factors would seem to account for this phenomenon. The first concerns provisioning. During this period, France's colonies in the Caribbean made it the leading sugar producer in the world. However, during the summer of 1791, slave rebellions had broken out in Santo Domingo, which was the main centre for sugar production. The situation on the island remained unstable, and it is probable that this island was no longer supplying the market with as much as usual. The rise in the price of sugar abroad, which, as Albert Mathiez emphasises,[3] was higher than the rise in Paris, shows just how rare this commodity had become on the world market by the beginning of 1792. The second factor behind the rising price of sugar in Paris was the depreciation of the *assignat*, which, at the end of the month of January, had lost 40 per cent of its nominal value. Prices tended, as we have seen, to reflect this depreciation, and this was true of sugar also. Another factor may have been involved. Since the *assignat* had depreciated even more overseas than in France itself, it is perfectly possible that, as Mathiez has also observed, merchants in London took advantage of the situation to make massive purchases of various commodities, including sugar, with paper money bought in England, and thus helped to push prices up even further.

During the last days of January, there was rioting in a number of the poorer quarters of Paris. Events took much the same course everywhere. Blazes were started, mobs invaded shops or warehouses and forced merchants to sell their sugar at the old prices. The demands put forward in the course of these incidents – some of which were violent, some not –

were reiterated by newspapers such as *Le Père Duchesne* or *Les Révolutions de Paris* and presented by petitioners at the National Assembly. They called for a return to the regulations and controls of the *Ancien Régime*, but with the addition of much harsher punishments for offenders. The underlying, thoroughly simple logic was as follows. The general belief was that the warehouses were piled high with sugar; the price rise was therefore due not to scarcity but to speculation; the hoarders engaged in such practices wished to line their pockets at the people's expense and had thereby taken the place of the old nobility; furthermore, these speculators were clearly a part of the plot hatched by the Court and the émigrés to starve the people and thus to foster regrets for the *Ancien Régime*; it was therefore necessary to punish this new aristocracy and force it to sell the hoarded foodstuffs at the old prices. There was a revival of the rumour, which had circulated upon several occasions during the reigns of Louis XV and Louis XVI, that there was a plot to cause famine in France. According to this rumour, some highly placed persons, possibly even the King himself, had been plotting, for reasons of self-interest, to bring about major subsistence crises.[4]

One can get a sense of the kinds of ideas that were current in the poorer districts by considering the demands presented to the Assembly by petitioners from the Faubourg Saint-Antoine:

We denounce all hoarders of whatever kind. Everything is in the control of the assassins of the people, whose greed is such that even basic commodities are not safe from them. These brigands talk of property; but is this property not a cause of *lèse-nation*? Upon hearing how terrible the wretchedness of the public is, does not the tocsin of indignation ring in your tender hearts against these eaters of men? Trade is stagnant and if anywhere it has shown signs of life, this is the result of hoarding. From every corner of the Empire the people, which has no other food than bread soaked in its sweat and tears, cries out to you: The death penalty for hoarders! The death penalty for functionaries who shield hoarding! Death to the conspirators who are plotting arson, looting and murder . . . !

One can thus see the idea gaining credence that the right to property, a primordial right as far as the Constituents, the authors of the Declaration of Rights of Man, were concerned, had to be curtailed, and that, more particularly, it did not entitle merchants to hoard and to raise their prices. A petition from the Gobelins section, presented on 23 January, even sought to justify this notion in terms of the Declaration itself:

We hear these vile hoarders and their wretched capitalists objecting that freedom of trade is enshrined in the state constitution. Yet can it really be that such a freedom requires a law destructive of the fundamental law which says, Article 4 of the Rights of Man: 'Liberty consists in the ability to do whatever does not harm another', and Article 5: 'The Law may rightfully prohibit only those actions which are injurious to society'? Now, we ask you, O legislators, you who are our representatives, is it not injurious to society to hoard basic foodstuffs in order to sell them when they are worth their weight in gold?

The demonstrations and demands of this period received a somewhat ambiguous response from the authorities. The Mayor of Paris made the astute observation to the mob that, if the unrest continued, the capital would starve, for fear of looting would stop 'any merchant from wishing to bring anything more [to market]'. But in the Assembly itself, the petitioners were assured that the law to which they had referred would be more closely studied. Since the Jacobins had declared that 'the men of the 14th of July do not fight for bonbons', the majority of the sections resolved to give up sugar in order to devote themselves to more glorious causes. It was still the case that very few responsible politicians were prepared to respond to popular demands over hoarding.

The unrest occasioned by the sugar crisis therefore died away, but other, graver troubles were already looming on the horizon. Bread, which, as we have seen, was the basis of the ordinary person's diet at the end of the eighteenth century, was in short supply. The harvest of 1791, good in the north but inadequate in the Midi, had on the whole not been too disastrous an affair. But in the autumn, corn riots broke out. In various areas, villagers tried to stop corn being transported to other regions. Their pretext was that they were legitimately opposed to the export of grain, which was forbidden, but they were manifestly concerned above all else to keep it where it was, in order to buy it at as low a price as possible. As the Minister Cahier de Gerville observed at the time, corn was more expensive in France than abroad, and it was therefore more profitable for merchants to sell in those departments where local production was insufficient rather than in other countries. The exports to which the rioters claimed to be opposed were therefore merely a pretext. However, the obstacles placed in the way of the free circulation of wheat made it more expensive not only in the departments where it was meant to be transported and where shortages were most severe, but also in the others, insofar as the grain trade was becoming a highly risky business.

When winter came, the troubles grew more serious. The authorities were forced upon several occasions to call out the National Guard in the north of the country in order to ensure that the grain intended for the Midi should actually set out for its destination. In February, at Dunkirk, the rioting lasted two whole weeks and ended in bloodshed. The mob set fire to the houses of the six most eminent corn merchants in the port; the authorities declared martial law and clashes left fourteen dead. But in the days that followed the troops refused to obey orders. The rioters then managed to seize the cargo from eighteen boats. At Noyon, on the Oise, the peasants held up several grain boats and unloaded them. The soldiers sent to restore order could not beat a path through the crowds, which were blocking the roads, and therefore fell back again. Deputies rushed to the scene by the Legislative Assembly to act as mediators agreed to pay compensation to the rioters, but they failed to have the corn restored to its owners; it was sold on the spot at the controlled price of fifteen *livres* per sack.[5] During this episode, the rioters had rendered the authorities powerless, as they were also in many other, similar occurrences, with the municipalities abdicating before the violence of the mob and accepting the controls on grain prices that were being demanded virtually everywhere.

One brave man proved an exception to the general rule. Early in March, armed bands were stirring up trouble around Etampes. They too were demanding that the price of corn be controlled. The Mayor, Simoneau, refused. Since the mob's threats were carried out, he declared a state of martial law, requisitioned troops, and having donned his tricoloured sash, marched forward to confront the rioters. But the detachment of cavalry serving as his escort deserted him when the first volley was fired, and an armed and frenzied mob murdered him, the cry 'Vive la nation!' on their lips. If *Le Moniteur* of 9 March 1792 is to be believed, there was no looting or theft of corn after the murder had been committed. The patriots were fighting for power as much as for bread.

After the murder of the Mayor of Etampes, the first intimations of repression can be discerned. The Assembly, and even the Jacobins, honoured the memory of a man who had died in defence of the law (in this case, free trade in grain). A pyramid ought, they said, to be raised in his memory. All France paid homage to Simoneau on the day of his funeral. Yet this adherence to principles which had been dear to the Constituents, and of which Simoneau's death had been a tragic reminder, was to be short-lived. Soon voices in the Assembly itself were to be raised in defence of the return to the *Ancien Régime* price controls that the rioters, their leaders and the popular press had demanded. The attitude of the Jacobins was also to alter quite rapidly. They were reluctant to honour the memory of Simoneau, even though he had been one of their own, and pleaded indulgence for the rioters. The spread of the rioting gave those who claimed to embody the will of the people pause for thought. Would they not be well advised to adopt as their own the ever more clamorously expressed demands of public opinion?

This is in fact what Robespierre did. In order to justify the controls over property rights that he was now advocating, he showed no hesitation in blackening Simoneau's name. 'He was not in any sense a hero', Robespierre wrote, 'but a citizen generally regarded as a speculator whose greed led him to profit from public provisioning, keen to wield against his fellow-citizens a terrible power, that humanity, justice and even the law prevent one from using with impunity; he was a guilty party before he was a victim'.

The unrest occasioned by the food shortages of early 1792 was but one expression of the general anarchy of the period, which Marcel Marion has described as follows:

The general population became increasingly prone to looting and to acts of violence; private and national lands [*biens nationaux*] were subject to the most terrible devastation, and the people, now that it was used to going unpunished, wreaked an awful revenge upon anyone resolved to defend the few remaining vestiges of public order . . . An unbridled *jacquerie* spread desolation and terror in Cantal . . . The Ardèche, the Hérault Aveyron, the Gard and the Tarn were in the most alarming state of upheaval . . . In the Bouches du Rhône . . . the rule of law no longer prevailed. Actual expeditions of town against town, and of commune against commune, were organised, houses and properties were broken into, there were illegal house searches, seizure of title deeds, arbitrary taxation and war levies.[6]

The unrest spread so rapidly that the Assembly, at the session held on 6 March, refused to listen to those of its members, no doubt excessively numerous, who wished to present an account of the disorder unleashed in their own departments. It did, however, discuss the country's predicament in general terms. Several highly influential orators on the left, Cambon, Guadet, Isnard in particular, accused the Feuillant ministers of apathy and reproached them for not having used force (although the executive was actually no longer in a position to use force). They also expanded upon the thesis, which reflected their bellicose frame of mind, of a counter-revolutionary plot fomented abroad.

A few weeks later, when the Girondins had ousted the Feuillants and formed a new cabinet, Grave, their Minister of War, instead of acting with the authority his supporters had demanded, announced his intention of withdrawing the troops from the areas of unrest. He declared before the Legislative Assembly on 14 April:

The army would not enable us to restore peace, reintroduce free trade in grain, stop the château-burning in the Midi and, lastly, maintain respect for property and genuine love of the Constitution everywhere. You will find the strength needed for re-establishing these things and ensuring their continuance only in citizens who have banded together to form a part of the National Guard, acting at the request of the constituted authorities.

Faced with the spread of popular demonstrations, those in power were reluctant to use force, and left it to the local authorities, who were often hand in glove with the rioters, to restore respect for the rule of law. Their attitude was similar to that adopted by the Girondins, who wished neither to lead the popular movements nor to oppose them and often advocated the withdrawal of central government from local affairs.

Did the Jacobins[7] sincerely believe that the depreciation of the *assignats*, the food shortages, the riots and the prevailing anarchy were the outcome of counter-revolutionary agitation orchestrated from abroad? Did they really think that a military victory over the enemies of the fatherland, which they imagined would be an easy matter, would by itself resolve the crisis at home? Did they naively suppose that it was enough to have triumphed over the enemies of the Revolution for citizens to recover their respect for the law? Or did they instead regard the war quite cynically, seeing it as a supremely effective way of seizing power and of distracting public opinion from domestic problems that they were wholly incapable of solving? No matter how one judges this issue, one is bound to agree with Albert Mathiez that 'the war of 1792 was up to a certain point an economic war'. But we will of course never know to what point, for no texts survive which give us an account of the deeper motivations and secret calculations of the Jacobin ministers and deputies.

The return of price controls

In the first few months after the opening of hostilities against Austria, the temporary recovery of national cohesion helped to check the food riots and the demonstrations in support of price controls. However, the situation did not remain calm for very long. Many of those who were ambitious for power rallied to the cause of economic interventionism, which was clearly an easy way of appeasing public opinion and thus of assuaging the deep sense of discontent aroused by the first military defeats. The troubles returned with renewed violence after the insurrection of 10 August 1792, which unleashed the passions and the violence of the populace. From 11 August, corn boats were stopped on the Canal du Midi. The armed mob murdered an official and transported the grain which they had just seized to Carcassone.

The insurrection of 10 August 1792 was directed solely at the person of Louis XVI. Its instigators wished to replace the constitutional monarchy, and the principle of property ownership upon which it was based, with a direct democracy founded upon the popular assemblies and the sections. The insurrectionary Commune formed in order to lead the uprising remained in existence and allowed them to continue their struggle for power. They fought within the Provisional Executive Council, which had just been established, and the Legislative Assembly, which now seemed doomed.

Towards the end of the summer, the fall of Longwy (29 August), followed by that of Verdun (2 September), led to the fear that a military débâcle was imminent. The possibility of a counter-revolutionary triumph and the fear of reprisals let loose all the furies. The terrifying massacres of prisoners were only the most extreme expression of the complete and utter disorder and anarchy which now reigned throughout France. Military defeats and the lack of basic foodstuffs occasioned a fear and a hunger so extreme that the most base instincts were aroused. Whether through political calculation (as was very probably the case with the insurrectional Commune of Paris) or through fear, the authorities gave free rein to the bands of looters or assassins which were springing up on all sides. Patriotism served as an excuse for the sacking of churches, châteaux and even state warehouses. In this way public wealth of inestimable value disappeared, including, for example, the Crown Jewels. Persons were as much at risk as property. Passers-by were often robbed in broad daylight. House searches and random arrests became ever more common. The course of justice was suspended, and no one respected the law any more.

By the autumn, notwithstanding a fairly good harvest, the supply of food had still not improved, and the markets were still empty. The civil disturbances which broke out in virtually every department gave rise to another set of problems. At Lyons, for example, the supplies that the merchants had ordered were no longer getting through, for the municipalities situated on the banks of the Saône were intercepting the convoys of corn. But, as Marcel Marion has observed, 'the people of Lyons blamed their wretchedness upon the rich, the "monopolists" and the counter-revolutionaries rather than upon those responsible for these attacks'.

Almost everywhere, the local authorities, being subject to the violence of the populace, agreed to control the price of corn and held hoarders up to public obloquy. In the frenzy caused by the enemy advance, the Assembly gave still more ground to the masses and amnestied persons who had been earlier condemned for breaking laws in relation to the free circulation of corn. The provisional Executive Council, under conditions which have remained obscure, even ordered emergency measures obliging those owning grain to sell it to representatives of the army. The Legislative Assembly, in its turn, yielded and passed laws, on 9 and 16 September, which actually marked a return to forms of price control that had been in force under the *Ancien Régime*. These laws granted the departments the authority to draw up an inventory of the corn held by private individuals and to requisition it, in order to 'guarantee the provisioning of the markets'. However, this authority did not include the right of price fixing and was only supposed to be exercised within the boundaries of the department in question. Yet, wherever rioting broke out, commodity prices were invariably regulated, and generally speaking, the spiralling rise in prices caused public opinion to demand that they be controlled.

Indeed, the ever severer economic crisis, caused either directly or indirectly by inflation, prompted demands that were far more radical than a mere return to the regulation of trade. At Lyons, the mob set up a guillotine opposite the Town Hall, for the purpose of executing hoarders. In Normandy, some of the commissioners of the Executive Council distributed, upon their own initiative, the text of a new Declaration of Rights of Man, which promised an 'agrarian law' and the redistribution of farmland. A sector of public opinion thus seemed prepared to accept the undermining of property and 'economic terror'. Certain Jacobins, Robespierre in particular, adopted as their own the new conceptions of right which were becoming current in patriotic circles, and revived conceptions that had been entertained by theoreticians of regulation such as the ex-priest Dolivier.

On 21 September 1792, the property-owning constitutional monarchy, which the Constitutional Assembly had sought to establish, was officially replaced by a republic. A Convention, elected by universal suffrage (but under conditions which allowed only a minority of the population to make a choice), was given the task of formulating a new constitution.[8] During its year of holding power, the Legislative Assembly had proved incapable of correcting the mistakes of the Constituent Assembly. Indeed, it had aggravated them. State expenditure had risen yet higher, income had fallen and monetary circulation, far from being reduced, was swollen by 900 million *livres'* worth of *assignats*, without taking into account the *billets de confiance*.

Since they had been unable to restore the rule of law or normal economic conditions, the men of the Legislative Assembly had chosen to divert the fury of the populace by lending credence to ever wilder rumours of counter-revolutionary plots, involving émigrés, the Court, refractory priests, foreigners, hoarders, the rich and so on. They were led by the logic of their accusations to combat those whom they identified as the enemies of the Revolution. In the virtually universal excitement, they had begun in April 1792 by declaring war on their external enemies. Yet the same logic could not help but drive the deputies to employ the same force against the supposed enemies within, by instituting the Terror and imposing strict price controls. The majority of the Legislative Assembly had rejected these extreme solutions, in spite of the more and more pressing calls for them. But the Convention, heedless of the principles cherished by the Constituents, was to show no such hesitation.

7

The seizure of power by the Mountain

The Convention met on 20 September, the same day as the Battle of Valmy was won. The tide of war seemed definitively to have turned a few weeks later, when success at Jemmapes (on 6 November) left Belgium in revolutionary hands. The Executive Council, together with a majority of the new Assembly, took advantage of this turn of events to consolidate their authority. But from this point on a remorseless struggle was waged between those who advocated a restoration of order and the leaders of the Commune and of the sections.

The trial of the King made plain just what contradictions and oppositions there were within the Convention itself. The Mountain, although in a minority, triumphed over the Girondins, who wished to restore order, and for the most part to save the neck of Louis XVI. It managed to eliminate its rivals once and for all during the insurrections of 31 May and 2 June 1793, when it made the rioters' demands its own. It paid a price, however, for allying with the sections, for certain of its most eminent representatives reneged upon their convictions regarding economics and accepted the principle of a Maximum for grain.

While those dramatic events which led from the fall of the monarchy to the seizure of power by the Mountain were unfolding, anarchy, and fiscal anarchy in particular, continued to prevail. In spite of a few lucid but isolated protests, the Convention proved no more capable than the earlier Assemblies had been of resolving its financial problems, except of course by recourse to *assignats*. A continually expanding circulation meant that the value of paper money was bound to collapse, with the same tragic consequences for provisioning and for the purchasing power of ordinary people. The distress suffered by the latter inflamed passions still further. As the troubles continued, new leaders, with more radical demands, emerged. They identified new targets for the obloquy of the masses, so that now not only genuine aristocrats but also the rich, hoarders and all those suspected of belonging to the 'merchant aristocracy' were at risk. From now on the Revolution was to be directed against the latter grouping.

The (provisional) return to free trade in grain

We saw in the previous chapter that in September 1792 the Provisional Executive Council, and subsequently the Legislative Assembly, had, under pressure of events, accepted serious limitations upon free trade. Departments had been granted the right to make censuses and even to requisition grain. Although the right to introduce price controls had been refused them, in practice the rioters forced this upon the merchants in virtually every area where incidents had occurred. So it was that bands of 'regulators' (*taxateurs*), often several thousand strong, had been at work in November, in the Beauce, the Loire, the Eure and the Sarthe, as well as in numerous towns, such as Chartres or Tours.

The Convention, like the Constituent Assembly and the Legislative Assembly before it, was dominated by lawers and advocates. Their interest in economic problems was very slight, and they imagined that it was in their power to resolve them by means of political decisions. The deputies with some experience of trade or business were few in number. Nevertheless, the majority of members of the Convention were sufficiently up-to-date in their thinking to grasp that the cause of the high price of basic foodstuffs was the plethora of *assignats*, and that the regulation of trade would merely make such commodities even scarcer and would recoil in the face of those very people who had so passionately advocated it.

Roland, the Minister of the Interior, was especially imbued with Turgot's ideas. He knew that restrictions upon the free trade in grain would cause the food situation to deteriorate. Disturbed by the events which he was witnessing but which he was unable to have any influence upon, he wrote to the Convention to warn it of the dangers it was courting. In his letter, which was read out on 27 November, Roland explained:

There are virtually no citizens left who either can or dare to devote themselves to trade. If they transport grain, they are accused of hoarding; mobs are forming in several departments, which make their way to the markets, control the price of grain and even seize it without paying.

In the course of this same letter, Roland also demonstrated that, under cover of patriotism, some municipalities in the Paris region were intercepting grain and flour convoys headed for the capital and were therefore posing a threat to its provisioning. He also made it quite clear just how absurd the interventions of the municipality of Paris had been:

Since the latter is causing flour to be sold in Les Halles at below the price it fetches in the surrounding areas, we find people coming in from the neighbouring districts to stock up; trade no longer feeds them in their own district, because it cannot sell at the same price. Now, it is easy enough to grasp that, with consumption increasing as the overall quantity of basic foodstuffs shrinks, we are fast approaching the time when, if no remedy is found, famine will be inevitable.

Finally, Roland asked the Convention to declare:

1. that the trade in grain be open to every citizen, and that circulation of grain be wholly unrestricted; 2. that those who make even the slightest attack upon free trade and upon the free circulation of grain shall be regarded as disturbing the peace and shall be charged with that offence . . . 3. . . . . that the Commune of Paris . . . will from now on be obliged to sell basic foodstuffs at the price for which it has bought them.

Roland's report inaugurated an important debate, in the course of which supporters and opponents of a free trade in grain came face to face. The latter condemned the activities of the big merchants and called for the state to intervene and to impose strict price controls. One of these men gave a very clear formulation of the statist point of view, asserting that 'it is not . . . the dealers in corn, but rather the administrators and the legislators who should provide for the French'. This same speaker did however defend himself against the charge of undermining the right to property by denying that this right could exist when famine raged: 'Is there a virtuous citizen who, in such circumstances, would keep something to himself, when his brothers were dying of hunger?'

Another deputy, Lequinio, responded by stating the case for free trade in grain. He quite rightly explained that 'any violent measures that might be taken to make grain circulate by force will in fact have the effect of preventing it from circulating'. But it was the speech given by Saint-Just which captured everyone's attention. The young deputy from the Aisne, who but a few months later was to become one of the main organisers of economic Terror, set out a wholly convincing defence of ideas that were liberal through and through. He began by declaring that he had no love for 'violent laws concerning trade'. He then went on to try to demonstrate that the high price of basic foodstuffs was due to the plethora of money in circulation, whose unregulated issue had 'since the

Revolution overturned the grain-trade system in France'. Upon this occasion, Saint-Just did not resort to demagogy, and gave a clear and lucid explanation of the origin of the subsistence crisis:

There is no money-saving going on nowadays. We have no gold, and yet a state must have gold; otherwise it is basic commodities that are piled up or kept back, and the currency loses more and more value. This, and nothing else, lies behind the grain shortage. A labourer, having no wish whatsoever to put paper money in his nest-egg, is very reluctant to sell his grain. In any other trade, one must sell in order to live off one's profits. A labourer, however, does not have to buy anything, for his needs have nothing to do with trade. This class of persons was accustomed to hoarding every year, in kind, a part of the produce of the earth, and nowadays it prefers to keep its grain rather than to accumulate paper.

By contrast, Robespierre, whose ideas Saint-Just would very soon come to share, took a firm stand against free trade. His arguments, or to be more precise, his peremptory assertions, took no account of the case argued earlier by Saint-Just.

Everything required to preserve the subsistence of men is the common property of society as a whole: only the surplus is individual property and is abandoned to the industry of merchants . . . Why did the law not stay the murderous hand of the monopolist, as it does that of the ordinary assassin?

This great debate ended on 8 December 1792. In spite of the pressure exerted by the Commune, the sections and certain of the departments, and in spite of the petitions which flooded into the Assembly and which denounced 'a new aristocracy, which seeks to raise itself upon the ruins of the old one through the fatal ascendancy of wealth', the Convention ruled in favour of a completely free circulation at home (although the export of grain was still prohibited), and stipulated the death penalty against the leaders of mobs impeding the free circulation of basic foodstuffs. It seemed as if the problems concerning the grain trade had been resolved, that the temptation to resort to interventionism had been resisted and that the right to property had been reaffirmed. But the Convention's firm attitude was something of an illusion; the free circulation proclaimed by law simply did not exist and, indeed, was never to exist. While awaiting an official return to price regulation, the taking of inventories, requisitioning and even price fixing continued to be practised in numerous towns and districts. It was not long before the Convention went back on its word and let itself be caught in the toils of *dirigisme*.

The first 'assignats' issued by the Convention

At a time when it was still relatively unaffected by pressure from the Paris mob, the majority of the deputies in the new Assembly had demonstrated, through their vote, their sincere attachment to the principle of free trade. Numerous deputies seemed to have a clear understanding of the harmful role played by paper money in aggravating the subsistence crisis. Indeed, Saint-Just was not alone in entertaining this point of view. Even Marat, who was generally only too prepared to espouse the popular cause, was in agreement with him. He wrote, on 1 March: 'The scourge which is laying waste to our lives consists, first of all, in poverty, which is ever increasing. It is caused by the vast quantity of *assignats*, whose value falls the more of them there are.' Roland and Clavière, while they were still ministers, echoed the Assembly's anxieties, and appeared before it at regular intervals in order to plead for measures serving to restrict the quantity of money in circulation. But the Convention was to prove just as careless in economic matters as the Constituent Assembly and the Legislative Assembly had been. Although it acknowledged how harmful the *assignats* were, it fought shy of introducing measures that would reduce the number in circulation or of acting with the severity advocated by the executive.

Since the income from taxes was still low – and, in the absence of rigorous constraints, how could it be otherwise? – the resources which the government could call upon were inadequate. Its expenses, on the other hand, continued to grow, because of the rising prices, the war and the subsidies doled out to the municipalities. The municipality of Paris, in particular, a town which made itself out to be patriotic but was none too prompt in paying its taxes, was constantly demanding hand-outs. We saw above that Roland complained about this behaviour. It is worth noting that, during the winter of 1792–3, the Commune spent around 500,000 francs a day in subsidising sales of flour (whose artificially low price brought buyers from neighbouring areas flocking in); that the *fédérés'* camp, whose creation had precipitated the conflict between the King and the Girondin ministers, had turned into a national workshop, and that by the time it was finally closed down, it had brought about an out-and-out loss of 900,000 francs; finally, that the (fraudulent) deficit of the Paris *Maison de Secours*, which issued *billets de confiance* without holding *assignats* of equivalent value as security, had by itself risen as high as two million francs.

At the end of 1792, the Emergency Treasury was 'lending' the state more than 100 million francs a month (the abolition of this Treasury was soon to put an end to the fiction of loans which, as was perfectly plain, were never to be paid back). Given this rate of expenditure, the *assignat* issues were rapidly exhausted. On 24 October, the Convention decided to create 400 million francs' worth of paper money; the quantity in circulation thereby rose to 1,972 millions, which was very close to the official limit, which was thereupon pushed up to 2,400 millions. Then, on 1 February 1793, 800 million more *assignats* were voted, and the ceiling was fixed at 3,100 millions. The public was then in possession of some 2,387 millions in *assignats*, a sum very close to the value originally reckoned upon for the surety in land.

Although the executive was reluctant to create yet more *assignats*, and although certain deputies expressed a wish to limit their circulation, the Committee of Finance knew no such scruples. Speaking in its name, Cambon displayed the utmost optimism. He sought to prove that tax returns were improving, that the state had access to new resources and that the sureties upon which the *assignats* depended were multiplying.

I have already had occasion to note that, in actual fact, tax yields were still just as disappointing as ever. Clavière mounted the Assembly tribune on 25 February, and in a display of some courage, argued unsuccessfully for measures to be taken against those who were late in paying (including, of course, the town of Paris). There were, he claimed, no less than 851 millions in arrears still outstanding. The fate of the Revolution depended upon this sum being recovered. As for the new resources that Cambon was counting upon, they would come from countries that the revolutionary armies had conquered.

After the victory of Jemmapes, at a time when the Revolution was sweeping all before it, it had simply seemed to be a question of 'lending help to all peoples wishing to recover their liberty'. But as France's economic troubles persisted, this generous attitude was quickly forgotten. Nice, Savoy, Belgium, the Rhineland and soon, it was hoped, Holland, had to make war contributions, maintain revolutionary armies, surrender the properties of their clergy and their nobility to the government of the Republic, and finally, to use *assignats* as official currency. Unfortunately for the Convention, things were not so straightforward. The conquered countries tended to reject the 'benefits' offered them by France. They failed to supply the expected booty and seemed in no particular hurry to pay the price demanded of them by the revolutionaries in order to be 'delivered from tyranny'. It turned out to be difficult, as Georges Lefebvre put it, to 'make the peoples happy without consulting them, and at their own expense'. In order to exploit the occupied territories more effectively, the Convention then decided to annex them, in accord with the new theory regarding 'natural frontiers' (that is, the Rhine) that had just been formulated by Danton.

France's expansionist policies were beginning to worry London, although the British government had at one time envisaged staying out of the conflict. Pitt began to prepare his country for the commencement of hostilities. War, which was seen by the Girondins as a solution to France's internal problems, was declared upon England on 1 February 1793. The death of the King shortly afterwards brought Spain in also. The alliance against France, which was considerably strengthened by these developments, quickly put the Republic's troops on the defensive. A highly costly military effort would be needed if the new coalition was to be confronted. A levy of 300,000 men was immediately decreed. It was in reaction to this decision that the Vendée revolted on 10 March.

The financing of the war effort was managed, as we have seen, by the issue of *assignats*. The property of the émigrés, which had been requisitioned in October 1792, constituted additional sureties which, as far as the Committee of Finance was concerned, justified the further proliferation of paper money. Their value, which is a matter of dispute, seems to have been at the beginning quite considerable, somewhere around two to three billion francs. Unfortunately, theft and vandalism reduced this value considerably. In addition, it was generally not fully realised at the moment when the sales took place, for these were frequently held under fraudulent conditions (whereas, in 1790 and 1791, the sales of *biens nationaux* had been perfectly above board).

Regrettable though it may have been that the nation's wealth was frittered away in this fashion, the real problem did not so much concern the value of the so-called surety, but rather the sheer speed with which the quantity of notes in circulation was growing. Contrary to what several observers of the time were claiming, the value of the *assignat* only depended for a very short time upon the public's confidence in the stability or solvency of the revolutionary government. This value in actual fact depended fundamentally upon the ratio of the quantity of paper money to the volume of goods that it enabled one to buy. Now, this ratio was increasing more and more rapidly. This is explanation enough of the rapid deterioration of economic conditions in France, and more particularly, of the food situation.

The 'Enragés'

In December 1792, the *assignat*'s value started to plummet. In the space of a few weeks, paper money lost around a third of its purchasing power. At the beginning of 1793, its real value corresponded to no more than about a half of its face value. Since wages had not risen to the same extent, because of the low demand for manpower, this strong and rapid depreciation could not help but aggravate still further the already acute problem of subsistence and exacerbate the reactions of the populations most affected. With the coming of winter, there were further, more pressing demonstrations in favour of price controls and the Maximum. In contrast to the situation the previous year, this time such demonstrations were led by leaders with a flair for organisation and capable, if not actually of theorising, at any rate of giving an explicit formulation of, and justification of, popular demands.

The most influential of these leaders was undoubtedly Jacques Roux. This ex-priest had become famous in the section of Gravilliers, thanks to the radical positions he had adopted and the bloodthirsty proposals he had put forward. In spite of all the local support which he enjoyed, he had failed to get himself elected to the Convention, for he was an impatient and clumsy man. His failure had left him with a chip on his shoulder, which may perhaps have caused his subsequent anti-parlia-mentarianism but in no way checked his revolutionary ardour. A violent harangue delivered on 1 December 1792 before the section of the Observatoire served to make him extremely popular. This discourse reiterated all the most pressing demands of the Paris mob, namely, the death of the King, the hunting down of speculators, hoarders and traitors and the lowering of the cost of living. It marked the political début of the most determined element of the sans-culottes, the *Enragés*, and the beginning of their struggle to achieve their main demand, the establish-ment of the Maximum.

The sans-culotte movement was exclusively urban, indeed Parisian. Its rank and file in the capital consisted of small artisans, workers, domestic servants, journeymen and all those who were out of work, perhaps 250,000 people in all, if their families are included.[1] Since their living standards depended to a large extent upon the scarcity of bread or upon the high price of other basic necessities, these ordinary people never conceived of the possibility that after the Revolution they might be even worse off and in even more adverse circumstances than before. Their preoccupation each day was simply to find sufficient food to stave off starvation. They also believed that the fundamental rights of man were those of life, work, welfare and education. They were not in principle opposed to the right to property, and very probably aspired to an egalitarian society of smallholders; but the rich, the big merchants and the financial dealers, in short all those who had what they themselves so cruelly lacked, were now in their eyes the enemies and scapegoats that the aristocrats had been before. Since it was through force that 'the tyrant and his lackeys' had been overcome, the same means seemed appropriate for bringing down the 'mercantile aristocracy'. As their wretchedness and hunger grew worse, so did the harshness of their attitude towards those who, in their view, were depriving them of the fruits of the Revolution. The Convention, however, seemed too respectful of protocol and of the laws to govern according to their desires. They therefore did not place their trust in it and in its deputies, many of whom anyway seemed to them somewhat suspect. What they desired was a system in which the popular assemblies were in permanent session, so as to dispense justice or to confirm or withdraw the mandates of their representatives. Being unsophisticated, relatively uneducated people, they had neither the time nor the knowledge to understand that, in the long run, the measures which they demanded would end up by rebounding against them, both politically and economically. François Furet and Denis Richet have given what seems to me a very accurate account of their state of mind:

The belief in the virtue of coercion as an instrument of justice, a kind of magical solution to social problems, was one of the most permanent features of the long martyrdom of the lower classes. This traditional aspiration of Frenchmen, buried and apparently forgotten when the stability of society, or of the nation, was not in jeopardy, always reappeared in a crisis.[2]

Towards the end of February 1793, a series of incidents akin to those of the previous winter took place in Paris. For several days, the mob overran the shops, and where it did not loot, it caused the goods to be handed over at prices which it had itself fixed. Its behaviour was so much of a piece that one might have supposed that the operation was planned. Pache, the new Mayor, in order to calm things down, tried to follow the example of Pétion, whom he had just ousted. He addressed the rioters himself and attributed the agitation, as he was bound to do, to the enemies of the Revolution. But he failed to re-establish order, for the *Enragés* in the streets had no fear of repression. Indeed, they had friends within the Commune itself, and Jacques Roux, who was a member, was quite prepared to strike a deal with them.

The members of the Mountain, whose domination of the Jacobin club was increasingly reflected in the Assembly itself, rejected the *Enragés'* policies. Indeed, their own intellectual convictions led them to be opposed to the regulation of trade, and therefore to the Maximum. The majority of them agreed with Saint-Just and Marat that the economic difficulties of the moment were due to the excessive number of *assignats*, and they therefore wished to reduce the quantity in circulation, where the *Enragés* favoured the withdrawal from circulation of the coinage and the establishment of the paper money as a compulsory currency. Furthermore, the members of the Mountain regarded all the violence and unrest as especially inopportune, at a time when confidence was needed if the sale of émigré property, which had just been decided upon, was to be effected under favourable circumstances, and if the levy of 300,000 troops was to proceed without a hitch.

Since the *Enragés* were effectively challenging the Mountain for the confidence of the populace, the latter responded by attempting to discredit their rivals, whom they made out to be yet another group of counter-revolutionaries. Yet they too needed to put forward a 'social' programme. Their programme, which was designed to rally the most deprived categories of the population, the natural constituency of the *Enragés*,[3] to the Revolution, depended in the main upon two series of measures, namely, the taxation of the rich and the punishment of hoarders. It should be pointed out that the second of these measures reflected a concern of a strictly moral or political order and had in fact no basis in law. In spite of the fact that no law defined hoarding or the crime it involved, Marat showed no hesitation in demanding that the Committee of General Safety be vested 'with the power to seek out the principal hoarders and deliver them up to a state tribunal . . . in order that they be judged as traitors to the fatherland'. He also demanded that the solution to the problem be adopted in haste:

The simplest ideas are those which occur first to a well-formed mind, such a one as is only concerned with the general welfare, and has no thought for itself: I therefore wonder why we should not turn against these public brigands the same means that they themselves employ to ruin the people and destroy liberty. Consequently, I would make the observation that, in a country in which the people's rights are not simply empty titles bestowed for reasons of pomp alone in a mere declaration, the looting of a few shops, and the hanging of a few hoarders at their doors, would very soon put a stop to these malpractices.[4]

The taxing of the rich

During the early days of March, the fortunes of war again turned. Dumouriez was forced to quit Holland. Defeat at Neerwinden, and then at Louvain, made the evacuation of Belgium necessary too. At loggerheads with the Convention, and more particularly with Cambon, Dumouriez went over to the enemy, having at one time entertained the notion of marching on Paris. In the following weeks and months, northern France was overrun. During this same period, the Prussians crossed the Rhine and laid siege to Mainz. These military disasters forced the Convention to adopt harsher policies. It therefore set up the Revolutionary Tribunal (10 March), passed a series of draconian laws on emigration and founded the Committee of Public Safety (6 April).

The financial situation seemed no rosier than the military one. The Assembly, for all that it had declared property sacred, introduced a progressive tax on the rich which made a mockery of its former declaration. This did not benefit it greatly, however, so chaotic was the fiscal situation in the country, but the fact that it was voted through at all shows the sort of contradictions with which the deputies were having to deal. The crucial sales of the *biens nationaux* were proceeding more and more slowly, so that the original rate of some eight to eleven millions per week had fallen to one million. Under these conditions, how was it possible on the one hand to reassure potential buyers, that is, the propertied classes, and on the other hand take stock of the point of view of the sans-culottes, who were the declared enemies of the 'rich'?

At the beginning of spring 1793, the Treasury seemed to have fallen into an irredeemably difficult situation. Large expenditure, and especially the urgent military expenses, could only be arranged in coin, which was the only kind of money accepted by the army contractors and by some of the troops. Yet the reserves were virtually exhausted. There was only 600,000 francs' worth of coin left in the coffers; whereas the state's expenditure at this period was close on fifteen millions a month. What was to be done? It was becoming more and more difficult to do as the government had developed the habit of doing, and buy coin with paper money, given the extent to which the *assignat* had fallen in value. At any rate, we know that the large majority of the deputies, including those whose allegiance was to the Mountain, was basically opposed to further issues of paper money. This majority quite rightly believed that in the last analysis the only solution to the country's economic problems consisted rather in a rapid withdrawal of the *assignats* from circulation. But the sales of *biens nationaux*, the only available means (short of sudden payment of all the taxes in arrears) of returning the paper money to the Treasury, were drawing to a halt. Then, on 8 and 11 April, the Convention was persuaded to have recourse to yet another expedient. It decreed that all citizens were obliged to accept *assignats* in payment at their face value and prohibited any trading in coin, as if a law could by itself confer the value of metal on mere paper. This was a massive concession to the *Enragés*, made more through immediate necessity than through deliberate choice, and one which involved an alliance with the then most active element in the sans-culottes. From this point on, the official sanction given to a fiduciary finance policy meant that every attempt, or indeed, every desire, to restrict the quantity of paper in circulation was abandoned.

Without further delay, in May, the Committee of Finance demanded of the Assembly a new issue of 1,200 millions. The quantity in circulation at that point stood at 3,100 millions and the proposal, which was accepted, meant increasing it by a third. The justification for a decision of this kind, whose harmful effects were well known, depended upon the so-called 'assets of the nation'. The nation's wealth was thus reassessed at 7,700 millions (taking into account an optimistic estimate of the value of the property of the émigrés, and of the arrears in taxes, which they pretended would soon be recovered), a figure well above that of its liabilities, if one added the 1,200 millions corresponding to the redeemable debt to the quantity of money actually in circulation. These calculations were erroneous, but even if they had been accurate, they would still not have provided a justification for the decisions which were taken. So drastic an increase in the quantity of notes was bound to lead, notwithstanding the decrees of 8 and 11 April and the real or exaggerated value of the surety, to a considerable drop in the value of the *assignat*.

The local authorities were likewise in financial difficulties, but the expedients to which the Convention had had recourse were not available to them. The issue of municipal paper money, the celebrated *billets de confiance*, which were so much abused, was now in effect closed to them. The department of Hérault had to find a means of raising finances that was at once speedy and popular. It therefore raised a forced loan of five millions from the rich, the proceeds of which were meant to equip 5,000 men and to 'relieve' their families. The Commune of Paris adopted this same procedure and in its turn decreed a forced loan of twelve millions. Other towns and departments followed suit. Everywhere, revolutionary committees appointed by the sections drew up lists of tax-payers, who were then obliged within the month to pay the sums which, all of a sudden, were reckoned to be owing (a third had to be paid in under forty-eight hours). There was thus no need to delay over the drawing up of registers and the determination of the precise size of incomes, nor to wait upon the good will of the tax-payers. Indeed, this new method turned out to be far more profitable than the classical system of taxation had been. Yet it still did not seem efficient enough to satisfy certain of the Paris sections, which demanded (successfully) that the Convention pay them advances against the loans which their own 'rich' would be paying.

There was thus one way of saving the Revolution, coming to the assistance of the poor sans-culottes and financing the war, namely, taking the money of the rich. Everywhere, whether in the sections, the clubs or in the Assembly itself, people outdid each other in dreaming up ever more ingenious ways of achieving this aim. At the Convention, Cambon came straight to the point, and on 20 May, proposed that a forced loan of one billion be levied on 'the rich, the egoists and the apathetic'. This was accepted in principle, in spite of the opposition of a number of the Girondins, who pointed out how arbitrary such a procedure would be. Yet they were not heeded, for the alliance between the Mountain and the *Enragés*, in favour of a new economic policy, had already been sealed. This did not stop the Jacobin club, whether out of cynicism or naivety, and anyway wholly ineffectually, from swearing unanimously, on 30 May, to 'perish rather than to suffer attacks on property'.

The alliance of the Mountain with the 'Enragés'

A series of military defeats wrecked the projects of the Girondin government. Brissot's friends had counted upon conquest to relieve the pressure on the Treasury, to calm the disputes occasioned by the trial of the King and to restore the credit of the *assignat*. At the beginning of April, Dumouriez's treachery put an end to their illusions. From this time on, the struggle with their opponents within the Convention, those aligned with the Mountain, was conducted without mercy.

The Mountain constituted the left wing of an Assembly in which it was in the minority. If its viewpoint was to prevail, the support of the Plain and of the uncommitted was necessary, but it was only the fear provoked by popular demonstrations and threats that could rally them to its cause. Its strength therefore depended in large part upon the militancy of the masses which it claimed to represent. However, from

February on, the emergence of the *Enragés* as a political force, who were a product of famine and economic crisis, deprived it of its popular support and of a part of its legitimacy. In order to win back the Paris sections, which were being stirred up by Girondin propaganda and by the ideas of the *Enragés*, the Mountain opted for an alliance with the latter.

Jacques Roux, the leader of the *Enragés*, had also very probably come to realise that, if he were to win the power to which he aspired, his skill at stirring up the mob was not sufficient. The support of the Convention, the new seat of republican legitimacy, was also necessary to him, for it did not seem possible as things then stood to overthrow the representative system by force. He therefore muted his anti-parliamentarianism and strove to win the sympathy of the Mountain by attacking *en bloc* the hoarders, the mercantile aristocracy and those who were accused of having wished to save the King, namely, the Girondins. More radical still was Varlet, Roux's admirer and rival, who tried unsuccessfully, on 9 and 10 March, to unleash an insurrection, the aim of which was to expel the Girondins from the Convention.

The shift of the Montagnards within the Convention towards the *Enragés'* demands became clear around the beginning of April. On 2 April, Marat revolted against the 'sufferings of the people' and announced a new social programme. This programme was initially somewhat restrained, for even a (relatively) moderate figure such as Danton adopted a 'social' tone in his speeches. He demanded that the price of bread be everywhere subsidised by taxing the rich, so that their condition would be 'in a just proportion to the wages of the poor'. The former Minister of Justice wanted to have the protective state intervene without therefore, at any rate in appearance, impeding the laws of the market. This proposal was accepted in principle, but no law actually applying it was passed, for it was quite plainly impracticable. One of the demands of Jacques Roux and his friends was anyway soon to be met, for, as we have already had occasion to note, the decrees of 11 April made the *assignat* a compulsory currency. This left the problem of the Maximum.

For several months, the Assembly had been inundated with petitions and deputations from the provinces and the poorer quarters. The demand was invariably for the punishment of hoarders and the setting up of a rigorous system of price controls in the grain trade. On 11 February, petitioners claiming to represent the forty-eight sections of Paris and the eighty-three departments demanded: 'Decree six years in irons for a first offence, and the death penalty for recidivists, for any farmer or merchant who sells a 240-pound sack of corn at more than twenty-five francs.' The demands rapidly became still more insistent. On 18 April, a deputation from the department of Paris, led by its procurer-general syndic,[5] solemnly declared:

When, in '89, the French people won back its liberty, it lived in the hope that it might enjoy all the goods that such liberty promised. For four years now, there has been no limit to the sacrifices that it has made. Money, soldiers, it has given of its all and as a reward it asks for bread. In every department, grain is now at such a price that the poor cannot afford it ... The right to property must not involve the starving of one's fellow-citizens. The fruits of the earth, like the air itself, belong to all men.

In the days succeeding this intervention, a long discussion of the Maximum took place in the Convention. Barbaroux, a Girondin, gave a clear account of the disastrous effects price control would have upon the citizens in whose name such a measure was being proposed. He very lucidly explained the dilemma in which the legislators would shortly be caught:

You are proposing to fix a maximum price for grain. But, either this maximum will be high, or you will bring it down lower than the present rate. If the Maximum is high, you will have done nothing whatsoever for the people; on the contrary, you will have sacrificed it; for no farmer will willingly hand over his corn at below the Maximum ... If, conversely, the Maximum is low, here is what will happen: the consumers will hurry to increase their share, and they will lay hold of as much corn as they can readily store.

His predictions as to the effect of the proposed measures upon law and order were equally prescient:

Do you wish house searches to become commonplace in town and countryside alike, with a bushel of corn being sought for, just as in former times they looked for a pound of salt or of tobacco? Do you want to arm the French against each other and to win the subsistence of one group to the detriment of the other ...?

Finally, Barbaroux raised an objection which was to prove well founded, as the interventionists were soon to discover to their cost. In effect, he explained, if a uniform Maximum were imposed, no producer would have any interest in adding the costs of transportation to his own costs; the corn would therefore tend to stay where it was and the towns would starve. If, on the other hand, local Maxima were established, the arbitrary and complex calculations involved would create an impossibly difficult situation, ripe for swindlers and damaging to the ordinary consumer.

Philippeaux, a Montagnard, was one of those presumptuous spirits who imagine that the state's intervention can circumvent the natural laws of economics. He therefore answered Barbaroux by acknowledging that a simple tax on foodstuffs would be harmful, but he went on to propose a method which, in his view, would eliminate its more damaging effects. It consisted in adopting a Maximum that would decrease with the passage of time. He thus claimed that it would be in each person's interest to sell the commodities he had produced as quickly as possible, for fear that any stockpiling of them would force him to surrender them at a lower price in the following month. The influx of these commodities would then immediately bring down the prices and the law would quickly become redundant.

The uncommitted were convinced not so much by Philippeaux's arguments as by the appearance before the Assembly, on 1 May, of a deputation from the Faubourg Saint-Antoine. It called for the Maximum, the annulment of leases, the paying into a fund intended for the relief of the needy of half of all incomes in excess of 2,000 francs, and the drafting of the rich into the army. But, above all, this deputation brought before the Assembly 9,000 men ready to revolt if they did not receive satisfaction there and then.

The following day, under threat and very probably against its own wishes, the Convention adopted the principle of a regulation of the grain trade, and on 4 May voted in the decrees regarding the application of this principle. The departments were thus vested with the authority to fix Maxima calculated according to the average prices for the first four months of the year, to demand declarations, to requisition, to conduct house searches and to oblige growers of grain to sell on the markets alone. Furthermore, in line with Philippeaux's proposal, the Maximum for the price of bread and for that of flour was to be lowered each month.

The effects of the first Maximum

It was not long before the harmful effects of this legislation made themselves felt. Far from answering to the *Enragés'* expectations or functioning as Philippeaux had imagined, these effects bore out the point of view of those who persisted in believing that, in the general interest, trade should never be regulated.

During the traditionally difficult months of May and June, which were immediately prior to the harvest, the departments showed varying degrees of zeal in establishing their respective Maxima. Furthermore, the Maxima that were in the end fixed differed greatly one from the other. This divergence meant that those departments in which the Maximum was relatively high, or else those in which the prices were still uncontrolled, attracted the grain, which, indeed, disappeared altogether from those departments in which regulation was especially restrictive. In a very short period of time, those local authorities whose markets were wholly empty reacted by prohibiting the exit of grain from their jurisdictions, even though it was against the law. These measures seriously isolated the departments which were short of grain and which could no longer provision themselves. However, even in those zones which traditionally enjoyed a surplus, hardship was commonplace. Indeed, it was not in the producers' interest to move their grain into the interior of a department where the Maximum, being uniform, did not allow them to take their transportation costs into account; at best, they would deliver it solely to the very nearest markets.

A further unanticipated difficulty emerged. The legislators had left it up to the departments to define which grain would be subject to the Maxima. Corn was invariably regulated, but oats, for example, were not. The price of this latter cereal, being uncontrolled in many places, rose steeply so that it was up to twice as high as that of wheat, which was usually more costly. This anomaly encouraged the producers of corn to use it to feed their livestock rather than to sell it at the Maximum.

In order to tackle the problem of empty markets, the local authorities could have recourse to house searches and requisitions. They were reproached at the time for being somewhat reluctant to pursue these options, and their mildness was ascribed to their political sympathies, which were often Girondin in nature. However, it should be borne in mind that this first law of the Maximum did give the producers some ways of sidestepping the arbitrary powers of the local authorities. The peasants employed these strategies to resist requisitions. Indeed, the latter were only supposed to be applied to quantities in excess of that needed for the family's own consumption. But it was an easy matter to make a family's basic needs seem much larger than they really were, and thereby to claw back substantial quantities of grain from the authorities. If surpluses still existed, they were then sold (really or fictitiously) to non-cultivators of the same region, who were granted the right to draw their provisions for a month in advance directly from the producers. After this, there really was not very much left to confiscate.

In Paris, the town for whose benefit the regulation of grain had been instituted, the situation was really not much better than in the provinces. The authorities had however waited until the Maximum in the neighbouring departments was known before fixing that of the capital, which they placed at a high enough level to attract deliveries from outside. Yet it was still not high enough to guarantee the town's provisioning. A further difficulty was that the few convoys that were destined for Paris were often intercepted en route by the starving people living along the way.

The famine, although it was general, was especially virulent in certain poor regions, such as the Massif Central. The petitions and supplications that flooded in to the Convention testify to the sufferings and the wretchedness of people who were sometimes reduced to eating grass. Everywhere the cry went up for the abolition of the 'murderous law' of the Maximum. The Convention did not abrogate it, but simply failed to enforce it; in some provinces it was suspended, in others it was merely circumvented. A disaster was thus avoided. Unfortunately, this experiment was not to prove instructive, for the interventionists quickly found an explanation for its failure. The problems which had arisen derived, in their view, not so much from too much but rather from too little regulation. They therefore persisted in attributing economic difficulties to the counter-revolutionaries, to the rich and to the mercantile aristocracy, whose egoism they wished to punish.

It is perfectly clear, as Barbaroux's speech once again testifies, that at the time of the French Revolution, enlightened spirits had enough knowledge of economic mechanisms to predict accurately what the effects of a regulation of trade would be. The Montagnards, save for a number of notable exceptions, such as Robespierre, were opposed in principle to the imposition of the Maximum. If they nevertheless accepted it, it was out of political opportunism, as the price they had to pay in order to win power. Later, faced with the disastrous consequences of such a decision, they held their ex-allies, the *Enragés*, to blame.

In its early stages, the alliance between the Mountain and the *Enragés* bore fruit. The Paris sections organised the insurrections of 31 May and, above all, of 2 June, this latter involving tens of thousands of sansculottes pointing their cannon at the Assembly. The representatives of the people yielded to the threats of a faction which laid claim to actually being the people. They allowed twenty-nine Girondin deputies and two ministers to be arrested. Once their adversaries had been eliminated, the Montagnards and their friends became masters of the Convention.

Since the calling of the Estates-General, a permanent struggle had ranged the official executive power, represented, at various different periods, by the King and his ministers or by the provisional executive committee and the Girondin ministers, against the Constituent or Legislative Assemblies or the Convention. From now on, a single group, the Montagnards, and a single institution, the Committee of Public Safety, were to hold undivided executive power.

8

Economic dictatorship

The power of the Mountain, which Robespierre's allies had ended up by appropriating, was to last for fourteen months. On the military plane, this period began very awkwardly for the French government. The summer of 1793 saw the federalist uprising, the victories of the rebels in the Vendée, and the advance of the armies of the Coalition. However, in the course of the following autumn and winter, foreign enemies had to beat a retreat, while domestic enemies were annihilated. Only the economic crisis withstood the Committee of Public Safety, which no longer showed any hesitation in imposing the regulations, controls and interventions which the popular movement demanded.

The *dirigiste* policies failed, just as could have been anticipated by the very persons who had put them into operation, and who had in the past spoken out in favour of free trade. It only served in the end to worsen the subsistence crisis. This being the case, confrontation between the Convention and the Parisian sans-culottes seemed inevitable, for the latter felt that their deepest aspirations had been thwarted at every turn. This confrontation was not to be, however, for the representatives of the sans-culottes at this juncture, the Hébertists, the successors to the *Enragés*, were eliminated in the spring of 1794, as a preventative measure. Their disappearance did not, however, put a stop to the economic interventionism which they had championed. The logic peculiar to regulation, which seemed to call always for yet more measures, combined with what seemed to be the imperatives of war, led the Committee of Public Safety to place still more emphasis upon interventionism. On 9 Thermidor, Year II, the French economy was almost entirely under state control. How did this situation arise?

Sans-culotte pressure

In the period running from the fall of the Gironde to the insurrections of 4 and 5 September 1793, the pressure exerted by the sans-culottes on the

Convention grew ever more intense. Under the combined effect of the famine and of despair at the sequence of military defeats, the most active part of the population of Paris attempted, employing the means it had employed so successfully in the past to impose its principal demands; namely, a purge of the army and of the administration, repression of suspects, regulation of the sale of basic necessities, and needless to say, a strict application of the Maximum.

During the insurrections of 31 May and 2 June, the *Enragés* had honoured the obligations which, through a tacit agreement, bound them to the Mountain. Once the forced value of the *assignat* and the Maximum decreed on 4 May had failed to bring the expected relief, they demanded, after the elimination of the Girondins, still more radical measures. In their disillusionment with parliamentary power, which they accused of waging an insufficiently resolute struggle against the rich, the *Enragés* calculated that the introduction of a direct democracy founded upon the sections and the local assemblies would ensure the triumph of their ideas. In order to wrest power from the Convention, they embarked upon a further trial of strength with it, just when the Constitution was being promulgated (24 June 1793).

This Constitution, which had been drafted in some haste and which was never to be applied, was a perfect expression of Jacobin thought. Egalitarian, deist and anti-federalist in inspiration, it repudiated the separation of powers and established universal suffrage (save for women). This constitution seemed at first to accord with the aspirations of the sans-culottes, for it bestowed all the powers upon a single Chamber, which was elected annually on a system of one man, one vote, and frequent recourse to referenda was also stipulated. But the sans-culottes wished to go much further down the path of direct democracy, through the election of representatives who would be permanently accountable to their constituents for their actions and would be at all times subject to recall by them.

On 25 June, Jacques Roux spoke quite bluntly to the Convention. He read out a petition from the sections of Gravilliers and Bonne-Nouvelle and from the Cordeliers club. The deputies were castigated for not having included clauses in the Constitution which specified the harsh economic measures and sanctions to be employed against the rich, who were charged with being the only ones to have profited from the Revolution:

Delegates of the French people, a hundred times this sacred enclosure has echoed with the crimes of egoists and rogues. The constitution is to be presented to the sovereign power, to receive its sanction; have you proscribed stock-jobbing therein? No. Have you pronounced the death penalty against hoarders? No. Have you given a precise definition of what free trade is? No. Well, then. We are telling you that you have not done all that you could for the welfare of the people.

The unfrocked priest continued his violent indictment in much the same vein, presenting justifications for all the measures advocated by the sans-culottes and rejecting in advance all the arguments raised against them. His reckless denunciation culminated in the claim that 'under the *Ancien Régime* it would not have been permitted for basic necessities to be sold at prices three times above their value'.

It is plain enough that the Convention could not tolerate its actions being represented as so much more dishonest than those of the monarchy. It reacted promptly to Roux's assertions, forcing the very people who had just provided him with his mandate to repudiate him. The abrupt volte-face forced upon the sections of Gravilliers and Bonne-Nouvelle by the Jacobin leaders shows just how easy it was to manipulate the 'popular will'.

Ironically enough, the ploys of direct democracy were in this way used against one of its main supporters. The Convention even managed to have its Constitution applauded by the sections and approved by the primary assemblies.[1] In its victorious struggle against the *Enragés*, it had enjoyed the support of the Commune, and more especially, that of one of its most important figures, Hébert, who, hugely popular because of his newspaper *Le Père Duchesne*, aspired to lead the sans-culotte movement. But he would need first of all to rid himself of his rivals, the *Enragés*, whose anti-parliamentarian and anarchist notions he did not share. This accounts for his alliance with the Committee of Public Safety against the *Enragés*.

After his outrageous speech before the Convention, Jacques Roux was imprisoned and then, after a few weeks of detention, released. This warning did not stop his friends from stirring up trouble in Paris in the course of the insurrections of 24, 25 and 26 June. A rise in the price of soap provided the *Enragés* with the occasion for an open struggle with the authorities. Their sporadic agitation was to last up until the beginning of September.

In the course of the summer of 1793, although the pressure from the street succeeded neither in changing the nature of the government nor in modifying the Constitution, it undeniably exerted an influence, through the fear that it aroused, upon the decisions of the Convention. Admittedly the deputies did not in the short term extend the Maximum to other products besides grain, nor did they attempt to make the May decrees effective. Yet they stuck to the principle of price controls, even though its harmful effects were daily becoming more evident. More seriously still, they passed a whole series of measures undermining free trade.

Thus, on 26 July, Collot d'Herbois' report was followed by the passing of a law on hoarding.[2] This law defined a whole series of commodities as 'basic necessities', namely, bread, meat, wine, vegetables, fruit, butter, oil, vinegar, brandy, soap, sugar, hemp, paper, wool, leather, cloth, fabrics, etc. Anyone in possession of such products was obliged to declare the fact before the municipalities or the sections within eight days. Monopoly commissioners had the power to put them immediately on sale, at cost price if need be. A trader who failed to make an accurate declaration might find himself charged as a 'hoarder' and as such sentenced to death (with, in addition, the seizure of his goods). Those who had made the denunciations would receive a third of what was confiscated.

Shortly afterwards, on 9 August, the Convention passed the law dealing with public granaries. The proposer of this measure was Leonard Bourdon, deputy for Gravilliers, and by the same token a rival of Jacques Roux. His proposals, which closely reflected popular prejudices, plainly represented a return to the price controls that had been in force prior to 1789. He was in fact reviving the *Ancien Régime* principle of the 'tithe barn'. Scattered throughout the country and operating upon their own initiative, these institutions used to buy corn when the harvests had been good and to re-sell in case of dearth. Under the new system, the granaries located in each district would have lost their independence. Leonard Bourdon suggested subordinating them to a central administration, whose job it would be to buy the whole of the nation's production and to re-sell it to consumers, with the actual growers having to surrender their entire harvests. This administration had to fix selling and purchasing prices that would be uniform for the whole of France, organise transportation between granaries and, of course, hold a monopoly over exports.

The success of such a project presupposed not only that the men running the public granaries were completely honest and disinterested, but also that they had access to information valid for the whole of France, concerning the needs of the population and the yields of the growers. It also presupposed that the latter would not react negatively to the administration's decisions by producing less or by failing to surrender the whole of their harvests if the prices allotted to them were not to their liking. We know that the majority of deputies were not so naive as this, and in fact believed in free trade. In spite of the threats issuing from the street, they did not follow Leonard Bourdon all the way, and although they did legislate for the creation of public granaries, they insisted that they be decentralised, administered by the districts and financed by means of an emergency credit of 100 millions to be levied from the rich. This return to the *Ancien Régime* constituted a first stage in the eventual subordination of everything to the control of the state.

In the course of the next few days, a number of relatively minor measures reinforced yet more the state's interference in the running of the economy and ended up by eliminating what little remained of free trade in grain. Thus, a decree passed on 15 August instructed the administrations to proceed with the threshing of the grain, for which workers could be requisitioned, and to undertake the general census which had already been stipulated in the law of 4 May. On this same day, another decreee authorised the representatives of the people to 'provision Paris by means of requisitions'. Then, on 19 May, the Convention established a Maximum for combustibles, and in the days that followed, for oats. On 23 August, certain arrangements respecting the decree of the *levée en masse*, which was passed on that same day, stipulated that payments be in kind. It was hoped by this means to replenish the public granaries and to put a part of the supposedly hidden corn into circulation. Finally, on 25 August, the tax on grain, which had lapsed, was reintroduced.

Vain attempts to reduce the quantity of 'assignats'

At the same time as it was reacting to popular agitation by regulating trade, the Convention was also confronted with the usual dilemmas regarding monetary and budgetary matters. On the one hand, the problem of the cost of living could be definitively resolved only through a drastic reduction in the quantity of *assignats* in circulation; on the other hand, issues of paper money still constituted the sole means of financing the state's expenditure, expenditure that was increased significantly by the war.

The selling of the Treasury's credits given to the buyers of the *biens nationaux* put only insignificant quantities of paper money into the public coffers. A premium offered to the purchasers themselves, in order to encourage them to settle their debts in advance, did not meet with much success either. Still more negligible results were achieved by obliging tax-payers to pay all the direct taxes due between 1791 and 1792 in the course of a few short months, for the lack of any real constraints meant that this obligation was a purely formal one. These ploys, although somewhat pitiful and hardly worthy of the government of a great country, at least had the virtue of according with the notion of a state keeping its word. This was not the case with two other measures adopted during that same summer.

The first of these measures, which was decided upon on 31 July, consisted in withdrawing those *assignats* which had the face of the King upon them. These *assignats*, either because they inspired more confidence than did the others (had the monarchy been restored, these were undoubtedly the only ones that would have been honoured), or because, being more carefully designed, they were harder to counterfeit, enjoyed, for the same face value, a higher purchasing power than did more recent issues. This premium upon the image of the dead King obviously seemed offensive to the revolutionaries. They therefore decreed that *assignats* bearing the image of Louis XVI would no longer have forced value and could be used only for purchasing *biens nationaux*, for paying taxes and for public loans. A number of the state's creditors were injured by the disappearance of the additional value of these *assignats*, without the quantity of money in circulation being significantly diminished, since the Treasury's debtors continued to hold them with a view to paying off their debts. This affair lost the state still more of what little credit remained to it.

The second measure had still more momentous consequences. It consisted in the creation of the Great Book of the Public Debt, in which all the state's debts were amalgamated. Admittedly, the loans mortgaged against resources such as *taille*, salt tax etc., which the Revolution had eliminated, had to be revised, since their sureties no longer existed. Montesquiou had already pointed this out in 1790. But there was now a new political justification for the unification of the public debt and for rendering all titles to debt uniform. Cambon gave a fairly rough formulation of this, in his report of 15 August 1793:

Those persons who still hope for a return to the *Ancien Régime*, when they have some money to invest, will always favour titles authorised in the name of kings, just as they used to speculate upon *assignats* with the royal head upon them ... Let us hope that inscription in the Great Book will be the tomb of old contracts and the single, fundamental title for all creditors, that the debt contracted by despotism will no longer be distinguishable from that contracted since the Revolution . . . You will then find that a capitalist who desires a king because he has a king for debtor, and because he fears to lose what he is owed if his debtor is not restored, desires the Republic, for it will have become his debtor, and because, losing it, he will fear to lose his capital.

Unfortunately, aside from its political interest, the Great Book of the Public Debt offered other, far less legitimate advantages for the revolutionary government. In a reaction against the practices current under the *Ancien Régime*, the Constituent Assembly had made a solemn promise to respect prior commitments and never to subject the public debt to deductions or reductions of any kind. The Convention, however, had no such scruples, for respect for the right to property had long since been jettisoned. It resolved, therefore, to cut the interest, premiums and shares which several royal loans bore, on the pretext that 'speculators, after having received the funds owed them by the nation, have used them to hoard foodstuffs and commodities'. As far as Cambon was concerned, the paying out of less interest to the state's creditors was therefore a blow struck against speculation. The Convention's great financial expert thus presented as an act serving the general welfare a piece of spoliation so brutal that even the monarchy in its closing stages would not have dared to commit it.

In following Cambon's recommendations, the Convention also decided to tax the annuities owed by the state by deducting the land tax when the interest on them was paid. The witholding at source of a tax which, like all others, was providing poor returns, was indisputably calculated to improve the overall fiscal yield. One might therefore suppose this decision to have been a necessary one; but unfortunately, it breached all the promises, reaffirmed by the Constituent Assembly, that state annuites would not be taxed and therefore constituted yet another violation of the right to property. As Marcel Marion observes, the law of 24 August creating the Great Book of the Public Debt was a 'bankrupt's law': 'the state was reneging upon very clearly defined commitments, entered upon under the *Ancien Régime*, but renewed since the Revolution'.

A loan, decreed at the same time as the above law, gave concrete form to Cambon's attempts to cut the quantity of money in circulation. Its subscribers were promised interest of 5 per cent payable in coin, on the nominal value of their contributions in *assignats* (which, by August 1793, had lost around 75 per cent of their face value). If they proffered a 100-

franc note, which only had a purchasing power of twenty-five francs, these subscribers might hope to get back each year five gold francs, which represented a real return of 25 per cent a year. Such a proposition could seem a very enticing one, if the subsequent payment of interest was made as and when promised, but it bore all the signs of being a fool's bargain, given the eventuality (which was altogether more probable) of paper money issues remaining the state's sole resource and of the servicing of the debt continuing to be in *assignats*.

The public would seem to have been wholly sceptical about any short-term improvement in the Treasury's finances. Cambon therefore had to try and make the conditions surrounding the new loan seem still more attractive, which prompted him to grant the purchasers of rents at 5 per cent an exemption from the obligation to subscribe to the famous compulsory loan of one billion which was to be levied from the rich. The *grand ressourcier* thus showed how little confidence he had in the success of this latter operation. Yet publicly he radiated optimism, announcing that he wished to withdraw from circulation, prior to the end of the year, one billion francs' worth of *assignats*.

Never short of measures which were in principle aimed at the 'rich' but which, in reality, ended up by harming the whole population, Cambon had stock companies banned and the Stock Exchange closed down. He justified these decisions in terms of the by now routine attacks upon the 'vile speculators', who were accused of intrigues against the Republic. This revolutionary rhetoric concealed a plan to suppress all financial operations that could rival state loans. As fate would have it, the suppression of the *Compagnie des Indes* gave rise to fraudulent ma-noeuvres on the part of a number of deputies, which were eventually uncovered. Fabre d'Eglantine, in particular, was compromised by this affair, and it was also to besmirch the reputation of his friend Danton at the time of their trial a few months later.

Just when the Convention was trying so hard to reduce the quantity of *assignats* in circulation, the only way it could find of laying its hands on the necessary resources was by resorting to further issues of paper money. However, in order not to undermine the confidence of the public, which had been assured that the state's finances would be put back on a sound footing, it decided, on 14 August 1793, that measures affecting the fabrication of money would from then on be decided in private by the Committee of Public Safety. Upon this same date, Cambon declared that the quantity of *assignats* in circulation totalled 3,776 millions, to which should be added the 559 millions withdrawn from circulation but still in public possession. This sum was a consequence of the issues of spring 1793, together with the 1,200 millions voted in May and a further 700 millions printed in June under the pretext that a mistake had been made at the time of the May issues. Because of the decision to keep monetary matters secret, it is hard for us nowadays to arrive at an exact estimate of the quantities put into circulation in the period after summer 1793.

Terror 'the order of the day'

At the end of August, the harvest promised to be a good one, but the markets were still empty. At Paris, in spite of all the efforts made by the Convention to provide for the populace, there was no flour to be had and one had to queue for hours at the baker's. The populace's hunger and exasperation made further revolutionary convulsions seem probable.

However, from June onwards, a significant change in the situation was apparent. The Convention, together with its temporary ally, the Commune, had managed to drive a wedge between the *Enragés* and the popular movement. The friends of Chaumette and Hébert had gained control of the Jacobins and of the majority of the sections. Like their ousted rivals, they favoured the reintroduction of price controls and the Maximum, and the showing of no mercy to those whom they termed the starvers of the people. They also advocated radical measures against hoarders and counter-revolutionaries of every kind. Their especial qualities did not lie so much in their 'economic' programme, which in every respect resembled that of the *Enragés*, as in their violent anti-Christianity, and above all in their conception of the Terror. Indeed, they did not wish it to be spontaneous and anarchic, as it had been in September 1792, but on the contrary, centralised and run by the government itself.

The Hébertists were behind the riots which finally broke out on 4 and 5 September 1793. In the course of these insurrections, the sans-culottes used petitions to give expression to their aims, which invariably included price fixing, the requisition of grain and the repression of hoarders. The Convention met once more with the Hébertists, exerting pressure upon them, to which they yielded, giving still more ground on political issues than they had done on economic ones. A major consequence of these insurrections was the decision of Barère, in the name of the Committee of Public Safety, to make 'Terror the order of the day' and to vote for the creation of a revolutionary army of 6,000 men and 1,200 artillery-men, whose task would be to spread the Terror throughout the country. A uniform Maximum for grain for all of France, which had been one of the rioters' main demands, was also adopted.

The events which had led to the institution of the Terror resulted in a degree of redistribution of power. The leaders of the *Enragés* disappeared from the political scene for good (Jacques Roux, who had once again been arrested, was to commit suicide in prison) and their influence waned. Hébert's influence, on the other hand, continued to grow. Collot d'Herbois and Billaud-Varenne, deputies who had become the insurgents' spokesmen, and who up until then had been very little known, now entered the Committee of Public Safety. By a curious paradox, Danton, who seemed too moderate for those who had won the day, enjoyed some success within the Convention at this period. He succeeded in pushing through a measure which restricted the length of meetings of the sections and thereby considerably reduced their influence. As a counterweight to this, a measure was passed that was very popular but highly costly for the state budget: needy sans-culottes were to receive forty *sous* for participating at each of the remaining meetings.

It was undoubtedly around September 1793 that the political influence of the popular leaders who sat on the Commune of Paris and who pushed the government towards interventionism and even towards economic dictatorship, reached its apogee. This influence lasted for several months more, and resulted in the majority of the sans-culottes' demands being met, before the Hébertists were liquidated in their turn. The innumerable speeches and writings of the period allow one to form a fairly precise notion as to the logic informing their programme. It may be summarised as follows.

The cause of the dearth which was affecting people almost everywhere was not a fault in the method of production but was attributable to hoarding. There was enough grain; the problem was simply that it was not circulating. The growers, like the merchants, were holding it back instead of putting it up for sale, either because they were selfish (and hoped to profit from the hardships of patriots) or because they were malevolent, that is, opposed to the Revolution. In either case, hoarding was a capital crime, the perpetrators of which should be hunted down and severely punished.

According to this viewpoint, the right to property could not be invoked in the hoarders' defence. 'Do liberty or property give me the right to murder?' asked Prudhomme in his paper, *Les Révolutions de Paris*.[2] He went on to explain:

What difference is there between someone who takes someone's life and someone who takes their means of existence; between someone who plunges a dagger into my breast, and someone who deprives me of basic necessities? ... if the law was capable of differentiating between two different kinds of death penalty, the crueller of the two ought to be reserved for hoarders.

As Cochin pointed out,[3] the fight against hoarding was, as far as the patriots were concerned, only one of the forms that the struggle against the aristocrats assumed. In their Manichean vision of the world, the concept of aristocrat no longer referred solely to the former nobles, but more generally to all those whom they took to be their enemies. This was especially the case with the 'mercantile aristocracy', which was composed of all the merchants supposed to have profited from the Revolution to make their fortunes, and of the henchmen of the monarchy and of enemies abroad, such as the émigrés, the federalists etc., all of whom were implicated, in the minds of the sans-culottes, in an abominable plot to starve the people ('the royalists are hoarding basic foodstuffs', declared Barère, in a revival of the well-worn motif of the *pacte de famine*). It is worth quoting Prudhomme once again on this subject:

Wicked persons who have no fear for themselves, but who use every means available to dry up the springs of plenty, presented themselves at the doors of several bakers in turn; they hoarded bread which they later, under cover of night, threw into the sewers, into the river or into the latrines.[4]

Or, again, Fabre d'Eglantine:

While the patriots have spared no efforts in the fight to defend our frontiers and our coasts and to crush domestic rebellions, another war is being waged on the republic, a silent, insidious and invisible war ... this war goes by the name of speculation.[5]

Whereupon Barère appealed for 'a revolutionary army which [would] sweep away the conspirators ... an army carrying out all measures necessary for public safety'.[6] In such a war, economic liberty was plainly out of the question. The government had to respond to the enemy's attacks with measures of constraint, which were no longer partial, as the Maximum decreed in May had been, but complete and total, so as to leave the 'aristocrats' no room for manoeuvre.

The General Maximum

On 11 September, the Convention passed a law fixing a maximum price, uniform throughout France, for grain and fodder. It was succeeded, on 29 September, on the basis of a report by Couppé de l'Oise, by a further law defining the maximum price for foodstuffs and commodities reckoned to be basic necessities, together with an altogether new factor, a maximum for wages. A list of forty articles was published (fuels were treated separately), whose prices were supposed not to go higher than those of 1790 'as recorded on the market price lists or by the current price in each department, and a third over and above'. Wages and salaries were fixed at 1790 levels, 'half over and above'. The public authorities in the districts had to draw up tables for the Maximum within a week, or else risk dismissal. Where this law was broken, it was stipulated that a fine be paid of twice the value of the object sold, affecting both parties to the transaction. This seemingly lightweight penalty was accompanied by an infinitely more serious one, namely, the recording of the names of offenders on the list of suspects.

With the passing of the laws on hoarding in July and those regarding the Maximum in September, the deepest wishes of the populace would seem at last to have been granted. The government had vested itself with the means to control prices and wages and to curb the refractory. All current foodstuffs had from now on to be sold at official prices, on penalty, as far as the merchants were concerned, of suffering the severe punishments meted out to all suspects. A revolutionary army, specially recruited to wage war on the hoarders and on other mercantile aristocrats, was particularly responsible for ensuring that this new republican discipline was respected. Under these conditions, would the poor sans-culottes finally profit in their turn from the Revolution, and eat their fill?

If the sans-culottes did imagine this, their illusions were to prove short-lived. Once the lists of the Maxima were published, the mob dashed into the shops and markets in order to buy at low prices foodstuffs which the day before had seemed completely out of their reach. But once these stocks were sold, the merchants could not refill their shelves at prices compatible with the Maximum. Their shops and shelves stayed bare. Certain of them, deprived of all custom because of the poverty to which the Maximum had given rise, risked provoking the authorities by shutting up shop. The latter threatened them with expropriation, organised house searches in order to make sure that nothing was being hidden, and treated them in general like suspects. Other merchants, where their line of business permitted it, cheated on the quantity or quality of the commodities sold. The Commune responded to these practices by appointing various inspectors (such as the commissioners whose job it was to taste wines and brandies), and this provided work for a few sans-culottes. Finally, after a few days of euphoria, and in spite of the quality of the recent harvest, the shortages grew worse and spread to products which up until then had escaped the crisis.

The difficulties arising out of the reluctance of producers to sell at the stipulated prices were compounded by those caused by the legal pillage perpetrated by the revolutionary army, or by the requisitions ordered by the more or less official committees or tribunals set up at different points along the transit routes of the basic foodstuffs. It was becoming clear that the next thing to be affected, after the circulation and the sale of victuals, would be their actual production.

Although wholly incapable of curbing the crisis which it had itself done so much to bring about, the Commune of Paris now undertook to organise the resulting hardship. Interminable queues formed before dawn in front of the bakeries, which were almost totally empty, in order to get a small piece of bread, which the authorities persisted in subsidising at three *sous* a pound. Instead of letting the rise in prices play its part in encouraging production, they introduced ration cards (29 October), which did nothing to increase the quantity of available foodstuffs. The use of these cards was very strictly supervised, yet frauds occurred nevertheless. Consumers were only supposed to use them in those bakeries where they were enrolled. The latter, in turn, could only have their stocks replenished through the mediation of officially designated wholesalers. By this means the Commune ended up by having total control of the bread trade and, shortly afterwards, that of other products also, including sugar, meat and even the bran fed to livestock, without thereby relieving the general wretchedness in the slightest.

Such methods were often imitated in provincial towns which, unlike Paris, were not the special concern of the Convention, and where the food situation was even more serious than in the capital. In many municipalities, the revolutionary committees, the sections or authorised representatives enforced their own measures for 'increasing available provision'. Throughout France there flourished ostensibly ingenious, but actually absurd or harmful ideas and proposals, which had however the advantage of flattering the prejudices and the ignoble sentiments of the ignorant masses. So it was that the authorities set about cultivating public or private gardens and disused land at a time when the *levée en masse* had made agricultural manpower so scarce that it was even inadequate for the purposes of working the most productive land. Potatoes were planted in the Tuileries and in the Luxembourg Gardens. War was declared on the vine. Lists of 'idle citizens' were drawn up. A decree stipulated that only one kind of flour and only one kind of bread ('the bread of equality') should be made. Because meat was in short supply, dogs and cats were sacrificed in great numbers. These measures, together with other, equally wayward ones, in no way served to relieve the general misery. Indeed, they show just how distressed were the politicians responsible for them, and how prone they were to demagogy.

The centralisation of the economy

The patent failure of the Maximum had soon to be acknowledged, at any rate in the form it had assumed on 11 and 29 September. Faced with the discontent of the sections, which were then at the height of their power, the Convention had to act without being in a position to revoke the interventionist politics upon which it had embarked. The only option open for appeasing the sans-culottes was to press ahead.

On 10 October 1793,[7] Saint-Just, speaking in the name of the Committee of Public Safety, announced the programme of a new system of government, which would be 'revolutionary up until the peace'. The June Constitution was suspended until the advent of better days and the existing institutions were placed under the dictatorship of the major committees. However, the administrative and political centralisation of the country, which they hoped to speed up, was turning out to be too complex a task for the meagre resources of the Committee of Public Safety. A Food Commission, consisting of three members, was therefore established. It was entrusted with 'the provisioning of the armies and the delivery of basic foodstuffs to those departments where they are in short supply'.

In the course of the debate surrounding the creation of this Commission, Barère described the law of 29 September, which had established the General Maximum, as 'a trap set the Convention by the enemies of the Republic' and as a 'present from London'. However, he did not argue that it be abolished; instead, like the other members of the Committee of Public Safety, he was quite prepared to see it consolidated.

In Barère's view, the law of the Maximum had suffered from two drawbacks. First of all, it had allowed local authorities too much leeway in the fixing of certain prices, and the districts had taken advantage of this to place private interests above the general interest. Secondly, in the calculations of the Maxima, no account had been taken of transportation costs and of the profits of tradesmen, whether wholesalers or retailers. In the light of Barère's observations, the Convention decided 'to tax at the centre' or, in other words, to entrust (on 1 November) the Food Commission with the responsibility for drawing up the price list, applicable to the entire nation, of all goods at the point of production. Transportation expenses and the profits of both wholesale (5 per cent) and retail (10 per cent) merchants were added to the costs of manufacture. In this way, it was claimed, the particular interests of the merchants being safeguarded, they would no longer act in an anti-social manner. This ambitious project involved nothing less than an attempt to calculate the 'right' price for the country's entire commercial, artisanal, industrial and agricultural production.

The Food Commission took three and a half months to complete this truly superhuman task as best it could. But, pending the publication, on 22 February, of the Maximum table at the 'point of production', many other tasks had still to be completed. These ranged from the drafting of an inventory of all the grain held by the country's inhabitants to the organisation of all the imports (especially, foodstuffs) and exports (above all, of luxury goods, for which revolutionary France had no further need), along with the draining of the marshes and the promotion of potato growing. It is also important to note that, on 12 February 1794, the Food Commission was granted sole right to proceed with confiscations and requisitions, which should, in principle, have put a stop to the anarchic and arbitrary manner in which these operations had up until then been conducted.

The right to requisition had been established at the time of the first Maximum. This right was exercised by the local authorities, and it concerned the supposedly superfluous quantities of grain held by the producers. In the following months, this operation was extended to cover other products reckoned to be basic necessities, and was vested both in the Minister of the Interior and in the authorised representatives. The sheer number of authorities empowered to requisition gave rise to massive confusion, led to every conceivable abuse (which only came to light after 9 Thermidor), and went unpunished. Agricultural production, which had already been weakened by the series of regulatory measures imposed upon it by the interventionist policies of the authorities, was reduced still further by the threat of requisitions. The Food Commission not only failed to put a stop to economically harmful practices, but also enjoyed extensive confiscatory powers. Indeed, on 15 November 1793, the Convention abolished the 'family reserve', which had previously placed some limit upon the interference of the authorities, and 'made the Republic's food reserves in their entirety into a sort of common stock'.

The fall of the Hébertists

The famine assumed dramatic proportions in the course of the winter. At Paris, thanks to massive expenditure by the Commune and the Convention, bakers still managed to sell some meagre rations of bread. The 250 grammes distributed per person per day in the capital actually represented a tiny amount, if one takes into account the dietary requirements of the period (one should bear in mind that bread constituted virtually the sole food of a large part of the population). In certain provinces, even these 250 grammes were not available, and other foodstuffs aside from bread had also become extremely scarce. The lack of meat was especially hard to bear. The lack of sustenance gave rise to sporadic rioting. Crowds would often attack and despoil peasants who ventured into the capital to sell their produce and buy whatever things they needed for their work or to eat. The situation seemed a potentially explosive one, and the fear was that further insurrections would break out at the first available opportunity, which, for want of any other enemies, would certainly choose the Convention as their target.

The worsening subsistence crisis showed just how inane the measures taken had been, and this knowledge could not help but deepen the divisions between the factions in power. The Hébertists in control of the Commune formulated demands which were at once simple and brutal, namely, that the economic Terror, as perpetrated by a strengthened revolutionary army, should be intensified still more. Their hostility towards tradesmen was further accentuated, and they even directed it at small merchants, some of whom constituted a part of their own following. As far as the Hébertists were concerned, only the threat of the guillotine could overcome 'the league composed of all those who sell against those who buy' and thus bring about the reign of plenty. Mercy and moderation seemed to them to be qualities eminently to be despised and they were violently opposed to the 'sleep-merchants', a term they used to describe Danton and his friends. They especially blamed the latter for having given fresh hope to the hoarders by broaching a discussion on the throwing open of the prisons.

In Ventôse (towards the end of February), bills were posted in Paris calling for popular insurrection. At the Cordeliers club, before an enthusiastic throng, Hébert showed so bold as to attack deputies, ministers (including Carnot, even though he was a member of the Committee of Public Safety), and even, in a gesture of supreme audacity, Robespierre himself. In the course of his harangue, he presented a justification of insurrection, which was for him the only practicable solution when the rights of the people were endangered. During the following days, the call to riot spread throughout the sections. The unleashing of an insurrection aimed at the Convention itself seemed imminent, notwithstanding the concessions that the Committee of Public Safety was granting to the sans-culottes and the new 'social' policies embodied in the famous Ventôse decrees, which were explicitly designed to placate them.

These decrees, which had been proposed by Saint-Just and passed on 26 February and 3 March 1794, ordered first of all the sequestration of all goods of persons known to be enemies of the Revolution, and secondly, the sharing out of such goods among needy patriots. The two categories of the populace referred to in these decrees were first of all to be inventoried, even though no precise definitions were given (the Committee of General Security was charged with investigating all persons who had been detained since 1 May 1789). This vast reform project, which was essentially agrarian in nature, prepared the way for a merciless struggle among patriots wishing to profit from the ransacking of the victims of their obloquy. It also represented a further restriction on property rights, or on what was left of them. According to its presenter, 'the wretched are the powers of the earth; they have the right to speak as masters to those governments which neglect them . . . he who has shown himself to be his country's enemy cannot be a proprietor there'.

Unfortunately for the Hébertists, who were not satisfied with these measures and who wanted power above all else, they were unable to carry the Commune with them in their subversive enterprise. The Committee of Public Safety, alerted to the danger that was threatening it, decided to make the first move. On 6 March, Barère informed the Convention that the dearth was the work of the very people who were complaining of it. He requested the public prosecutor to lose no time in denouncing, before the representatives of the nation, those who had posted the defamatory bills and those who had spread distrust of the merchants who were provisioning Paris.

A few days later, the Hébertists were arrested and accused, by a kind of tragic irony, of being party to a 'foreign plot' designed to starve Paris. On 24 March, they were executed. By now such events attracted little attention. Being thus rid of the faction which had posed the most immediate threat to them, Robespierre and those who were then his allies undoubtedly feared that they would no longer be able to control the influence of the rival faction, the 'Indulgents'. They therefore had its most eminent members arrested. Danton and those who appeared with him before the Revolutionary Tribunal were guillotined on 5 April.

Once the Hébertist leaders had been eliminated and the influence of the now leaderless sections much reduced, the forces which had worked the hardest to establish an interventionist policy and an economic dictatorship seemed to be on the wane. However, the Committee of Public Safety, now master of the situation, renounced neither regulation nor the Maximum. Through its suppression of the Provisional Executive Council and through its purge of local government, it in fact took advantage of its newly won freedom of manoeuvre to centralise its power, and its economic power in particular, still more.

The reforms which the Committee of Public Safety undertook upon this occasion were concerned with various excesses and abuses attributable for the most part to the Hébertists, but they did not affect the interventionist nature of the régime. Thus, the revolutionary army which, by its extortions, was terrorising the peasantry, was disbanded. A report drafted by Dudot, on 29 March 1794, led to a refinement in the penalties for hoarding. Requisitions, which were entrusted to the Food Commission (now the Commission of Trade and Supplies), lost something of their arbitrary character. In short, the Committee of Public Safety sought by kind words and a few relatively minor measures to win the cooperation of the tradesmen, who were no longer officially the enemies of the Revolution. But the counterpart to this very partial relaxation of the economic Terror was a reinforcement of the *dirigiste* and centralised character of the government.

Two decisions will give the measure of the policies pursued in the course of spring 1794. First, a decree of 30 May (11 Prairial) actually gave the state a monopoly over all foreign trade. On 26 June (8 Messidor), another decree stipulated that the whole of the harvest be requisitioned in advance. If one takes into account the other arrangements the state had already made, it is clear that, on the eve of 9 Thermidor, it was in control of virtually all production and distribution in France.

It rapidly became clear that the centralisation of the national economy could only be effective if the labour force were brought under control. The Law of the Maximum stipulated that wages should not be higher than 1.5 times their level of 1790. In reality, however, there was a great disparity between the different ways in which labour was rewarded. Those who were employed directly by the state, and more particularly those who were involved in producing armaments, were paid according to the Maximum, a fact which gave rise to much discontent and even strikes (which in theory were still prohibited by the Le Chapelier law). On the other hand, certain workers in the private sector, whose incomes the authorities found it hard to check, sometimes earned a good living. In the countryside in particular, the scarcity of manpower occasioned by the *levée en masse* had inflated actual wages well beyond the legal rate. In order to make the cost of labour compatible with the Maximum of the prices of products, the government, if it were not to abandon all attempts to control prices, had to ensure that the letter of the law was respected. Since the workers often refused to work for the Maximum, Barère forced through a decree on 4 May conscripting all those who played a part 'in the handling, transport and retailing' of products defined as basic necessities; those who participated in a criminal association (a strike) against the people's provisions were threatened with the Revolutionary Tribunal. On 30 May, another decree called upon all agricultural workers to bring in the harvest. On 19 July, Saint-Just had those workers who were on strike arrested as suspects. Finally, on 23 July, the Commune published a new schedule for wages in the capital.

The attempts of the Committee of Public Safety to regulate employment and to control wages indisputably resulted in Robespierre losing his popularity and in the Paris mob becoming disillusioned with him. As Albert Mathiez observed;

On 9 Thermidor, the workers of Paris, dissatisfied with the new schedule of wages that the Commune had recently promulgated, appeared to take no interest in the political struggle that was unfolding before their eyes. On 9 Thermidor itself, they demonstrated against the Maximum on wages.[8]

Two days later, when Robespierre and his friends were in their turn led to the scaffold, these workers cried out as they passed: 'Fuck the Maximum!' The instigators of the Terror had been led to their downfall by the logic of the system of controls which they had themselves introduced.

Financial arrangements during the Terror

In spite of the centralisation imposed by the government committees, public accounting during this period was in a state of utter chaos. It would seem an impossible task to reconstitute the Treasury's outgoings and incomings, especially for the few months prior to Thermidor. Cambon's declarations before the Convention, and the figures that he presented, clearly cannot be regarded as an accurate reflection of the real situation. Expenditure was far from having been brought under control, and the *assignats* (new issues of which were no longer announced) were more and more used to supplement a by and large inadequate level of receipts. Their issue so swelled the quantity of paper money in circulation that, on 9 Thermidor (27 July 1794), it amounted to 6,400 million *livres*,[9] whereas on 15 August 1793 it had been 3,217 millions. In spite of all the withdrawals that Cambon strove to effect, it had doubled in the space of eleven months.

During the summer of 1793, the *assignat* had plummeted to around a quarter of its face value. The government of France under the Terror used every available means of constraint to bolster its price. A veritable hunt for precious metals swept the country. Coinciding with the dechristianisation campaign, it resulted in the systematic looting of the churches, which did not always work to the state's advantage. The gold which was dishonoured both as a symbol of monarchy and as a corrupter of souls was actively sought by agents of the state, who withdrew it from circulation so that it might no longer compete with paper money. The same authorities that forbade citizens to use gold greedily seized it, so plain was it becoming that it was the only stable value left. The draconian measures taken had a few results, which, however, could not help but be transitory. In Thermidor, year II (July 1794), the price of the *assignat* had climbed back up to 35 per cent of par after having touched 50 per cent in December 1793.

The upkeep and provisioning of the armies was a serious drain upon the revolutionary government's budget. Since neither authorised representatives, nor ministers nor government committees, nor the Commission of Trade, were required to keep accounts regarding these transactions, the bills were even higher than they might otherwise have been. Given these huge expenses, taxation, which was normally the state's principal resource, was still plainly not providing adequate funds. In order to lay its hands on the sums of money needed, the Convention had laid great store by the sale of émigré properties which, it was claimed, was going very well. The real situation was quite otherwise. These properties had lost a great deal of value in the period when they were up for sale, and as we shall see, the actual selling of them was badly handled. The people living in the vicinity showed no compunction in overrunning them, and there was no one to stand in their way; the farmers who occupied them refused to accept responsibility for their upkeep; the municipalities took advantage of the fact that their owners were absent to allocate to them the largest share of the land tax for which they were answerable, which reduced their value still more. When, finally, these properties were put on the market, few potential buyers came forward, partly because resources were scarce and partly because those who still had them tended to hide the fact, for fear of being regarded as rich. In addition, collusion between purchasers and local authorities gave rise to innumerable frauds, which brought the selling prices still lower. The truth is that the sheer length of time accorded for payment (ten years), together with the option made available to purchasers of paying off their debt in *assignats*, meant that, by the time the Terror was upon France, the *biens nationaux* were being sold off for derisory amounts.

The victories of the Republic's armies, and their entry into the Palatinate and Belgium, brought the Treasury some relief. These two countries were in fact subjected to systematic looting. Philanthropic designs, and the project of liberating all the peoples of Europe, were soon forgotten. It was now a question of laying one's hands not only on whatever supplies were to be found in the conquered countries but also on every object of any value whatsoever. The instructions given by Carnot on this topic were perfectly explicit:

Carry out useful expeditions, bring back supplies, arms and any clothing that might be used by our armies; strip our enemies of all their resources, all their means of existence. It is a great misfortune that we have to plunder, but it is still preferable to take destruction elsewhere rather than suffer it on one's own territory.

The war of the patriots against the rich

The *Enragés*, and after them the Hébertists, had claimed political power in the name of the Revolution, in order to make the sans-culottes happy or, more precisely, to allow them to benefit from economic advantages. Even after these two movements had disappeared, 'patriotism' continued to serve as a screen for official looting and for the redistribution of the accumulated wealth of the country.

Centralisation led to a greater development of the revolutionary bureaucracy. A huge staff, recruited solely on the basis of political criteria, invaded the Ministry of War and the Trade Commission. Places were the reward for opinions, whereas competent but lukewarm functionaries were purged. A blind eye was turned to incompetence, negligence and even connivance, just so long as civic virtues were paraded at the same time. The result was, as Boissy d'Anglas recorded a little later, that 'the French nation has seen the treasures of public wealth escape and be dispersed in almost equal measure among greedy rogues and well-intentioned but unenlightened men'.

Many patriots benefited from state hand-outs without actually becoming functionaries. They could profit from the public manna by receiving the forty *sous* granted to sans-culottes who attended their section meetings, or the three *livres* a day granted to citizens guarding suspects in their homes. Or again, they might have a share in the funds allocated by various municipalities to the revolutionary committees in order to 'research into the plots of evildoers'. A Book of National Charity was even established, in order that the needy might be compensated with goods taken from the enemies of the Revolution. It was Barère who had to justify the creation of such a book (on 11 May 1793): 'It is up to the Convention to repair the injustices of monarchical laws, to eliminate the extreme inequality of fortunes and to efface the word "poor" from the annals of the Republic.'

The Revolution gave many 'patriots' the opportunity to participate personally in the 'destruction of the inequality of fortunes'. The most effective weapon used by them in the war against the rich was without a doubt local taxation. Such taxes, although forbidden, were nevertheless levied, not only by authorised representatives but also by the popular societies, the revolutionary committees or even by ordinary individuals girt with a tricolour scarf, and, suddenly and quite arbitrarily, under the pretext of serving for the equipping of the armies or for the help of the needy, they affected all the rich or everyone suspected of being so.

The ultimate weapon in the war against the rich was, of course, the scaffold. In a period at which economic mechanisms were so unregulated that a large part of the population depended for their survival upon the black market, it was no longer possible to put a number to those guilty of a breach of the laws in force. Therefore sentences for economic crimes were relatively scarce. To be more precise, recent studies[10] suggest that the Revolutionary Tribunal had pronounced 267 sentences of this sort, 181 of which were for hoarding or for failure to respect the maximum, and eighty-six for passing counterfeit money or for trading in *assignats*. But one should not be deceived by this apparently 'lax' attitude. It is in fact difficult to discern, on the basis of the most frequent indictments (seditious talk, uncivic behaviour, etc.) and the collective judgements of groups composed of persons often having no relation with each other, just what the real reasons for arrests were. One should add that, by the end of the Terror, the prisons contained thousands of suspects, who could, thanks to the Prairial laws, be sentenced faster and faster. Many condemned for potential economic crimes owed their lives to the fall of Robespierre. On 9 Thermidor, if Louis Madelin is to be believed,[11] Fouquier-Tinville ordered the executioner to cut off forty-two more heads, 'all of them belonging to quite ordinary people, virtually all shopkeepers'.

The scaffold, which was no respecter of social distinctions, also played a more direct part in filling the state's coffers. Since the property of those executed actually reverted to the state, it sometimes happened that judges sitting on the tribunals or authorised representatives would, confidently believing that they were acting in the nation's best interests, have well-to-do persons condemned so that their goods and property could be confiscated.[12] A popular expression of the period ran: 'they are coining money in the Place de la Révolution [which is where the scaffold was]'. As for Lebon, an authorised delegate, no one could have put it more plainly:

Considering that among those charged with crimes against the Republic we should do our utmost to cut off the heads of rich men who are generally known to be guilty, the criminal tribunal established at Arras will first of all judge in a revolutionary spirit those charged who are notable for their talents or for wealth, and the other cases will be adjourned until the first have been tried.

Under the Terror, patriotism had become a highly lucrative profession. Some of the most famed heroes of the Revolution, Mirabeau and Danton at their head, had undoubtedly proved the truth of this axiom and enriched themselves to a scandalous extent. Moreover, although Robespierre and Saint-Just, as the supreme heads of the state, had shown themselves to be incorruptible, or so it was said, the régime which they had established was one where corruption was rife. Since property rights had been almost wholly displaced by the interest of the nation or that of the poor, anyone acting in the name of such interests could do as he wished.

During Ventôse, Saint-Just had declared that 'Force of circumstance may perhaps be leading to consequences which we could not have imagined.' This admission, which was meant to explain how it was that the policies of the Terror had arisen, also undoubtedly shows why it was that economic regulations were not only maintained in operation after the fall of the Hébertists but were even reinforced and extended. The men who had been heads of state since the spring of 1793 tended to think that trade should remain free. But their political opportunism had led them to yield to popular leaders. When the latter had gone, the interventionist system was already too complex and its ramifications too numerous for it to be abolished without giving rise to serious difficulties in the short term. Anyone whose thinking was imbued with the concepts of the Physiocrats or of Adam Smith, and who was confident of the long-term benefits that the whole country would derive from the suppression of the Maximum, of requisitioning and of the other forms of regulation of trade and production, would not have been afraid to tackle them. However, the economic convictions of men like Saint-Just, Barère, Carnot, not to mention Robespierre, were not sufficiently firm for them to accept the risk entailed, in their view, by the 'liberalisation' of exchange.

In fact, the Committee of Public Safety let itself be drawn into the logic of regulation. The control of the price of a single commodity, such as grain, automatically entailed that of all the products used by the producers of grain also; it then required the control of the prices of the products for which grain might be substituted; finally, it involved that of the cost of manpower, it being a factor common to all production. Agricultural producers, manufacturers or tradesmen could adopt one of two attitudes: either they could submit to regulation, lose money and end up by closing down and falling idle, or else they could brave the Maximum and sell at black market prices with all the risks and potential rewards attendant upon such behaviour. Given those circumstances, shocking imbalances emerged between the poverty of workers caught in the vice of controlled wages and expensive foodstuffs, and the fortunes won by a few individuals who were more or less unscrupulous or who were anyway prepared to brave the state's prohibitions. The authorities were thus faced with a growing scarcity of supplies, with the closing down of numerous businesses and with runaway real prices. The more they paraded their determination to succour the needy, who were in fact the victims of their own measures, and the more urgent it seemed to equip their armies in the field, the more they were tempted by the interventionist escalade.

The Thermidor government found itself at the head of a country in the grip of an extremely serious crisis and of a wholly state-controlled economy. It no longer had any other choice but to take advantage of the discouragement suffered by the Parisian mobs, and of the euphoria produced by the victories won by the armies of the Republic, and to relax the regulatory constraints imposed in the past few years.

9

'Dirigisme' in retreat

The history with which we are concerned ends at 9 Thermidor. It has enabled us to pursue, against the backdrop of a period rich in events and characterised by the lack of a stable system of government, an analysis of the behaviour of politicians. Given the extreme conditions of the revolutionary period, this behaviour appeared in something like its pure state. It may be summarised as a merciless struggle for power, and as the exercise of that power in the name of the citizens, even when they were its victims. Now, in this period those who held power owed their legitimacy, and ultimately their actual survival, to the mob. The rulers' policies had therefore to be approved by it. So it was that decisions were taken which seemed to be beneficial in the short term, even if in the long run they had disastrous consequences or were in fact contrary to the convictions of those who had made them.

The mechanism by which, from 1789 to summer 1794, the Revolution's basic dynamic was established, thus becomes plain. The gears were engaged when, in an attempt to guarantee their own popularity and to consolidate their power, the men who were in the majority in the Constituent Assembly undertook to honour all the debts incurred under the *Ancien Régime*. At the same time and for the very same reasons, they in fact dismantled the much-loathed fiscal system of the *Ancien Régime*, while also refusing to employ the force necessary to raise new taxes. These men promised, not always sincerely, to find a way out of the dilemma they had just created for themselves, without thereby undermining the right of property which they had declared was sacred. Thus they confiscated the property of the Church and issued paper money. The *assignats* resolved the Treasury's short-term difficulties but gave rise to yet trickier problems in the following months and years. It was after summer 1791, in particular, that the inflation triggered off by paper money began to wreak real havoc. The men who dominated the Legislative Assembly, which had been elected but a short time later, had neither the courage nor the far-sightedness to halt the issues of *assignats* and revert to a more orthodox fiscal policy. They wished to preserve their popularity by blaming the subsistence crisis upon the plots of émigrés and counter-revolutionairies.

The rhetoric of the Girondins led quite naturally to war against foreign enemies, and subsequently domestic ones. The deterioration of the economic situation, a foreseeable consequence of decisions taken in the past, worked to the advantage of the Montagnards, who became the spokesmen of the mob, whose wretchedness was by now so intolerable that it was in a state of open revolt. Once they had won power, they found themselves obliged to satisfy popular demands and to pursue the sorts of *dirigiste* policies favoured by the *Enragés*, and after them by the Hébertists. The intrinsic logic of regulation of, and interference in, the economy resulted in virtually all of it being subjected to state control, to the Terror and to famine.

Since it seemed impossible to go any further down the path of authoritarianism, the Thermidoreans, and after them the men of the Directory, had no choice but to revert to a more liberal form of government. This is what, gradually, the proceeded to do. They abolished the Maximum, relinquished requisitioning to a certain extent, and curbed those measures of constraint that had proved most damaging to the economy. Since, however, they too were reluctant to exert a sufficient degree of fiscal pressure to balance the budget, they continued to finance their policies with issues of paper money, up until the point at which this method had wholly outlasted its usefulness. It was their good fortune, in fact, at a number of critical moments, to receive booty which their generals had seized from the countries which they had overrun.

I want now to give an account of how it was that the difficult business of returning to a less constrained form of economy was effected, and how the lamentable paper money episode came to an end.

The gradual reintroduction of free trade

The men who overthrew the Terror, and who had been implicated in the economic policies pursued at that time, in full cognisance of their perverse nature and their deleterious consequences, did not really have any project of government. They seized power in order to save their own necks and they were none too sure as to how to wield it. Their somewhat chaotic economic policy consisted in gradually scrapping the most harmful elements of state regulation and state interference in the economy. To their lasting credit, they also attempted to stop public wealth from being exploited in the name of a supposed patriotism by unscrupulous minorities, as had been the case since the founding of the Republic.

The abuses of the Commune of Paris, which was dismantled and replaced by twelve *arrondissements*, were denounced from the tribune of the Convention. The decree of 5 September 1793, which had granted forty *sous* to any poor citizens who attended the meetings of their sections, was revoked. Those listening upon this occasion learnt that commissioners often registered as present up to four times as many persons as were actually in attendance at the section meetings, and that they lined their own pockets first, then went on to distribute money to their protégés.

The government itself paid the wages of countless 'patriots', and offered what were plainly sinecures in offices and ministries. The sans-culottes were especially keen to secure the post of watchman of suspects under house arrest, a job which earned them three *livres* a day. The excessive expenditure of the administration had in fact been somewhat curbed, after Cambon had demonstrated the extent of it:

One of the great vices of a democratic state is the huge number of public and salaried functionaries, and this is not the least of the charges one might lay at the door of persons who had set about creating an army of some 40,000 watchmen, who had been promised three *livres* a day, which resulted in a daily expenditure of 1,620,000 and an annual expenditure of 591,300,000.

The sale of *biens nationaux* posed the new government a serious problem. It still represented, in theory at any rate, the Treasury's main resource. But, as we saw in the previous chapter, prevarication had seriously reduced the value of this patrimony. Furthermore, the confis-cation of the property of the émigrés, or of those who were claimed to be such, had given rise to massive despoliation. A strict regard for justice would have required that the propriety of certain transactions be looked into more closely. However, a fair number of representatives in the Convention feared that an annulment of sales already effected might sow seeds of doubt in the minds of subsequent buyers as to the validity of their purchases, and that this doubt would prejudice any future auctions and thereby damage the standing of the *assignat*. Recourse was therefore had to a series of half-measures. A few reparations were made, but they remained limited, and nothing was done to ensure that a better running of the national patrimony bolstered its value. The sale of *biens nationaux* therefore went on, without the Treasury receiving payments even close to their real value.

Once free of pressure from the sections, from the Commune, and from the Jacobins, whose club had been shut down, many members of the Convention now felt free to express their real convictions. Since their education had been by and large an Enlightenment one, they did not believe in the virtues of regulation; they therefore called for free trade, not in order to advance the interests of those involved in it, but for the 'general good'. Unfortunately, in this area as in so many others, in spite of the cogency of the arguments that were employed, the Assembly preferred to make compromises rather than opt for the total and immediate suppression of the interventionist measures of the previous period. Requisitions were still authorised, albeit more limited and better controlled ones; in particular, penalties were stipulated for those who diverted them to their own profit.

The Trade Commission had been a key mechanism in the Robespierrists' far-reaching plan to bring the economy under state control. Its ostensible object, the guaranteeing of supplies, seemed to be above criticism. In reality, it had done precisely the opposite, and bore a heavy responsibility for the aggravation of the famine. The requisitions which it ordered actually represented hoarding in the strict sense, since the commodities that had been confiscated often lay unused for months in warehouses, prior to being handed over by inept or venal commissioners to speculators, who re-sold them at a huge profit. The members of the Convention were coming to realise that the Commission was primarily serving the interests of those who, in the name of patriotism, were only concerned to further their own interests. As Tallien wrote,[1] regarding the way in which the personnel for this Commission had been recruited:

If someone of real merit applied, he was set aside as suspect. The men that were chosen were totally untried, but by the same token, prone to intrigue, prompt at undertaking transactions that were to their own advantage, ever prepared to hoard in the name of the Commission, to harry merchants and tradesmen in the departments, and finally to ruin trade and bring about famine under the pretext of guaranteeing plenty.

The bureaucracy created by the centralisation of the economy posed a problem of a far greater magnitude than the one occasioned by the Trade Commission. 'If you cast your eyes over the various commissions,' cried Thibault, 'you will see a swarm of clerks more insolent and more spendthrift than those of the *Ancien Régime*, who are never to be found in their offices, and who are incompetent at their jobs.' In spite of numerous accusations of this sort, made from the tribune of the Assembly, the Thermidoreans did not suppress the Trade Commission; displaying yet again a tentative and hesitant approach, they simply reduced its powers. The Maximum, which was universally agreed to be harmful, was not abolished either. Testimonies as to its baneful effects, often popular in origin, flooded into the Convention. They proved, above all, that the Maximum on grain was the sole one that the authorities could to a certain extent enforce. But, since the cost of labour and that of the majority of foodstuffs had increased by five or six times since 1790 (the year to which reference was made when calculating the Maximum), the cultivators would stop producing rather than sell at a loss. The Maximum, far from satisfying the needs of the 'people', was therefore contrary to its interests. As one member of the Convention put it: 'If you destroy the Maximum, everything, it is true, will be dear; but if you keep it, there will be nothing left to be bought.'² What point was there in having low prices, if the desired commodities did not exist?

The opposition to a return to free trade was led by a number of deputies, such as Robert Lindet, who acknowledged the disadvantages of the Maximum in the form that it had been decreed, but who claimed that it ought to be reformed rather than scrapped. Other members of the Convention, although they declared themselves opposed in principle to the Maximum, feared that any too sudden a disappearance of it would lead to prices running riot. These two lines of argument caused the Assembly to equivocate. In November 1794, it altered the system governing the calculation of the official agricultural prices, in such a way as to benefit agricultural producers. However, this partial reform, as rapidly became clear, had no tangible effect upon production. Finally, men such as Cambon and Tallien exerted so much pressure that, on 24 December 1794 (4 Nivôse, Year III), the Convention abolished the Maximum altogether. This (in principle) salutary measure unfortunately came too late. The disastrous effects of price controls, combined with those of inflation and extremely poor weather, had already affected the production and distribution of the harvest of 1794.

The famine of Year III

Since the summer of 1794 was so unusually dry, the peasants had to broach their reserve supplies, especially their fodder and their salt fish,

even before winter had begun. It turned out to be the bitterest winter
since the beginning of the eighteenth century. Since the freezing conditions made communications and transport difficult, and since the
meagre resources of the peasants quickly ran out, as they ate larger
quantities in an attempt to ward off the cold, circumstances conspired to
produce a serious subsistence crisis. The freakish weather joined forces
with modes of regulation and interference invented by man to bring
about a truly terrible situation.

We have already seen how even a depreciation of paper money of
around 10 per cent per year had been sufficient in 1791 to make the
growers cut back on the quantities of grain that they were delivering to
the markets and thus provoke a subsistence crisis. Whereas, in July 1794,
the *assignat* still held 33 per cent of its face value, a year later it had fallen
to 3 per cent. The consequences of a depreciation of 90 per cent in the
space of a year, amplified by the effects of the Maximum, of the
requisitions, of centralisation and of the Terror, which had reduced the
country's economy to total chaos, could not help but be catastrophic and
bring about a disaster of a kind altogether without precedent in the
history of modern France.

There are many eye-witness accounts of the famine of Year III. The
most heartrending of such testimonies tell of the corpses of peasants
being found by the wayside with their mouths full of grass or hay. In my
view, however, it is a more recent article that best allows us to get the
measure of this catastrophe.[3] Its author, Richard Cobb, has drawn up a
table of the deaths recorded month by month by the civil authorities of
the town of Rouen, during the period which runs from Year III to Year
X. Figure 5 (p. 169) shows the relation between the monthly death rate
from Year II to Year IV, and the average death rate, for the same months,
during the six subsequent years. Closer examination of the information
drawn from Richard Cobb's tables indicates that mortality was exceptionally high between the month of Vendémiaire of Year III (October
1794) and the month of Thermidor of Year IV (July 1796). For the
whole of Years III and IV it was, respectively, twice and 2.6 times higher
than the average value for the following years. But it is also of interest to
note that the conditions which occasioned this rise in mortality began to
exert their influence before the terrible winter of Year III and that they
continued to have some impact during the following summer (which
was also a very dry one) and winter (which was likewise cold). Natural
conditions therefore merely served to exacerbate a crisis which was
brought about by interventionism and which only came to an end with

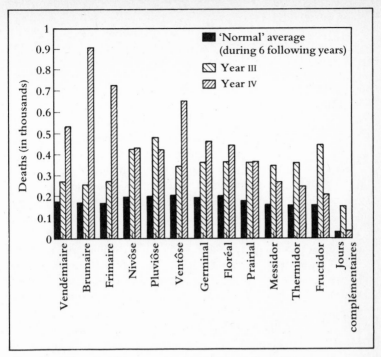

Figure 5 Monthly death rate in Rouen (source: R. C. Cobb)

the good harvest of 1796, at a time when the partial liberalisation of the economy was finally bearing fruit.

Furthermore, figures for births corroborate the conclusions which may be drawn from the data regarding mortality. Indeed, Richard Cobb shows that there was a sharp fall in conceptions during the terrible winter of Year IV (winter of 1795–6). Finally, it is worth bearing in mind that Richard Cobb is convinced that the excessive mortality he has identified was not due to an epidemic but actually to the terrible condition of wretchedness brought about by the lack of foodstuffs and the extreme destitution of the poorest communities.

Numerous historians have seen the change in economic policy and the partial abandonment of interventionist measures as responsible for the outbreak of the famine of Year III, which continued into Year IV, as we have seen. Richard Cobb, for example, says of the death rates recorded in his article that they 'serve as a condemnation of the subsistence policies of the Thermidoreans, which represented a sudden return to a free

economy and to the lifting of restrictions from the primary producers'.[4]
Georges Lefebvre likewise observes that 'the abandonment of a managed
economy . . . necessarily provoked a frightful catastrophe. Prices soared
and the rate of exchange fell. The Republic was condemned to massive
levels of inflation, and its currency was ruined.'[5] Albert Soboul uses
virtually identical terms when he declares that, with the suppression of
the Maximum, 'a terrible crisis ensued'.[6]

The most elementary economic theories teach us, in my view, that
allegations such as these rest upon a confusion between the causes and the
consequences of the phenomena under observation. The famine of Year
III took place because *dirigisme*, requisitions, war, the Maximum and,
above all, inflation had reduced agricultural production to chaos.
Weather conditions had served to exacerbate a crisis that in actual fact
had begun well before the terrible winter of Year III. The belated
abolition of a number of constraints served to check any further
worsening of the crisis but was not enough to bring about an immediate
return of prosperity. During the winter of Year III, and the months that
followed, people were not able to find food, for the simple reason that it
had not been produced in sufficient quantities. The lifting of restrictions
upon prices merely served to reveal the scarcity to which the Maximum
had given rise. As Marcel Marion has pointed out, 'for the poor to have
bread, the first and crucial requirement was for France to be producing
corn, and with the advent of the Maximum, the moment was fast
approaching when it would stop producing any at all'.[7]

Moreover, nothing could be more absurd than to claim, as some of
the historians quoted above have done, that the inflation of 1795 was
brought about by the abolition of the Maximum. The fall in the value of
the *assignat* preceded the scrapping of price controls, and as I shall try to
demonstrate in chapter 10, may be perfectly satisfactorily explained by
the ever-increasing quantities of paper money that the government put
into circulation.

As in the earlier periods, so too in 1795, the people of Paris benefited
from the solicitude of the authorities. The meagre amounts of cash still
held by the state were used to distribute bread rations. Yet these soon fell
to six, then to four, and then to as little as two ounces per person per
day.[8] These rations, although higher than those consumed in many of the
provinces, represented the sum total of food available to a good part of
the population and were plainly inadequate to sustain normal levels of
nutrition. Finally, in spite of their exhausted condition, the disappoint-
ments they had suffered and the disappearance of all leaders of any real

stature, the faubourgs rose up and besieged the Convention. The insurrections of Germinal (1 April) and of Prairial (20–3 May 1795) echoed to the cry 'bread or death'. These were the last and most pointless convulsions of the poorer quarters; they provided a pretext for the arrest of the last of the main figures of the Terror who were still at large, and of a few Jacobin deputies. These uprisings had of course no effect upon the pitiable living conditions of the ordinary people, and were merely a dramatic consequence of the inflationary, and more recently interventionist, economic policies pursued in the past few years.

The subsistence crisis very probably also lay behind the famous 'Conspiracy of Equals', the leaders of which, Babeuf and Buonarroti, were arrested on 10 March 1796. The conspirators, who were the spiritual heirs of Marat, thought that the Terror had failed because it had not been taken far enough. In theory, they wished to establish a society in which actual equality and a communism of property reigned. The socialists therefore consider them nowadays to be their real precursors, with the *Enragés*, Hébertists and other Robespierrists being regarded as ideologically impure, their aspirations criticised because they would have led to a society of smallholders.

After the terrible Year III, the living conditions of the people, which are to be distinguished from those of the various sorts of profiteer (who were adept at exploiting the innumerable opportunities for lining their pockets that a deregulated régime offered unscrupulous persons), slowly improved. The credit for this must go in part to François de Neufchâteau, a minister under the Directory, whose most significant measure consisted in the reintroduction, on 9 June 1797, of free trade in grain. However, if contemporary accounts are to be believed, it was not until 1799 that agricultural production was once again at the level it had reached prior to the Revolution.

The end of the 'assignats'

When the Directory was established, on 31 October 1795 (9 Brumaire, Year IV), the *assignat* had fallen to one-hundredth of its face value (a gold *louis* was worth 2,400 *livres-assignats*), and its depreciation was still accelerating. Eighteen billion *livres* of paper money were now in circulation. In its last days, the Convention had once more resorted to printing money. It had conducted long debates as to whether it was appropriate to maintain the fiction that a *livre-assignat* represented the same value as a *livre* in coin. For as long as this fiction lasted, creditors were scandalously short-changed by their debtors, who, thanks to paper money, ended up by paying back but a tiny fraction of their real debt. The state itself, because it had sold the *biens nationaux* on credit, and because it allowed taxes to be paid off in *assignats*, was seriously affected by such transactions. Finally it admitted what everyone had known for a long time, namely, that it had failed to keep its word and that a paper franc was not worth as much as a gold franc. This admission resulted in the setting up of a sliding scale, which tied the purchasing power of the *assignats* to the quantity in circulation (21 June 1795). The consequence being that issues continued at a fine old rate.

As the value of the paper money in circulation fell, it became necessary, even if needs remained constant, to issue ever larger amounts. However, closer inspection reveals that the issues of the autumn of 1795, which came close to two billions a month, were only equivalent in value to twenty millions in the notes issued in 1790 and 1791. Appearances notwithstanding, the Thermidoreans were far less guilty or less lax than the members of the Constituent Assembly, who, if one takes real values into account, had issued more paper. Yet past errors weighed heavily upon the Thermidoreans and very soon the *assignat*, which had proved so convenient a source of finance for the Treasury, was to prove unusable. As Jean Morini-Comby observes, 'the daily needs of the state exceeded the available means of fabrication of the notes'.[9]

During the first months of the Directory, the issues of *assignats* continued, as did their depreciation. The new government was loath to jettison a source of finance which, in spite of its harmful consequences, had proved so convenient. In a desperate attempt to shore up the paper money, it resorted to a series of tried and trusted ruses, although by then it was perfectly plain how ineffectual they were. The Stock Exchange, which had been closed in August 1793, and then reopened in April 1795, was closed yet again in November of the same year, the accusation being levelled once more that trade in gold and silver had brought down the value of paper. A forced loan of 600 millions, which was theoretically payable in coin or in corn, enabled the rapid withdrawal from circulation of a huge quantity of paper money, since contributors were also able to pay in *assignats*, which were taken in at one-hundredth of their face value. This venture was initially very popular, for it was hoped that those who had enriched themselves through the Revolution would bear the costs of it. However, as could have been anticipated given the chaotic state of France's administration, the forced loan met with stiff resistance, so that the terms governing it were modified and, by the end of March

1796, it had only yielded the equivalent of 116 millions in coin. The *assignats* recovered in the course of this operation, instead of being burnt, as had been stipulated, were put back into circulation.

After the failure of this last attempt to prop up the *assignats*, they were worth little more than the paper upon which they were printed (this was literally true in the case of the hundred-franc denominations). The government no longer had any option but to stop producing them. The blocks which had been used to print the *assignats* were solemnly destroyed on 19 February 1796. They had served for the printing of 45,581,411,618 *livres* of paper money, a little over thirty-four billions of which was still in circulation.

The lamentable episode of the 'mandats territoriaux'

The sales of *biens nationaux* now represented the Treasury's principal resource. Unfortunately, however, they were going ahead too slowly to match the government's needs, which were estimated as being of the order of 1.5 billion francs in coin per year. The Council of Five Hundred was then won over by a new proposal, namely, that areas of forest be auctioned to the sum of 1,200 million francs, so as to withdraw some *assignats* from circulation, and that, at the same time, 600 millions of the state's debt be redeemed by means of drafts which could be directly exchanged, without auctions, against public lands whose value would be fixed (assessed through the application of a multiplicative coefficient of the revenues produced in 1790).

The Directory was financially so hard-pressed that it adopted this scheme, but in an altered form. It held on only to the idea of a new paper money, which could be launched in place of the *assignats*. The law of 18 March 1796 thus created the *mandats territoriaux* and established them as compulsory currency. A stock of 2,400 millions was to be issued, rather than the 600 millions originally stipulated. This currency, which in its turn was declared to be of equal value to gold, was to be exchanged for *assignats* in the ratio of one to thirty. At a time when the *assignat* was worth a mere 0.33 per cent of its face value, this was in effect to give to the franc *mandat* which was tied to it a value of thirty times 0.0033 or 0.10 francs in coin, which in no way corresponded to official parity. The extremely rapid collapse of the new paper money should therefore occasion no surprise. This collapse was in no way checked by the official speeches singing its praises, for the general public had long since lost faith in them.

Once aware that the value of the *mandat* was falling fast, the government resolved, first of all, to shore it up with authoritarian measures. This proved to be in vain, for by 4 April the new currency had already lost 80 per cent of its value, and two weeks later, 90 per cent. The use of coin, although prohibited, was common practice, and the authorities themselves used the *mandat* at its market value in a good number of operations. Public opinion was especially scandalised by the fact that the members of the legislature had indexed their own remuneration against the inverse of the value of the paper money while continuing to affirm parity with the coinage. During this period, junior functionaries received salaries whose nominal value was fixed, but whose real value, so to speak, was next to nothing. These circumstances reduced them, and the majority of *rentiers* also, to the direst poverty and sometimes even to death by starvation.

The Directory's grand plan, that of pegging the value of the new money to that of the *biens nationaux*, worked against the state's best interests. The public lands serving as a surety for the *mandats* were valued at 4,840 millions. This figure is open to dispute because it rests upon incomplete knowledge of the revenues of 1790 upon which the estimates are based. The original values in *livres* for 1790 were very probably underestimated, but from another angle, the corresponding properties, since they belonged to the state, had suffered serious damage. However, no matter what the real values in coin, the sale prices, as expressed in *mandats*, calculated at a rate of one for one, represented but an infinitesimal part of them. The public grasped this immediately and hurled themselves at the lots put up for sale, so as to profit from this unbelievable windfall. Since the prices were fixed, all the demand for property could not be satisfied, and schemes of the most dubious sort were set up.

Dupont de Nemours, elected to the Council of Elders after his imprisonment during the Terror, showed as much hostility to the *mandats* as he had done to the *assignats*. The *Historien*, a newspaper published by him during this period, recorded some of the incredible abuses arising out of the sales of *biens nationaux*.[10] It may be worth quoting a number of typical examples. In Bordeaux, a mansion which had cost 500,000 *écus* was sold for 127,000 francs' worth of *mandats*, which, at the going rate, was no more than 10,620 *écus*; in Provence, a new house worth more than 6,000 livres in coin was sold for 540 *livres'* worth of *mandats*, that is, twenty *livres* and sixteen sous in coin; in the Gers, a wood of 130 acres was sold for 63,000 *livres'* worth of *mandats*, or

3,000 in coin, and its new owner immediately made 25,000 francs in coin by cutting it down, while holding on to his ownership of the soil; in the Basses-Pyrenées, the purchaser of a château which cost him 21,000 francs immediately made 8,000 francs by selling the railings and the balustrades; at Bordeaux again, a fine house which brought in a rent of 7,000 *livres* a year under the *Ancien Régime* was bought for the equivalent of 8,379 francs in coin and then resold two months later for 20,000, a figure still well below its value; at Lyons, a theatre bought for 20,000 francs in coin was leased out two days later for 25,000 francs.

No one could dispute the sheer scale of the catastrophe that the government had brought upon itself. The authorities, however, were reluctant to revoke the decisions they had taken, for fear of reversing their own judgements, and also because they included deputies representing private interests, those whom Dupont de Nemours called the 'redeemers' faction', who took advantage of the situation to speculate and to line their pockets. The legislation designed to bolster the *mandats'* status as currency was not repealed until 5 May 1796. On this same day, the prohibition upon holding gold was abrogated. Then, as late as 17 July, citizens were given the freedom to engage in cash transactions and to use the currency of their choice. Finally, on 31 July, the Assemblies decided, very belatedly, to call a halt to the losses that the sales of *biens nationaux* were inflicting upon the state. Upon this occasion a measure was passed which was both unconstitutional, because retroactive, and unjust, because contrary to the terms of contracts which were already in operation. The purchasers, who, because of the terms of payment granted them, still owed a quarter of the price of the *biens nationaux* they had bought, were requested to settle their debt on the basis of a scale of prices decided upon by the Treasury. A few days later, the payment of functionaries and of annuities was itself partly pegged to the value of the *mandat*. It was only in November 1796 that the sale by auction of the *biens nationaux* was resumed.

After a few more half-hearted attempts to shore up the *mandat*, it became clear that it no longer served the government's interests and that it was just one more expedient that had become null and void. Calculation of taxes had been readjusted upon the basis of the current value in coin. But the state, in its financial distress, had no use for the paper money which it was receiving, and which no one else wanted either. In order to encourage tax-payers to pay in coin rather than in *mandats*, the value of the latter had to fall sufficiently low for them to go out of circulation and for gold to recover its monetary function. This painful episode saw the government behave in a wholly infamous manner, for it entrusted private interests with the task, which it dared not carry out itself, of destroying the little credit that still attached to the *mandats territoriaux*.

The *Compagnie Dijon*, which consisted of three partners with close links with the local governments, launched an operation which, in the weeks after 11 December 1796 (the date upon which its agreement with the state was signed), involved it advancing the sum of 2,695,000 francs in coin to the Treasury, interest free. In return for which, it took delivery, through six departmental tax-collectors chosen by itself, of the *mandats* which were to be found in each department. In this way it collected 661 millions in *mandats*. The sheer size of this sum, far in excess of what the Treasury believed it held in its coffers and therefore also in excess of what it had intended to grant to the *Compagnie Dijon*, shows precisely what sort of state the Republic's finances were in. These funds were immediately put into circulation and brought about the desired fall in value of the *mandat*. The *Compagnie Dijon* took advantage of the situation to buy back gradually, without forcing prices up higher, and therefore cheaply, the 661 millions of paper money that it was supposed to give back to the state. It then recovered its original advance, having made handsome profits. This affair created a major scandal. Surprised by the scale of the operation, the state sought to renege upon its commitments towards the *Compagnie Dijon*. The Company, guilty of forging documents, was taken to court by the Treasury, but ended up by winning its case.

The government had achieved its objective. The *mandat*, which had lost virtually all its value after less than a year in existence, was officially withdrawn from circulation on 4 February 1797. It could be used for one month more, at the rate of one per cent of its face value, for the payment of tax arrears. Once the date of 21 March 1797 had passed, it had to be exchanged, still at the rate of one per cent, against drafts received in lieu of coin in payment for public lands.

The history of the revolutionary currency thus ended in bankruptcy and scandal. Conceived of in a climate of euphoria, initially in order to give the state the means to honour its debts, it had been the instrument of a despoliation which even the *Ancien Régime*, whose fiscal practices had actually brought about the Revolution, could not match. As Marcel Marion observes: 'Forty-five billion *assignats* were sunk in 2,400 million *mandats*, which in their turn were reduced to 240,000 francs in coin. If one of the state's creditors had received 3,000 francs' worth of *assignats* in

1791, and if he had held on to them religiously (actually an unrealistic hypothesis, for no one in his right mind ever hoarded *assignats*), they would have been turned into 100 francs' worth of *mandats*, and then into one franc in coin.'[11]

The Directory's financial distress

Once deprived of the special facility of issuing paper money, the Directory was obliged to live from day to day and to resort to the most shameful expedients. The affair of the *Compagnie Dijon* is a good instance of the kind of agreement that the government would often come to with the most suspicious characters, especially where military supplies were involved. The state's creditors, never knowing when or how they might be repaid, demanded positively usurious conditions. Payment for their services consisted of *biens nationaux*, wood-cutting concessions, crown jewels, not to speak of promises of the most diverse kind. Dubious suppliers and dishonest lenders set up shady operations, which were usually oiled with bribes and underhand commissions. The most reprehensible *Ancien Régime* practices, such as having recourse to advances on taxes, were current once more.

In spite of the reform of the fiscal administration, and in spite of the tracking down of tax-payers who were in arrears, tax returns were lower than ever. Being unable to fill its coffers with the returns from already established taxes, the government proceeded to invent some new ones, including the notorious levy on doors and windows. The indirect taxes which had existed under the monarchy, although universally despised, were reintroduced.[12] Yet all of these measures proved wholly ineffectual. Military conquest was the only means whereby the Directory could gain access to the resources it needed for its own survival.

The wretched army which Bonaparte, through his genius, managed to organise and restructure financially, and subsequently to lead to victory in Italy, was to become the Republic's chief treasurer. The conquered country had to pay onerous contributions. By August 1796, the victorious general had already dispatched fifteen millions in cash to Paris, not to speak of the money he held on to or sent to the other revolutionary armies. Heartened by Bonaparte's victories in Italy, the other armies triumphed in their turn. By 26 March 1797, the government in Paris had received fifty-one millions from the army of Italy,[13] ten millions from that of Sambre-et-Meuse and a little over two millions from the army of the Rhine. These sums, to which one should add 100

million florins paid by Holland, together with the sums raised by the
sales of the Belgian *biens nationaux*, were without a doubt substantial, but
represented only a part of the 240 millions in money or basic commodities which, according to Barbé Marbois,[14] the French army had taken
from the conquered countries.

Since the collapse of the *mandats territoriaux*, the Directory's resources
had mainly come from usurers and other speculators on the one hand,
and on the other, from the victorious generals of the revolutionary
armies. One cannot rule out the possibility that the *coup d'état* of 18
Fructidor (4 September 1797) was not so much ideologically motivated
as prompted by those who held the government in the palms of their
hands and were concerned to keep it in power. The *réacteurs* who, in
1797, won the elections to the Chambers, wished to restore the country's
finances to good order, and in foreign policy, wanted peace. The
Directory ousted 177 of them, even though their election as deputies was
above reproach, because they represented a threat both to the 'financiers'
and to the war chiefs.

Yet a few weeks after this crime against democracy, the executive was
guilty of an attack upon property rights, known as the 'bankruptcy of
the two-thirds', which was reminiscent of the worst exactions of the
Monarchy. On 30 September 1797, the Minister of Finance, Ramel, cut
the public debt at a stroke from 250 millions to eighty millions. A third
of the debt was maintained ('consolidated'), the bills which represented
it being acceptable as payment for taxes or for *biens nationaux*. The other
two-thirds, which were described as 'repaid', were in fact exchanged
against bearer bonds valid for the settlement of that portion of the *biens
nationaux* that was payable in paper money (*assignats*) and rapidly lost
almost all of their value. In 1800, these bonds were being exchanged at
one per cent of their face value; a year later, they were exchanged for
perpetual annuities at four-hundredths of their original value.

A short time before it disappeared, the Directory took one last
financial decision, which was wholly in keeping with the series of
expedients by which it had always lived. On 27 June 1799, it issued a
new forced loan. While waiting for it to be collected, a syndicate of
bankers granted the Directory an advance in the form of bills of account
against the future income from the loan. This latter again proved
disappointing, and on the eve of 18 Brumaire, functionaries were not
being paid and the state seemed to be staring bankruptcy in the face.

In the midst of the financial chaos which marked the last years of the
Republic, one can discern the slow emergence of the institutions which a

little later were to give France a central bank and an at least partly independent banking system. In the weeks leading up to the creation of the *mandats territoriaux*, a number of financiers had argued for the creation of a bank in order to sell off the *biens nationaux* and in order to supply the state with twenty-five millions a month, by means of its own paper money issues. At this point, the government, being under the influence of the Left, just as the Constituent Assembly had been when it had received a similar proposition, turned down this offer, preferring to leave it to the executive to create paper money, the outcome being as described above. But from 1796, a number of banks emerged; they issued their own paper money, which enjoyed a limited circulation, so that any depreciation of it would be wholly contrary to the share-holders' interests. For several years, these banks furnished industry and trade with the credit they needed. Privately issued paper money continued to be sought after, whereas state paper money, which had supposedly been created in the general interest, was altogether discredited.[15]

The post-Thermidor period saw the emergence of new forms of political and economic interaction. Governments were no longer made and unmade by revolutionary insurrections and by Parisian agitators. The street had lost its former power, and politicians took decisions in response to another set of interests altogether. Patriotism was no longer a means of lining one's pocket (save at the expense of the 'liberated' countries). Nevertheless, during its last months, the Convention was hesitant. The ideas inherited from the Enlightenment could not eradicate every trace of the checks on economic freedom imposed by the Terror. With the advent of the Directory, the behaviour of those in government changed, for they no longer owed their power to the mob but to military men and to 'financiers'. The decisions which they took reflected the changed situation. *Coups d'état* occurred within the Assemblies; financial manipulation, despoliations and bankruptcies became the standard practice of governments. Neverthless, the return of a degree of economic liberty allowed the French economy to recover slowly from the shock of the Revolution.

10

The French Revolution: economic considerations

Now that we have come to the end of this economic history of the French Revolution, I hope to have convinced the reader of the pertinence of the model outlined in its opening pages. This model advances an explanation of the processes of escalation and outbidding involved in the Revolution during the period running from the spring of 1789 to Thermidor, Year II. It fleshes out the otherwise intangible notion of 'the force of circumstances', which has been invoked for the past two centuries by historians, and brings out the interactions between politicians' decisions, whose objectives are very short-term, the unfavourable consequences of these decisions in the longer term, and the reactions to these consequences, whose beneficial consequences are once again immediate only.

Our model implies a fundamental relation, but one that we have frequently asserted but not yet demonstrated, namely, that the proliferation and only the proliferation, of the *assignats* may, for a period of several years, account for their depreciation and the corresponding rise in prices. The politicians of the revolutionary period understood this very well, but it would seem often to have been forgotten since. In order to make at last some progress on this old debate regarding the role of paper money, I propose that we resort to the modern methods of econometry. Since the results thereby obtained constitute a crucial part of our thesis, the reader will need, in spite of their technical nature, to pay especial attention to the proofs involved.

This quantitative analysis will be rounded off by a few reflections regarding a number of other economic consequences, apart from inflation and the subsistence crisis, of the policies followed in the course of the Revolution. Although we cannot provide definitive answers, we shall look into the redistributive effects of these policies and we shall consider the question of respect for property rights, in the name of which the Revolution was made. Finally, we shall address a classic question, namely, whether the Revolution held back or, conversely, favoured the development of the French economy.

The depreciation of the 'assignats'

As we have seen, the depreciation of the *assignats* was one of the main motors of the French Revolution. It began by aggravating the subsistence crisis to a great extent. The resulting hunger gave rise to rioting in the poorer quarters. In Paris itself, these riots weighed heavily upon the decision-making of the various Assemblies, and brought power to those men who undertook to satisfy the demands of the mob. The Committee of Public Safety's reintroduction of price controls for grain represented a revival of the interventionist practices of the *Ancien Régime*. In spite of the failure of the first regulatory measures, this government was tied by its policies and had no alternative but to press on with them, and finally, to introduce the economic Terror.

The statements and writings of the representatives on the various legislative bodies, including those of the most eminent members of the Mountain, such as Marat and Saint-Just, show without a shadow of a doubt that the most extremist members of the Convention understood perfectly well the part that the *assignats* were playing in the disorganisation of the French economy. It is therefore somewhat surprising to discover that, in studies of the topic written since, the majority of historians have actually neglected the part played by the *assignats*, and indeed have often gone so far as to distort it radically, by attributing the devaluing of the paper money to counter-revolutionary intrigues, and therefore to political rather than economic causes. Jaurès, for example, actually claimed that the *assignat* 'held up fairly well for four years', before concluding peremptorily that the '*assignat*-currency saved the Revolution'.[1]

In order to decide whether the depreciation of the *assignats* was indeed linked to the quantity in circulation (as represented in figure 6, p. 182), I have conducted a classic econometric test. This test depends upon the notion that the behaviour of all the economic agents may be summarised in terms of a stable function of demand for currency. In the present context, I have assumed (see Appendix v for a more exact formulation of my hypotheses and for the details of my results) that the real quantity (with constant purchasing power) of *assignats* that the public wished to hold, i.e., their nominal quantity m multiplied by their value v as expressed in coin, is, by a first approximation, constant. Any increase in

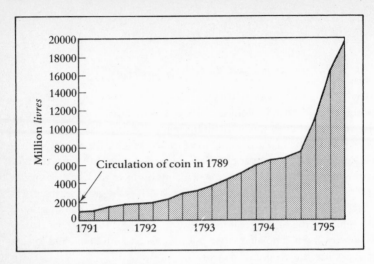

Figure 6 Circulation of *assignats*

the quantity *m* in circulation must therefore be compensated for by a proportional decrease in the value *v*. It is in fact generally admitted that, in the wake of new issues, economic agents who find themselves with more cash than they wish proceed to spend whatever is surplus to their requirements. The increased supply of *assignats* thereby made available on the market necessarily leads to a fall in the value of paper money.

I have tested this hypothesis by means of a technique known as linear regression, which is currently used for estimating the contemporary money demand functions. It involves finding the linear function of *m* which will minimise the sum of the squares of the deviations with the observed values of *v* (in fact, one employs the logarithms of *m* and of *v*). Using three-monthly data, for a period running from June 1791 to June 1795, we have found that the regression-line (that is, the function we are trying to determine) has a slope of −0.974, very close to the theoretical value of −1 representative of the constancy of the produce *mv*. In addition, we have found that the quantity of *assignats* in circulation accounts for 74 per cent of their value.

The results we have arrived at are illustrated in figure 7, p. 183, where we have represented both the observed value of the *assignats* (according to Pierre Caron's tables) and their theoretical value as given by the regression-line. What we actually find is that indeed, over a period of four years, the observed values and the theoretical values vary in relation

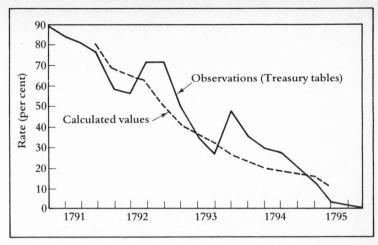

Figure 7 Observed and calculated values of *assignats*

to each other. However, over shorter periods, the *assignats* may seem to be over- or undervalued. Thus, the autumn of 1792 was a period of overvaluation (possibly due to the military victories of the time) and, conversely, the summer of 1793 saw an abnormal fall in the value of paper money (related, no doubt, to the series of defeats suffered by France). During the Terror, and the accompanying price controls, the *assignat* was once again overvalued, and this situation did not end on 9 Thermidor but persisted up until the end of 1794. Finally, after the spring of 1795, the *assignats* definitively collapsed as a currency, very probably because, having observed the accelerating drop in value of the paper currency, the public was less and less prepared to accept it. (When the public fears an excessively steep drop in the value of the *assignats*, the cost of holding cash in hand increases and their demand falls, and as a consequence the product *mv* must diminish; this phenomenon has been shown to be a feature of all periods of hyperinflation.)

It seems relatively unimportant to me to establish just why it was that the value of the *assignat* fluctuated round the theoretical value that I have postulated, even though this has been a hotly debated question in the past. The crucial point is to have shown that, throughout the period of existence of paper currency, its depreciation may be perfectly well accounted for by the quantity theory (that is, by the quantity of money put into circulation), and therefore by strictly economic factors and not by counter-revolutionary activities or by any lack of confidence in the

Revolution, factors which are still invoked nowadays. Since it was in the interests of those men who were in power to continue with the issues of paper money, they did their utmost, in order to justify what they were doing, to bolster the thesis of psychological factors. It is somewhat strange, nonetheless, to note just how many historians have subsequently adopted this argument as their own. Contrary to what Jaurès was in the habit of asserting, the *assignat*'s loss of credit did not reflect 'the loss of credit of the Revolution in the minds of the people', but more simply the quantity of paper money that had been printed.

The 'assignats' and the redistribution of wealth

The question of the *biens nationaux* is intimately linked to that of the public debt and to that of the *assignats*. The Estates-General had met in order to find a solution to the difficulties of the Treasury, which had found itself unable to honour its commitments. A majority of the deputies in the Estates-General held that only the granting of a constitution could guarantee that, in the future, the kingdom's finances would always be in good repair. This same majority sought to be the guarantor of the property rights of the *rentiers* and of the other creditors of the state, while at the same time planning to set up a new fiscal system, which would be more just than the *Ancien Régime* one had been.

Formulated in this manner, the problem faced by the Constituents could not be given a genuinely satisfactory solution. Indeed, in order for the state's creditors to escape despoliation and receive what had been promised them, the Treasury had to resort to taxation (or to other far more suspect forms of appropriation), and therefore to raise funds from tax-payers who had been picked arbitrarily and who had probably gained absolutely nothing from the expenditure which had occasioned the initial public debt. As it turned out, it was the clergy as an order which was taxed by the nationalisation of its properties and thereby sacrificed, so that the Constituents might find a way out of the dilemma with which they were confronted.

If the estimates of the period are to be believed, this solution, which was actually contrary to the principles of August 1789, could at best only be a partial one. In the course of presenting the report of the Finance Committee to the Assembly on 27 August 1790, Montesquiou reckoned the constituted debt to be 2,339 million *livres* and the redeemable debt to be 1,902 millions. His total of 4,241 millions, although very probably exaggerated, represented a sum that was much higher than the generally agreed value of the church property, which was 2,000 millions. Under these circumstances, only a part of the state's debt could be repaid, and that gradually, as and when the sales of *biens nationaux* were effected. For the immediate future, taxes would have to be levied on a regular basis, if the part of the *Ancien Régime*'s debt that remained due, prior to its total repayment, was to be serviced, and if (of course) the state's current expenses were to be met.

But the majority of the deputies lacked political courage, or possibly any sort of courage whatsoever, when faced with unrelenting pressure from the mob, which was present at their deliberations and refused to countenance any return to fiscal discipline. Because the taxes, even if less onerous than those of the *Ancien Régime*, would have been extremely unpopular, the state chose not to enforce their collection too stringently. Indeed, this lax attitude to taxation made it impossible to opt for the solution of rescheduling the public debt by means of *quittances de finances* (a kind of Treasury bond). The only way out of the impasse was to use *assignats* as a way of supplying the Treasury's current resources, the elimination of the redeemable debt merely serving as a pretext for the Assembly to vote for them. The issue of paper money held the advantage of being, in short, a tax, but a tax that was both invisible and delayed, for it was through its subsequent inflation that the citizens' contributions were in effect, levied.

This type of tax was of course among the least equitable that could be imagined. It affected the holders of *assignats* wholly at random, it was regressive (the rich usually holding, in proportion to their wealth, less actual currency than the poor), and it gave speculators with inside information the opportunity to make substantial gains. It was also uneconomic, because it had a profoundly unsettling effect upon the mechanisms of production and exchange. On the other hand, it was much appreciated by politicians, for whom it provided resources that seemed not to have been demanded of anyone and therefore could be obtained without opposition.

But the *assignats* were not simply a fiscal resource. Their issue was also tied to the sale of the *biens nationaux*. They were a part of a system set up with the declared intention of respecting the principles of 1789. I have shown above what sorts of destructive effect they had. It remains for me now to assess the redistributive effects of the Revolution's economic policies, of which they were an absolutely fundamental element.

Let us begin with the creditors of the *Ancien Régime*. On the eve of the Revolution, they held bills against the Treasury of a value which, although certainly less than the 4,241 millions announced by Montes-quiou, was all the same very probably close to three billions.[2] To a large extent, these bills took the form of perpetual or life annuities held by tens of thousands of *rentiers*. One should add to the *Ancien Régime* loans materialised by these debts the 625 millions[3] which the Constituents had undertaken to pay back to the owners of the venal offices which had been abolished, and the whole of the clergy's debts, taken on by the state.

Although it is hard to assess the total sum owed by the Treasury in 1790, it is still harder to estimate the real value of the repayments made subsequently. One can however assert that this value was very low, so that those who had trusted the revolutionary state to guarantee their rights were to a great extent despoiled. A part of the sums lent to the Royal Treasury or invested in offices were paid back in *assignats* that were to a greater or lesser extent devalued. Unfortunately, we do not know what the equivalent sum in coin was. The sums that were still owing when the Great Book of the Public Debt was established (on 24 August 1793) were arbitrarily reduced or even struck off the registers, and it was with massively devalued paper money that the state settled up with the last of the creditors it was actually prepared to acknowledge.

The whole of the *biens nationaux* were gradually put up for sale. How did the state profit from the huge fortune that it had seized? I have outlined the reasons why I believe that, around 1791, the bids corres-ponded more or less to the officially estimated value of the properties put up for sale, taking into account the conditions accorded to the buyers and an anticipated depreciation of the order of 10 per cent per annum, and that the auctions passed off more or less normally (see, on this subject, Appendix IV). The acceleration in the rate of inflation exceeded everyone's expectations and gave the purchasers a substantial profit that was, in fact, wholly legal, since it had been brought about by the government's own monetary policies. After the proclamation of the law on suspects, when patriotism became for some a profession or a way of lining one's pocket, countless frauds took place, since auctions no longer occurred under regular conditions.

Whatever the cause may have been, whether it was the depreciation of paper money or fraudulent bidding, the revolutionary governments squandered the immense wealth which they had confiscated. A necessar-ily crude estimate suggests that the greater part of the *biens nationaux*, worth around four billion *livres* in 1790 (two billions in church property, to which were added two further billions' worth of properties belonging to suspects, émigrés and those condemned to death), had been surrendered before 1797, whereas the sum total of payments received by the Treasury by this date amounted to no more than one billion. Sporadic sales continued up until the Empire, but after 1797, thanks to the return of the coinage, they would very probably have almost fetched their market value. Under the Restoration, those properties which had not yet been sold were restored to their owners. To sum up, in a relatively short period of seven years the state carried out, involuntarily and on an arbitrary basis, an extraordinary redistribution of wealth involving three billion *livres*, which comes to around double the national product of the pre-revolutionary period. Contrary to the purposes of Jacobin ideology, the beneficiaries of this massive wealth were not the poor, but rather, in varying proportions depending upon the region, well-to-do peasants,[4] bourgeois and even, through their use of catspaws, nobles and émigrés.[5]

Finally, one should not forget that it was the state itself, at least in the early stages, that had done best out of the issues of *assignats*, since it created, in terms of nominal value, a total of around 45.5 billions of paper money (even without taking into account the *mandats territoriaux*). In real value, they brought in resources estimated by S. E. Harris[6] at approximately seven billion *livres* of 1790 (four billions of which were from the pre-Thermidor period). Nor should one forget that in return the Treasury subsequently suffered considerable losses, as we have seen, on account of the postponed settlement of the purchases of the *biens nationaux*, and also because the taxes which it did in the end collect were paid in devalued *assignats*. In this case too, it is impossible to arrive at an accurate picture of the situation.

The question of property rights

Throughout the eighteenth century, as the economy slowly developed, a part of the population of France grew rich through trade and production (especially in textiles). In the large towns, it eventually joined up with the handful of financiers and bankers, whose trade consisted simply in advancing funds to the King. This section of the Third Estate, being the only category of person in the kingdom liable to build up savings, was naturally given to underwrite bills issued by a government whose greed for money grew ever greater. Furthermore, throughout the national territory, thousands of suppliers large and small were owed sums by a state which was gradually growing more centralised, and which was slowly increasing its interference in the economy.

In earlier times, the monarchy had shown no hesitation in declaring itself bankrupt and even in turning on its creditors, who would sometimes end their lives on the scaffold. Such days were now long past, and for two reasons in particular. First, the fact that the creditors, as we have just recalled, were now far too numerous meant that despoliation of them would have proved very unpopular and would have been fiercely resisted. The second reason was very probably connected to the first, and consists in the fact that the notion of natural rights, which John Locke had eleborated upon and which the Physiocrats had advocated in France, was universally accepted towards the end of the *Ancien Régime*, so that any violation, even by the state, of the property rights of individuals would have seemed a flagrant injustice.[7]

The Constituents were themselves inspired by the same motives as checked the *Ancien Régime* in its closing stages when it had sought to act in an arbitrary manner and despoil its creditors. Two of the articles of the Declaration of the Rights of Man, a document which they themselves had drafted, are particularly significant in this respect. Article xiv reads as follows: 'All citizens have the right, by themselves or through their representatives, to have demonstrated to them the necessity of public taxes, to consent to them freely, to follow the use made of the proceeds and to determine the amount, the means of assessment and collection and the duration', and Article xvii runs: 'Property being an inviolable and sacred right, no one may be deprived of it except for an obvious requirement of public necessity, certified by law, and then on condition of a just compensation in advance.'

The solution to the problem of financing the budgetary deficit that was adopted, namely, the nationalisation of church property, therefore created a severe split in the National Assembly. The Right opposed this solution, arguing, quite rightly, that it rested upon a legal subterfuge and that in reality it represented an attack upon property rights. The Left claimed that the reverse was in fact true, and if it won the day, it was very probably because a majority of deputies, whose convictions regarding such matters were somewhat superficial, voted with it, being content to save appearances and to find a solution to the thorny problem of finance.

A few months later, the Assembly was divided in much the same way over the issues of *assignats*. A deputy on the Right, the abbé Maury, echoed Mirabeau: 'What is one doing when one creates a paper currency? One is stealing at sword-point.' In his elaboration of this formula, he listed all the property rights which the *assignats* would violate. 'Every man in France who owes nothing, and to whom everything is owed, is a man ruined by the paper currency,' he declared, going on then to raise the question which the majority of deputies wished to sidestep: 'Have we the right to bring about the ruin of even a single one of our fellow citizens?'

The representatives of the Left dodged the moral issues much as they had the economic arguments, and once again managed to convince a majority of the Assembly, which was prepared to rally to any and every ploy that might in the short term get them out of the budgetary impasse.

Subsequently, when the harmful effects of the *assignat* issues began to make themselves felt, the demands for price controls made by the popular leaders raised the question of property rights once again. The Girondins, who had constituted the Left of the Legislative Assembly, opposed such controls, on the grounds that they were contrary to the spirit of the principles of 1789 (and also because they felt that they would prove ineffectual). They were overtaken, and thus driven to the Right of the Convention, by those of the Jacobins who, out of opportunism, ended up by accepting state interference in the economy – that is, the Montagnards. When the latter had gained control of the new Assembly, it became clear that their economic policies (Laws of the Maximum and requisitioning) and financial policies (forced loans, partial bankruptcy linked to the Great Book of the Public Debt) represented a breach of the principles underlying property rights. However, because public opinion was too attached to such principles, they did not openly renounce them, claiming rather to reformulate them.

Their new interpretation was that selling bread at a high price to a needy person, for example, was stealing from him, and in the most extreme case, where he was deprived of a food that he could no longer buy, one would be taking away his life, his most valuable possession.[8] Given this perspective, economic controls were a way of checking new forms of attack upon property rights, namely hoarding or speculation. Of course, if the idea that it is due to the inflation of paper money is ruled out, every price rise would obviously seem to be the outcome of motives which were selfish (such as lining one's pocket) or, worse still, ill-intentioned (harming the Revolution). Passing laws to prevent hoarding therefore came to seem moral, and the punishing of those who broke this law was a patriotic act.

It goes without saying that this interpretation of the nature of property was a misuse of words, and, in the last analysis, contrary to the interests of the poor that it was supposed to protect. To deny a merchant the right to fix as he sees fit the price of the goods which belong to him, and which he wishes to sell, is both to prevent him from exercising one of the essential prerogatives of his property rights over these goods and to deny to third parties the right to enter freely into contracts with him. It prevents this merchant (or producer) from acting rationally, from planning his transactions with his own suppliers, from undertaking business (or production) deals by anticipating the profits which justify the investment he has made and the risks he has taken; it therefore leads him either to abandon (voluntarily or because of bankruptcy) an activity which has ceased to be lucrative, or to defraud, or to engage in black-market activities in order to release the necessary profit margins. In either case, goods become scarcer and prices rise, the very things that price controls were in fact supposed to prevent.

As far as property in land is concerned, we find a development similar to that of the idea that the representatives of the people had concerning property rights. The Constituents abolished the 'feudal system' but suppressed only the personal rights (such as the *corvée*) to which the peasants were subjected. Real rights, that is, those which applied to property in land, were, in 1789, simply put up for repurchase. However, the Convention, in July 1793, abolished them without compensation. One should further add that the members of the Convention also flouted property rights whenever it was a question of increasing the state's possessions. The properties of suspects and émigrés, or at any rate of those considered to be such, properties amounting to a total value of around two billion *livres*, were quite simply confiscated. This legal theft was justified by equating the government's political opponents with its foreign enemies.

Considered from the point of view of property rights, the history of the French Revolution is tragic and paradoxical. When it began, the intention was to include the principle underlying these rights in a Constitution, and more particularly to safeguard the rights of *rentiers*, but with each succeeding Assembly, the pressure from the Left increased, and this principle was repudiated time and time again. It culminated in a total betrayal of the principles of 1789, in the despoliation of individuals who should have been protected from arbitrariness and in an haphazard redistribution of the wealth of the nation.

It is worth pointing out here that, in the eyes of contemporary marxists, the men of the revolutionary Left cannot be regarded as precursors of socialism. Indeed, these men, in spite of all the attacks they managed to unleash against property rights (economic regulation, interventionism, requisitions, confiscations, bankruptcies etc.), were not opposed to the principle of property itself. It is reasonable to suppose that they hoped for the advent of a society of smallholders who were more or less equal. Because the rich were selfish and had grown rich in the first place by putting their own interests above the public good, they would be excluded from this society. On the other hand, neither the Jacobins nor the *Enragés* nor the Hébertists envisaged the collectivisation of land or of the means of production. Yet, in practice, the kind of wholly controlled society which emerged under the Terror left as little freedom to individuals as if it had been in the hands of genuine collectivists. Given this, a distinction resting upon the theoretical conceptions of the leaders is of little real interest and one can date the birth of totalitarianism from the French Revolution, even if, subsequently, it was to be given a number of different ideological packagings.

The economic consequences of the Revolution

At the end of the *Ancien Régime*, France was producing less *per capita* than England. As François Crouzet has shown,[8] this lag can be traced far back into the past, the relative growth of the two countries having been practically identical in the course of the eighteenth century. One is tempted, in such circumstances, to wonder whether the Revolution, that is, the period running from 1789 to 1799, saw this gap close or, on the contrary, increase, and whether the events which took place during this period had a positive or a deleterious effect upon the subsequent development of the French economy.

The first part of this question may be relatively easily answered. Without being able to quote precise figures, it seems obvious that *per capita* agricultural production fell during the period with which we are concerned, with a veritable collapse occurring between 1792 and 1795, and a very slow recovery in subsequent years. It was only by the end of the Empire that French agriculture recovered the levels it had reached in 1789.

Industrial production, which had been similarly hard hit, was in 1800 not yet back at the level it had reached in 1789. The decline of the textiles sector (with the exception, very probably, of cotton), was especially clear, with the number of looms in operation falling by a half over a ten-year period (but with an improvement towards the end of 1794, after the trauma of the Terror). François Crouzet has presented a very interesting explanation of this profound and enduring crisis, which he attributes to a contemporary eye-witness, Sir Francis d'Ivernois.[9] This Genevan counter-revolutionary, an émigré in London, used statistical data collected by the prefects under the Consulate to draw up a very sombre picture of the state of the French economy at the dawn of the nineteenth century. What was behind the crisis, in his view, was a fall in the price of land, a fall attributable to the glut caused by the sale of church and émigré property and also by the general insecurity of the period. Since capital was more profitably invested in agriculture, it tended to be diverted from industry. Since, at the same time, there was a rise, in real terms, in the prices of raw materials and of wages, industrial prices were bound to rise too, causing French industry to lose its foreign outlets and also contributing to a cutback in domestic demand. Yet one should also point out that the excessive expenditure of the state had squeezed out industrial investments, the sale of *biens nationaux* being merely one of several means the Treasury was employing to attract the funds from the private sector which it was diverting from productive uses.

If one treats the period of the Revolution and of the Empire as a whole,[10] some advance does however emerge, but at an average rate over a twenty-five year period that was much lower than that recorded for the decade 1781–90 and which still further emphasised the lag with respect to English industry, which was then at the height of its expansion. In spite of a situation that was in general unfavourable, special factors permitted the development of a number of branches of the French economy, such as heavy industry (because of the war), the production of beet sugar (encouraged by the interruption in sugar cane imports) or the cotton industry (thanks to outstanding technological developments and to the temporary suspension of English competition).

In the longer term, structural mutations occurring during the revolutionary period undoubtedly had a more varied effect upon the development of the French economy. One may suppose that some of the mutations observed would have happened anyway, even without the upheavals characterising the period. Yet, because the writing of history as fiction seems a basically sterile exercise, I shall simply draw up a brief balance sheet of the changes which did in fact take place.

The deepest of such changes were certainly those affecting the countryside. Once rid of feudal dues, the peasants had become full owners of their lands or, through the sale of the *biens nationaux*, had acquired new ones. The forms of taxation introduced in the revolutionary period, although they still weighed heavily upon agricultural revenues, had shed the arbitrary, and most crucially anti-productive, character of the old system. The scrapping of price controls on grain, and of internal customs tolls, because it permitted a better allocation of resources, should, as the Physiocrats had so clearly understood, have been a powerful stimulant to agricultural production.

But, alongside these consequences favourable to economic development, one should add others which were much less so. As Jean-Charles Asselain has emphasised:

the crucial consequence of the Revolution was the consolidation, for the next hundred and fifty years, of a régime of small farms and peasant smallholdings ... What one in fact finds, after the Revolution, is a slowing down in rural emigration (and, as a consequence, a slowing down in the formation of an industrial proletariat). Demographic growth also slowed down, for a voluntary reduction in the number of births made it possible to avoid a still more extreme fragmentation of farms. Above all else, there was a slowing down in the rate of growth of agricultural production and productivity: the Revolution permitted the survival of countless farms that were too poor to afford to invest or to overhaul their methods of cultivation.[11]

Industry and trade were also affected in a more subtle manner by the reforms of the revolutionary period. These reforms undoubtedly put an end to the guild system, which had done so much to impede economic modernisation under the *Ancien Régime*, and, agriculture aside, they established a relatively unoppressive system of taxation. As in the case of agriculture, so too with industry and trade, the unification of the national market certainly played a positive role, just as did the introduction of patents and of a metrical system. On the other hand, the free trade desired by certain Constituents, and apparently introduced to some extent towards the end of the *Ancien Régime*, was never fully enforced. It was in the interests of certain producers to put pressure on the government to make widespread usage of tariffs and customs barriers, prohibitive measures which were very much strengthened as a consequence of the Napoleonic Wars. The protectionist tradition, which the Revolution might well have broken with, was in fact definitively established during this period, and was to last, with incalculably destructive consequences, up until the present time.

This balance sheet, which, up until this point, has been solely concerned with traditional economic factors, ought also to include some reference to the various wars, both at home and abroad, which, since they continued up until the collapse of the Empire, had a powerful effect upon the productive capacity of France. The physical destruction they wreaked may have been relatively limited, but the losses in human life they caused have been assessed at 1.5 to two million individuals. It is naturally very hard to weigh up the economic consequences of a hecatomb on this scale.

The French Revolution also had a crucial impact upon the structures of public institutions, which can still be felt at the present day. It is worth recalling, for example, that, at the end of the *Ancien Régime*, the bureaucracy (which was so admirably described by Tocqueville) still dominated the French economy. At the beginning of the revolutionary period, many wished to dismantle this bureaucracy and to establish an extreme decentralisation of authority. The Constitution of 1791, and also the one which Condorcet drafted at the beginning of 1793, actually reflected these tendencies. However, the outbidding occasioned by inflation and the subsistence crisis meant that centripetal forces, incarnated from then on by Jacobinism, carried the day. The organisational forms that such forces imposed upon France, although cut back to some degree after Thermidor, anticipated those that the Empire was to bequeath to the France of today, which, although more organised and more moderate, were nevertheless strongly *dirigiste* in character.

In this respect, developments in the administration of taxes are especially instructive. At first, the intention was to dismantle it and to make it less oppressive. Yet, ten years later, the financial world had recovered its prerogatives. As Michel Bruguière has observed, 'the centralisation of the monarchy was thus restored, if not reinforced, with corollaries that have stood the test of time, including surveillance, use of informers, homogeneity of documents throughout the national territory.'[12]

Our present view as to what is desirable and what is undesirable in politics rests in large measure upon the perspective we have upon the history of our own society. But this history can only be the interpretation of past events summarily and imperfectly known. It is written by men who decipher the facts of the past that they uncover in the light of their own ideas, and more particularly, in the light of their own political ideas. The history of the French Revolution, which has been based as much upon myths as upon facts, has up until now been especially vulnerable to the prejudices of those who have interpreted it. It still serves to bolster erroneous notions and to justify the perpetuation of damaging policies.

In the introduction to a collection of essays entitled *Capitalism and the Historians*, Hayek has written: 'if it is too pessimistic a view that man learns nothing from history, it may well be questioned whether he always learns the truth'.[13] This observation would seem to be especially applicable to the economic 'model' of the Revolution. How often has it happened, in recent history, that countries have fallen prey to totalitarian régimes through having accepted, albeit with a few minor variations, the same destructive cycle of crisis–inflation–price controls–nationalisations–Terror, set in motion in the name of the noble ideals of liberty, prosperity and social justice?

Is it not time that we changed our attitude towards our own history? Ought we not to go back to the close analysis of historical reality, which rests upon the analysis of the protagonists' motivations (their self-interest, their ideals and their ideologies) and of all the consequences of their actions? Is it not time that we jettisoned those theories which Karl Popper has termed 'historicist', and which claim to account for the behaviour of social classes? Should we not, by the same token, stop according special privileges to what François Furet calls 'explanation in terms of actors' intentions'? For, whereas the immediate and visible consequences of political decisions are generally in accord with the actors' declared intentions, the more distant, diffuse and hidden consequences are usually not so at all. The art of being a good historian, like that of being a good economist or a good sociologist, surely consists precisely in the understanding of the invisible and unanticipated consequences of human actions.

Appendices
I
The final budget of the 'Ancien Régime'

The final budget of the *Ancien Régime*, that for 1788, was partially reconstructed in 1936 by F. Braesch,[1] on the basis of the *Compte rendu au roi* and other documents left by Necker. I have presented the main results of his investigation below. They make it only too easy to understand 'the profound causes of the ill the Estates-General was called upon to remedy'.

Total of the state's budget for the fiscal year 1788: 629 million *livres* divided up as follows:

Expenses

Finances (costs of collection etc.)	6.04%
Court expenditure	5.67%
Administration, justice, police, highways	3.03%
Welfare in state regions, towns and districts	2.80%
Public economy	3.68%
Public education and welfare	1.94%
War	16.83%
Navy and Colonies	7.18%
Foreign Affairs	2.28%
Servicing of the regular debt	29.59%
Various expenses linked to this debt	5.03%
Repayment of capital	11.70%
Pensions	4.32%

Income

Loans	21.37%
Lotteries	2.62%
Various items	4.20%

Direct taxes (including the *taille*: 154.7 millions)	24.60%
Indirect taxes, including *Fermes Générales* (150.1 millions) and customs dues (51 millions)	32.47%
Monopolies and industrial ventures	2.23%
Produce of [royal] lands	7.86%
Dues from state districts (direct taxes)	4.64%

II

The grain trade

Under the *Ancien Régime*, regulation of the grain trade undoubtedly checked the development of agricultural production. Although the Physiocrats had pointed out just how damaging such regulation was, the general populace was not aware of this. So much was this the case that, during the Revolution, when a catastrophic economic policy brought about a serious subsistence crisis, the patriots called for a return to the old price controls.

Marcel Marion, in his *Dictionnaire des institutions de la France aux XVIIe et XVIIIe siècles*, under the heading 'Grain trade', gave the following description of these controls:

Under the *Ancien Régime*, famine was an ever-present threat, because of the low levels of production of the soil, difficulties in communication, and the paramount importance of bread in the diet of the less well-to-do classes, especially in the towns. As a consequence, it had been thought necessary to impose a whole series of restrictions upon the grain trade, which were more or less in abeyance under normal conditions, but which once again became realities once the rumour of a failed harvest, whether true or false, was spread abroad. The principal controls were: 1. the obligation to sell only at markets and not in granaries; 2. the prohibition upon growers to keep their grain for longer than two years; 3. the obligation to declare the quantities harvested, with visits by commissioners serving as a check upon these declarations; 4. grain merchants or *blatiers*, being perpetually under suspicion, were also obliged to make a whole series of declarations and to swear oaths; they had to get authorisation from the magistrates; they were forbidden to enter into any partnership, or to stockpile grain; they had to be neither labourers nor gentlemen, nor officers nor tax-collectors nor tax-farmers or officials responsible for the collection of royal funds; 5. the markets were also hedged round with irksome restrictions: one had to undertake sales oneself and not by commission, one had to declare one's asking price and not raise it; one was not supposed to carry back the grain that one had brought, the sale of which became compulsory at the third market; up until midday, sales were reserved for ordinary people, and bakers and tradesmen only had the right to buy afterwards, the quantity purchased also being strictly limited; 6. within a radius of eight (subsequently ten) leagues around Paris, all purchases of grain were forbidden to the bakers and tradesmen of Paris (save at Limours, Brie-Comte-Robert and Mennecy); all the grain that had come within this privileged zone could not leave it again, with the result that, if Normandy was suffering from shortages, Burgundy was forbidden to come to its assistance, and vice versa; ... 7. finally, it sometimes happened that, as, for example, at Rouen, the monopoly of the buying or selling of grain belonged to a chartered company. Rouen had one comprising 112 merchants enjoying a monopoly of this sort, even on the markets of Normandy, and another consisting of eighty porters, loaders and unloaders of corn.

The free circulation of grain from province to province was sometimes permitted and sometimes forbidden, but virtually always rendered impossible in practice by the overwhelming reluctance of the local populations to watch corn, which they would prefer to keep jealously to themselves, leaving their canton, and by the support these passions received from the local authorities, and more especially from the magistrates and the police.[1]

III

The life of Dupont de Nemours

Dupont de Nemours (see chapter 3) played a prominent part in the events of the pre-revolutionary period, prior to becoming an influential deputy in the Constituent Assembly. Strangely enough, this figure is virtually forgotten today.[1] If so few have sought to honour his memory, it is very probably because he belongs to a liberal tradition whose supporters have always been in a minority in France. It seems to me appropriate to review here the main stages of his career.

Pierre-Samuel Dupont (or Du Pont) was born in Paris in 1739. His parents, who were Protestants, had each a very different influence upon him. His mother belonged to a family of minor, impoverished nobility; his marked taste for literature and the arts derived from her. His father, a clockmaker, had an authoritarian and somewhat introverted character, and shared all the prejudices of his day against literary men. He opposed Dupont's aspirations and his penchant for study, and wished his son to follow in his footsteps.

When Dupont was seventeen, his mother died, and life became hard for him. Left to his own devices, in conflict with his father, he found it hard to invest his existence with any meaning. He began training for a military career, then for a medical one. After a serious illness, he again became an apprentice clockmaker and finally, having dreamed of various chimerical projects, he resolved to consolidate his situation in life, in order to be able to marry his sweetheart, Nicole Le Dée de Rencourt.

From an early age he had been attracted to the social sciences. Some of his early writings were already informed by a few Physiocratic ideas, which he seems almost unconsciously to have anticipated. He does not seem, however, to have attracted any attention until 1763, when his rebuttal of the arguments in a celebrated book advocating the introduction of a progressive tax finally brought him to the notice of Quesnay. Once a part of the closed circle to which most of the economists belonged, Dupont was to become in turn assistant to the Intendant of Soissons, to Turgot and to Trudaine. During the following decade, he published two Physiocratic essays and wrote a large amount. Intellectually, this was the most fruitful period of his life. His fame was now such that the Margrave of Baden asked him to become his personal adviser, and the King of Poland entrusted him with the education of his children. He was not an expatriate for long, however, for after the death of Louis XV Turgot, once appointed Minister of Finances, summoned him to be his secretary.

The collaboration between the two men was very close and should have given rise to the numerous economic and fiscal reforms that were needed if *Ancien Régime* society was to emerge from stagnation. The *Mémoires sur les municipalités*,[2] which they wrote together, contained the principles for these reforms, since it advocated the introduction of a constitutional monarchy, the election of representative assemblies and an end to privilege. Unfortunately, before Turgot had had the opportunity to persuade the King to agree to these reforms, his enemies, realising their own interests were under threat, managed to engineer his downfall. Dupont shared in his mentor's disgrace, retired to the property which he had bought at Nemours, and, good Physiocrat that he was, devoted himself to agriculture for several years. In 1779, Necker, appointed Minister in his turn, summoned Dupont to join his administration, at the prompting of Vergennes, for he had no special liking for him. When Calonne supplanted Necker, Dupont stayed on, and as Inspector of Manufactures he was entrusted with a series of sometimes very unrewarding tasks, prior to becoming the real inspiration behind the Treaty of 1786 between France and England, which liberalised trade between the two countries.

In 1787, when Calonne convoked the Assembly of Notables, in order to win from it the increase in taxes needed to stop the state going bankrupt, Dupont was appointed its secretary. If he was keen to hold this post, one which Mirabeau coveted also, it was because he wished to conduct in person a defence of the very radical projects put forward by Calonne, which were to a large extent his own creation. But his enemies ousted Calonne, and Brienne, who was his successor, although a former friend of Turgot, kept Dupont out of the government. He very probably bore him a grudge for having participated in an ephemeral Fourqueux Ministry and thus delayed his own nomination. Dupont used his new-won leisure to play a part in the intellectual ferment which was preparing the ground for the Revolution, and it was this that secured him election as deputy of the Third Estate in the *bailliage* of Nemours.

When in the Constituent Assembly, Dupont devoted all his energies to advancing the principles of liberty and to sustaining a resolute defence of property rights. In all circumstances, he strove to emphasise forms of reasoning based upon sound economic theory and he was invariably opposed to proposals which advanced instant solutions to the problems posed at the cost of harmful consequences in the long term. Unfortunately, in an Assembly preoccupied with courting popular approval, he was often defeated. The Jacobin Left regarded him as an adversary, with Marat even going so far as to class him among 'those who should be stabbed'.

After the dissolution of the Constituent Assembly, Dupont, with the assistance of his friend Lavoisier, the chemist (but also economist and former *fermier général*), became an industrialist, founded a printing works and opened a bookshop. He also founded a paper in order to defend his central ideas (opposition to the war, curbing of the powers of the Assembly, objection to the creation of the *fédérés*' camp) and in order to challenge the influence of the Jacobins upon public opinion. On 10 August, he took up arms in defence of the King. So courageous was his behaviour that he was actively persecuted by those who won the day. Fleeing from one hiding-place to the next, he eluded their revenge for a time, being finally arrested in June 1793.

Freed after Thermidor, Dupont was prepared to accept the Republic, on condition that it was able to guarantee security of persons and liberty of opinions. With the advent of the Directory, he entered the Council of Elders, where he continued to express the economist's point of view and opposed the expedients upon which the régime depended. During this period, he also published a paper, *L'Historien*. At the time of the *coup d'état* of Fructidor, he just managed to evade the prison hulks, where a number of his friends were in fact sent. Sickened by political life in France, he decided to emigrate to the United States. There he drafted a programme of public education for Jefferson. But, as the bank which he had founded there went bankrupt (through the fault of the French authorities), he returned to France. Under the Empire, which he detested, he held a number of different official posts. Appointed to the Council of State by Louis XVIII, he was forced, after the return of Napoleon, to set out for America once more. An indefatigeable man, he went on writing up until his death, caused by a conflagration in his son's gunpowder factory which, in spite of his great age, he had helped to extinguish.

So ended, at seventy-seven years old, the life of a man who had participated intensely in both the intellectual and the political life of his time. Earning the unanimous respect of his contemporaries for his devotion to his friends, his uprightness and his unswerving attachment to his principles, he is all but forgotten by history, although he was often armed with better arguments than were his opponents, to whom posterity has proved far kinder.

IV
Value of the bids for the 'biens nationaux'

As I have indicated in chapter 5, the auctioning of the *biens nationaux* saw higher bids being made than had been officially estimated. The conclusion drawn at the time was that these sales were a great success, and this was itself interpreted as a vindication of the new régime and its doings. A few years later, it had to be acknowledged that, if calculations were made in real currency, which had a constant purchasing power, the sums which had been collected were in actual fact much lower than had been anticipated. The universally agreed explanation for the losses suffered by the Treasury in this affair pointed to, on the one hand, the staggering of payments across a long period and, on the other, the severe depreciation of the *assignats* during this same period.

This explanation, though it takes into account everything that could have been known once events had taken their course, is in need of further refinement. More particularly, one must question whether the process set in motion by the Constituent Assembly was really capable of getting full value for the public lands, at any rate during the period when the first sales were held, that is, towards the end of 1791. To answer this question, suppose we adopt the point of view of a potential purchaser, for example, during the summer of 1791, and ask ourselves what sum he could offer in *assignats* for a property whose value, correctly assessed, had been 100 gold *livres*.

At this time, with the *assignat* already having lost around 20 per cent of its value vis-à-vis the coinage used in the estimates (see figure 4, p. 96), the buyer who pays in paper money can offer up to $(100 / 0.80) = 125$ in settlement. But one should bear in mind that it was possible to make a deferred payment. Let us suppose, taking account of the conditions prevailing at the time, that one can pay 80 per cent of the sum owed over twelve years, with an annual interest of 5 per cent. If the buyer, having observed that, in the course of the previous year, the *assignat* has lost around 10 per cent of its value, thinks that the depreciation of the paper money will continue at the same rate of 10 per cent per year, he will take this into account when bidding. His reasoning would be as follows:

If x is the amount of the bid, $0.2x$ is made in a down payment and $0.8x$ is payed in twelve annual payments, the sum outstanding accruing the additional annual interest, of 5 per cent. A present value calculation shows that these annual payments are $[0.8x / 8.8632]$ *livres*. Since the payments are made in a currency which is depreciating at a rate of 10 per cent a year, one can calculate its present value by applying a discount factor of 15 per cent (10 per cent inflation + 5 per cent real interest). The present value of the bid x is then equal to the down payment ($0.2x$) plus the present value of an annual flow of $[(0.8x) / 8.8632]$ paid over a period of twelve years and discounted at 15 per cent, giving as a total $0.69x$. If one also takes account of the fact that the current value of a property worth 100 gold *livres* is 125 *livres-assignats*, a bid could be made at the officially estimated real value if $0.69x = 125$, giving 181 *livres-assignats*. When the auctions were hotly contested (which seems generally to have been the case with first-generation properties), offers therefore had to be 81 per cent higher than the estimates (if one allows the latter to have been accurate), without therefore implying that the transaction was an especially successful one.

What really happened? Marcel Marion gives examples of the contrast between estimated values and values at auction for lands sold in seventeen departments or districts. There was on average an excess of 70 per cent, which is close to the figure we have arrived at, taking into account its imprecise nature. Of course, the sales referred to in Marcel Marion's sample did not all take place in circumstances of the kind we have posited. Indeed, the majority of them are scattered up until around the end of 1791. Nevertheless, if we treat our figures as representing averages for the sales realised under the Constituent Assembly, our conclusion must be that such sales were made in the equivalent of gold *livres*, for prices extremely close to the official estimates. The extraordinary loss the Treasury suffered over the sales of public lands only occurred later, from the moment when the depreciation of the *assignat* became even faster than bidders had anticipated. The success of these sales is just one more illusion we should ascribe to the *assignats*.

V

Econometric study of the depreciation of the 'assignats'

In my attempt to account for the depreciation of the *assignats*, I have had recourse to a simple econometric technique. It consists in positing a demand function of money and then testing it (by means of a linear regression) on the revolutionary paper. Additional problems peculiar to the *assignats*, some of a theoretical nature, others arising out of the data available to us, further complicate an otherwise classical test.

Theoretical problems

It is traditional to posit that economic agents desire to hold cash in order to make transactions. The real quantity of currency required for this purpose (independent of variations in price) is therefore proportional to the volume of exchanges occurring in the economy, i.e. to production. Since, in a relatively primitive situation such as that of the French economy at the end of the eighteenth century, the holding of currency for the purposes of financial speculation must have been minimal, I shall disregard the effect of interest rates (which are anyway unknown to us). On the other hand, forecasts of the rate at which depreciation accelerated may have played an important role, especially after the beginning of 1795. As I have no way of assessing such forecasts, I will bring this study to a close at June 1795, the date at which they probably became a crucial factor.

Coin did not disappear all of a sudden from transactions. During a period whose duration cannot be specified, coins and paper money were used simultaneously, the public's total demand for money then including both of these two means of payment. Under these conditions, the *assignat* would have been less in demand than if it had been used alone, as our model presupposes. Consequently, our model will overestimate the value of the *assignat*, for as long as coin continued to be used in current transactions. For this reason, our test will cover the period from June

1791, the date at which the lack of low denominations proves that coin has disappeared from circulation.

Problems of measurement

We do not have precise knowledge regarding the quantities of *assignats* in circulation. Taking into account the paper money put into circulation and the paper money withdrawn after the sale of national lands and fiscal returns on the one hand, and official declarations of the period on the other, different authors have arrived at different estimates of the changes in the circulation of the *assignats*, or the quantity of money they represented. These estimates cannot take account of the quantities of counterfeit money and of *billets de confiance*, which were nevertheless increasing the quantity of money in the hands of the public. I have used Professor Robert Besnier's estimates here.[1]

The value of the *assignat* poses a still harder problem. For want of a price index in *assignats*, I have used the values for paper money vis-à-vis coin which Pierre Caron[2] has published. These are based upon reports made in Paris by the agents of the Treasury. Now, as S. E. Harris[3] has shown, depreciations in the provinces are not only different from those identified in the capital but also different from one another.[4]

Taking into account the delicate problems referred to above, I shall now test a model which, though simplified, nevertheless retains the essential characteristics of the theory. This model in fact supposes that the *supply of real money mv* (which ought to contain that part of the coin which it is difficult to incorporate into the model) *is equal at all times to a constant demand* (which must in fact be treated as dependent upon national production y, which is impossible to estimate). A regression of log (v) upon log (m) should give for the independent variable log (m) a coefficient which statistically does not differ from minus one. With the data specified above, we have the following results:[5]

$$\log (v) = 11.48 - 0.974 \log (m)$$
$$(9.64) \ (-6.62)$$

with the following statistics:

$$R^2 = 0.745 \ \text{DW} = 0.753 \ F(2.15) = 43.8$$

These results confirm the hypothesis that the value of the *assignats* is adjusted in such a way that the supply of real money is always equal to a demand assumed to be constant.[6]

Notes

Introduction

1. A. D. White, *Fiat Money Inflation in France* (New York, 1959).
2. It is obviously anachronistic to use a term such as 'politician' to describe men of the revolutionary period, but I shall use such a term here to refer to persons who during this epoch held, or aspired to hold, political power that was elective. Their behaviour, which essentially consisted in satisfying the immediate demands of the masses, resembled that of present-day politicians.
3. I shall frequently refer below to the first three volumes of his *Histoire financière de la France*, which was published between 1914 and 1921.
4. E. Labrousse, *Esquisse du mouvement des prix et des revenus en France au XVIIIe siècle* (Paris, 1933), and *La Crise de l'économie française à la fin de l'Ancien Régime et au début de la Révolution* (Paris, 1944).
5. A. Soboul, *The French Revolution 1787–1799*, translated by Alan Forrest and Colin Jones (London, 1974), pp. 204–6.
6. A. Soboul, *The French Revolution*, p. 21 (translation modified).
7. Sometimes called 'the economy of institutions' in France. The most celebrated representatives of 'public choice' school are Anthony Downs, Gordon Tullock and James Buchanan, the winner of the Nobel Prize for economics in 1986. Gordon Tullock has developed a general theory of revolutions, in his *The Social Dilemma: The Economics of War and Revolution* (Blackburg, 1974), but his theory is fundamentally different from the model presented in the present work.
8. See A. Soboul, *The French Revolution*, p. 22.
9. A. Cobban, *The Social Interpretation of the French Revolution* (Cambridge, 1964).
10. Ibid., p. 21.
11. See, on this topic, the works of the American historian George V. Taylor and, more especially, 'Noncapitalist Wealth and the Origins of the French Revolution', *American Historical Review* (January 1967), pp. 469–96.
12. In France, the most telling refutations of the marxist position were produced

in the 1960s, by François Furet and Denis Richet. These arguments were not economic in nature. Indeed, Furet and Richet deny that the Revolution constituted a unity at all, or that it was the outcome of a conflict between the rising bourgeoisie and the aristocracy. Their thesis was propounded in *La Révolution Française* (Paris, 1965; second edition, 1986). Geoffrey Ellis has summarised the debate over the marxist interpretation in 'The "Marxist Interpretation" of the French Revolution', *English Historical Review*, April 1978 pp. 353–76. For a historiographical account, see Alice Gérard, *La Révolution Française, mythes et interprétations, 1789–1970* (Paris, 1970).

13. F. von Hayek, *Law, Legislation and Liberty,* one-volume edition (London and Chicago, 1982), part 1, p. 26.

14. I hope the reader will forgive this neologism. I mean by 'anthropomorphicity' the tendency language has to attribute human behaviour to groups or other entities.

15. This was the definition given in 1560 by the Paris Parlement, as Marcel Marion records in his *Dictionnaire des Institutions de la France* (Paris, 1923).

16. My conception of ideology is close to that formulated by Jean Baechler in *Qu'est-ce que l'idéologie?* (Paris, 1976), or by Douglass C. North, *Structure and Change in Economic History* (New York, 1981).

17. So as not to weigh down my text with notes, quotations from this source are not referenced.

1. The fiscal crisis

1. On the institutions of the *Ancien Régime*, see Marcel Marion, *Dictionnaire des institutions de la France* (Paris, 1923; new edition, Picard, 1984); Guy Cabourdin and Georges Viard, *Lexique historique de la France d'Ancien Régime* (Paris, second edition, 1981); Albert Soboul, *La Civilisation européenne et la Révolution française* (Paris, 1970).

2. In the *cahiers* of the Third Estate of Nemours it is recorded that commoners paid the capitation tax at the rate of one-eleventh of their incomes, while the nobility and those not liable to *taille* paid one-eightieth. The *vingtième* was certainly the fairest of all the taxes of the *Ancien Régime*, but any attempts to extend it invariably ran up against the resistance of the privileged. On the eve of the Revolution, the two *vingtièmes* together yielded less than sixty million *livres* which would seem by all accounts to constitute less than 10 per cent of the kingdom's revenues.

3. It is hard to estimate what precisely the *dîme* yielded; if we follow what various authors of the period have written, the sum in question could be reckoned as being, on the eve of the Revolution, between seventy and 133 million *livres*.

4. See M. Marion, *Dictionnaire des institutions de la France.*

5. *De la Révolution française par M. Necker* (Paris, 1797).

6. M. Marion, *Histoire financière de la France*, vol. 1 (Paris, 1927), pp. 388–400.
7. H. Taine, *Les Origines de la France contemporaine*, vol. 1, *L'Ancien Régime* (Paris, 1876), p. 404.

2. The French economy at the end of the 'Ancien Régime'

1. On the subject of agricultural production in the course of the eighteenth century, see 'Tithes and Net Agricultural Output', in E. Le Roy Ladurie, *The Territory of the Historian* (Hassocks, 1979), trans. B. and S. Reynolds, pp. 193–203. In the course of the eighty years prior to the Revolution, the rise of the real agricultural product would have been from 25 per cent to 40 per cent.
2. An account of the regulations which weighed upon the *Ancien Régime* grain trade is contained in Appendix II.
3. According to J. Marczewski, as quoted by P. Léon, in F. Braudel and E. Labrousse, eds., *Histoire économique et sociale de la France* (Paris, 1970).
4. Of the many studies by George Taylor, see 'Noncapitalist Wealth and the Origins of the French Revolution', *American Historical Review* (January 1967), pp. 469–96.
5. See A. Soboul, *La Civilisation européenne et la Révolution française*, vol. 1 (Paris, 1970); p. 323.
6. J. Godechot, *The Taking of the Bastille*, translated by Jean Stewart (London, 1975), pp. 63–4.
7. A. de Tocqueville, *L'Ancien Régime et la Révolution*, in *Oeuvres, papiers et correspondance d'Alexis de Tocqueville*, vol. 2 (Paris, 1952), p. 132.
8. Tocqueville, *L'Ancien Régime et la Révolution*, Book II, chapter VI, p. 135.
9. E. Labrousse, *Esquisse du mouvement des prix et des revenus en France au XVIIIe siècle* (Paris, 1933).
10. E. Labrousse, *Esquisse du mouvement des prix*.
11. According to the studies by M. Toutain quoted in A. Sauvy, *De la Rumeur à l'histoire* (Paris, 1985).
12. G. Rudé, *The Crowd in the French Revolution* (Oxford, 1959), p. 33.
13. E. Faure, *La Disgrâce de Turgot* (Paris, 1961).
14. A. Young, *Travels in France*, ed. J. Kaplow (New York, 1969), pp. 376–89.
15. J. Godechot, *The Taking of the Bastille*, p. 122. According to J. Dupaquier, M. Lachiver and J. Meuvret, *Mercurials du pays de France et du Vexin français* (SEVPEN, Paris, 1968), the price of wheat at Pontoise (one of the main provisioning centres for Paris), which was around thirty *livres* a *setier* up until mid November 1788, then rose sharply, to reach 49–51 *livres* a *setier* by 11 July 1789 (a price which had not been exceeded since 1709). It then fell swiftly, until it was only 24–6 *livres* a *setier* on 8 August.
16. H. Taine, *Les Origines de la France contemporaine*.
17. On this subject, consult his *Histoire du climat depuis l'an mil* (Paris, 1983).

18. My own econometric studies show that the price of corn in June 1789 was inexplicably high with respect to that of November 1788, a fact which does not correspond to an exceptionally bad harvest. The factors determining prices at the moment of the supply gap of 1789 therefore postdate the previous harvest and the climatic conditions of the latter cannot be invoked as the sole cause. F. Aftalion, 'Le prix du blé à Pontoise en 1789', *Histoire, Economie et Société*, 1ᵉʳ trimestre (1988).

3. 1789

1. A. Cochin, *L'Esprit du Jacobinisme* (Paris, 1979).
2. For information on the composition of the Assembly, see G. Chaussinand-Nogaret, *Mirabeau* (Paris, 1982), p. 153.
3. H. Taine, *Les Origines de la France contemporaine, La Révolution*, vol. 1 (Paris, 1877), p. 13.
4. On the effects of the dearth upon the unfolding of the *journée* of 6 October 1789, see G. Rudé, *The Crowd in the French Revolution*, pp. 61–9.
5. Quoted by M. Marion, in his *Histoire financière de la France*, vol. 2, pp. 19–20.
6. It is possible that Mirabeau believed for a time that the Duke of Orleans would have proved a better king than his cousin and that he helped him in attempts to undermine the authorities, especially at the time of the *journée* of 6 October 1789.
7. Appendix III gives a brief summary of Dupont's life.
8. According to G. Schelle, Dupont's biographer, Dupont himself, because of his distrust for his former protégé, was the instigator of the decree of 7 November, which prevented the members of the Assembly (and therefore Mirabeau also) from becoming ministers.
9. Alongside speculators and foreigners, the abbé Maury ranged the Jews 'who came in the train of the former with their treasures in order to exchange them for territorial acquisitions. They finished revealing the conspiracy by asking from you, sirs, at this very moment, a civil state, in order to confiscate both the title of citizen and the church properties'. These words supplied Jaurès, in his *Histoire socialiste de la Révolution française*, with a pretext for unleashing a violent attack against the abbé Maury, which made him out to be the first anti-semite demagogue and a precursor of Drumont. This is to forget the kinds of concept that were current in the eighteenth century. Even Montesquieu, who was fair-minded in his attitude towards the Jews, associated them with money. As for Voltaire, the apostle of tolerance, he hounded them mercilessly, being quite ready to accuse them of ritual murder (on this question, see Léon Poliakov, *Histoire de l'antisémitisme*, Paris, 1981). It is, however, true that the abbé Maury was opposed to the emancipation of the Jews. But this was also the case with the deputies of the

'*partie gauche*', such as Rewbell, a future Montagnard. It is quite improper to try and associate the royalist Right with anti-semitism.

10. F. von Hayek, *Law, Legislation and Liberty*, vol. III, pp. 128–49.
11. B. Constant, 'Principes de politique', in *De la Liberté chez les modernes* (Paris, 1980).

4. The 'assignats'

1. Quoted by M. Marion, *Histoire financière de la France*, vol. 2, p. 103.
2. For further details, consult F. Braesch, *Finances et monnaie révolutionnaires* (Paris, 1934).
3. We know that a sudden increase in the quantity of currency in circulation can produce a revival of economic activity, but we also know that it is necessarily ephemeral and rapidly turns into a price rise. Which does not stop politicians even nowadays from calling for expansionary monetary policies.
4. Modern historians agree that Lavoisier's estimates are reliable and that those of Montesquiou are not.
5. When a currency is expected to depreciate, lenders in fact ask for high interest rates in order to compensate for the loss of purchasing power of their guarantee.
6. It was in vain that Dupont, together with a number of other clear-sighted deputies, strove to convince the 'people' that nothing could be expected of the *assignat* issues. When, a few weeks later, the Assembly voted in favour of the creation of paper money, Hébert, in his *Père Duchesne*, crowed over the fact that no one had been foolish enough to believe Dupont.
7. *De La Révolution Française par M. Necker.*

5. The finances of the Constituent Assembly

1. The elections were held in January, February and March 1790, and saw the triumph of the patriotic candidates.
2. F. Braesch, *Finances et monnaie révolutionnaires*.
3. See S. E. Harris, *The Assignats* (Cambridge, Mass., 1930), p. 61.
4. G.-F. Laennec, *Aperçu préliminaire du compte des revenus, des dépenses, des dettes et de la situation de la commune de Nantes*, read to the public assembly on 1 December 1790.
5. In what follows, I shall use the estimates for the values of the *assignats* supplied by Pierre Caron. See his *Tableaux de dépréciation de la monnaie* (Paris, 1909). These values can clearly only be approximations. Furthermore, at any given time, there are strong local disparities which I shall disregard here.
6. A *livre* was divided into twenty *sous*, which were divided in turn into twelve

deniers. A gold piece struck for the first time in 1380 under the name of 'franc' had the value of a *livre*. The equivalence between the two denominations was to continue. On 10 April 1795, a law made the franc and its metric subdivisions a compulsory monetary unit. On 7 April 1803 the 'Germinal franc' was defined, and this remained stable until the First World War.

7. See M. Marion, *Dictionnaire des institutions de la France . . .*, p. 35, S. E. Harris, *The Assignats*, and E. N. White, 'Free Banking during The French Revolution', Rutgers University Working Paper, 1987.

6. *The rising cost of living, anarchy and war*

1. E. Clavière, *De la Conjuration contre les finances* (Paris, 1792, probably January or February).
2. A period in which the effects of low-denomination *assignats*, as analysed in the previous chapter, were considerably lessened.
3. A. Mathiez, *La Vie chère et le mouvement social sous la Terreur* (Paris, 1927).
4. On the subject of the 'famine plot', see the works of Stephen L. Kaplan and, more particularly, *Bread, Politics and Political Economy in the reign of Louis XV* (The Hague, 1976).
5. For more information on these two episodes, the reader should consult A. Mathiez, *La Vie chère et le mouvement social*, pp. 60–2.
6. M. Marion, *Histoire financiére de la France*, vol. 2, pp. 310–13.
7. Or, to be more exact, the Girondins and the friends of Brissot, who was the main champion of the war against Austria.
8. Just one-tenth of the seven million electors who were registered took part in the vote. The procedures adopted would not be regarded as very democratic nowadays, since in many electoral districts people voted simply by shouting out their candidate's name.

7. *The seizure of power by the Mountain*

1. This figure is quoted in A. Soboul, *Les Sans-culottes* (Paris, 1968), and is based on an estimate given by F. Braesch. Even if one does not subscribe to this author's interpretation of the French Revolution, his work contains very rich descriptions of this popular movement.
2. F. Furet and D. Richet, *The French Revolution*, trans. S. Hardman (London, 1970), p. 184.
3. In the programme which he presented to the Convention on 27 February, Chaumette requested the poor to stop thinking of themselves as 'tenants in their own fatherland'. On this topic, see Mathiez, *La Vie chère et le mouvement social*, p. 160.
4. In *L'Ami du peuple*, no. 136.
5. The Constituent Assembly had decreed that each department should be

administered by a 'conseil général'. This elected assembly would in turn elect an eight-member 'directoire du département' which held the actual executive power. A 'procureur-général syndic' was also elected in each department and was supposed to represent the executive power (the King); his task was to ensure the law was enforced.

8. Economic dictatorship

1. The Constitution was subjected to popular ratification. It received over 1,800,000 'fors' and 17,000 'againsts'. The low levels of participation show that, in the kind of democracy in existence in 1793, only the supporters of those in power tended to have a voice and that they represented a minority of the population. The majority, through fear, was reduced to silence.
2. No. 211, vol. XVII.
3. A. Cochin, 'Sur la politique économique du gouvernement révolutionnaire', *Revue des Questions Historiques* (November 1933) pp. 267–76.
4. *Les Révolutions de Paris*, no. 211, vol. XVII, p. 153.
5. Speech to the Convention of 3 August 1793.
6. Barère to the Convention, on 5 September 1793.
7. The revolutionary calendar was introduced on 5 October 1793. I will refer to it only where events are generally known by it. In order to facilitate the reader's understanding of the chronology of the sequence of events recorded here, I will tend to use the dates from the Gregorian Calendar.
8. Mathiez, *La Vie chère et le mouvement social*, p, 605.
9. According to Jean Morini-Comby, *Les Assignats* (Paris, 1925); Marion gives a slightly different figure.
10. J.-F. Fayard, *La Justice révolutionnaire* (Paris, 1987); for an earlier survey of the same subject, see J. L. Godfrey, *Revolutionary Justice* (North Carolina, 1951).
11. L. Madelin, *La Révolution* (Paris, 1979), p. 370.
12. The death of the *Fermiers généraux* would thus, according to some estimates, have brought in between 130 and 400 millions to the state.

9. 'Dirigisme' in retreat

1. In his journal *L'Ami du Citoyen* of 27 Brumaire (17 November 1794).
2. Bérard, as quoted by Marcel Marion.
3. Richard C. Cobb, 'Disette et mortalité', in *Terreur et subsistances* (Paris, 1965).
4. Richard C. Cobb, 'Disette et mortalité'.
5. G. Lefebvre, *The French Revolution*, trans. J. H. Stewart and J. Friguglietti, vol. 2 (London, and New York, 1964), p. 142.
6. A. Soboul, *The French Revolution*, p. 435.

7. M. Marion, *Histoire Financière de la France*, vol. 3.
8. An ounce (*once*) represented around thirty grammes.
9. J. Moriny-Comby, *Les Assignats, Révolution et inflation* (Paris, 1925), p. 121.
10. See *L'Historien*, no. 208, of 16 June 1796, and the few subsequent numbers.
11. M. Marion, *Histoire financière de la France*, vol. 3.
12. In order to find the resources necessary for the repair of the roads, which were almost wholly dilapidated, the *droit de passe* was instituted. This tax, which was a hindrance to the circulation of goods, played its part in giving rise to frauds and helped to increase the price of basic foodstuffs.
13. It is worth quoting in this respect a confidence of Napoleon's: 'I came back from the Italian campaign, with no more than three hundred thousand francs to call my own; I could very easily have brought back ten or twelve millions instead, and they would still have been mine; I never kept any accounts, and I was never asked for any. I expected, upon my return, some great national reward; public opinion was all for bestowing Chambord upon me; I would have been very content to receive riches of this sort, but the Directory shelved the idea. Yet I had sent at least fifty millions to France in service of the state. This was the first time ever, in modern history, that an army had provided for the needs of the fatherland, instead of being a burden upon it.' Las Cases, *Le Mémorial de Sainte-Hélène* (Paris, 1842), vol. 1, pp. 105–6.
14. Quoted by M. Marion, *Histoire financiére de la France*, vol. 3.
15. In 1799, under the Consulate, when the Bank of France was created, the most important of them, namely, the *Caisse d'Amortissement*, the *Caisse d'Escompte* and the *Comptoir Commercial*, were incorporated into it.

10. The French Revolution: economic considerations

1. J. Jaurès, *Histoire socialiste de la Révolution française* (new edition, Paris, 1969), vol. 2, p. 131. In a more recent work, *A History of Gold and Money, 1450–1920*, translated by J. White (London, 1976), p. 304, Pierre Vilar asserts that 'the rapid devaluation of the *assignat* . . . was not so much connected with the excessive issues . . . ' [translation modified].
2. In the 1788 budget, 218 millions had been devoted to the payment of interest; capitalised at a rate of 7.5 per cent, they corresponded to a debt of this size.
3. According to J. Godechot, *Les Institutions de la France sous la Révolution et l'Empire* (Paris, 1968).
4. Many peasants acquired, by means of a formal purchase, land which they had merely leased in the past; in such cases, there was no change of owner in the strict sense but simply a change in the title to the property.
5. G. Lefebvre, 'La vente des biens nationaux', *Etudes sur la Révolution française* (Paris, 1963).

6. S. E. Harris, *The Assignats*, p. 53. His calculation involves multiplying the sums issued by their value in relation to the coinage as given in Pierre Caron's tables (see Appendix v).
7. On the emergence of the concept of property, see H. Lepage, *Pourquoi la propriété?* (Paris, 1985).
8. F. Crouzet, *On the Superiority of England over France*, translated by M. Thom (Cambridge, 1990).
9. F. Crouzet, 'Les conséquences économiques de la Révolution: à propos d'un inédit de Sir Francis d'Iverrois', *Annales Historiques de la Revolution Françaisé* (April–June 1962), pp. 186–217.
10. See on this subject J.-C. Asselain, *Histoire économique de la France* (Paris, 1984).
11. J.-C. Asselain, *Histoire économique de la France*, vol. 1; *De l'Ancien Régime à la Première Guerre mondiale.* It is perhaps worth adding that the consequences of revolutionary economic policies were, in this respect especially, further aggravated by the laws establishing the egalitarian division of inheritances (15 March 1790) and those abolishing the freedom to make one's own will.
12. M. Bruguière, *Gestionnaires et profiteurs de la Révolution* (Paris, 1986).
13. F. von Hayek, *Capitalism and the Historians* (London and Chicago, 1954), p. 3.

Appendix I. *The final budget of the 'Ancien Régime'*

1 F. Braesch, *Les Recettes et les dépenses du Trésor pendant l'année 1798, Le Compte rendu au roi, de mars 1788, Le dernier budget de l'Ancien Régime* (Paris, 1936).

Appendix II. *The grain trade*

1 Marion, *Dictionnaire des institutions de la France*, pp. 117–18.

Appendix III. *The life of Dupont de Nemours*

1 There are two biographies of him: one by Gustave Schelle, *Du Pont de Nemours et l'école physiocratique* (Paris, 1888; reprint Slatkine, Geneva, 1971), the other by Pierre Joly, *Du Pont de Nemours, soldat de la liberté* (Paris, 1956).
2 This was the same memoir which Mirabeau was to present to Calonne some years later, claiming it was his own work.

Appendix V. *Econometric study of the depreciation of the 'assignats'*

1 From an unpublished series of lectures. His estimates are close to Marcel Marion's.
2 Pierre Caron, *Tableaux de dépréciation du papier-monnaie* (Paris, 1909).

3 Harris, *The Assignats*, pp. 111–32.

4 Results obtained from regressions done with the averages of the local tables of S. E. Harris, or with the original values on foreign markets, are not significantly different from those published here.

5 Figures in parentheses are students' tests; they indicate that the null hypothesis (that one or other of the regression coefficients is zero) should be rejected; on the other hand, the hypothesis that the slope of the regression line is one cannot be rejected.

6 The low value of the Durbin Watson (DW) statistic indicates autocorrelation in the residuals; this does not invalidate our conclusions, but shows the presence of disturbances which caused temporary over- or undervaluation of the *assignat*.

Select guide to further reading

Compiled by Michael Sonenscher

Benedict, Philip (ed.), *Cities and Social Change in Early Modern France* (New York and London, 1989)

Bergeron, Louis, *Banquiers, négociants et manufacturiers parisiens sous le Consulat et l'Empire* (Paris, 1978)

Braudel, Fernand and Labrousse, Camille Ernest (eds.), *Histoire économique et sociale de la France*, vol. 2 (Paris, 1970)

Cabert, A., *Essai sur les mouvements des revenus et de l'activité économique en France de 1798 à 1820* (Paris, 1949)

Chapman, Stanley and Chassagne, Serge, *European Textile Printers in the Eighteenth Century: A Study of Peel and Oberkampf* (London, 1981)

Crafts, N. F. R. *British Economic Growth during the Industrial Revolution* (Oxford, 1985)

Crouzet, François, *Britain Ascendant: Studies in British and Franco-British Economic History* (Cambridge, 1990)

Dupaquier, Jacques (ed.), *Histoire de la population française* (Paris, 1988)

Ellis, Geoffrey, *Napoleon's Continental Blockade. The Case of Alsace* (Oxford, 1981)

Grenier, Jean-Yves, *Séries économiques françaises (xvie–xviiie siècles)* (Paris, 1985)

Jones, Colin, *The Longman Companion to the French Revolution* (London, 1988)

Jones, Peter, *The Peasantry in the French Revolution* (Cambridge, 1988)

Kaplan, Steven L. and Koepp, Cynthia J. (eds.), *Work in France. Representations, Meaning, Organization and Practice* (Ithaca, 1986)

Kaplow, Jeffry (ed.), *New Perspectives on the French Revolution* (New York, 1965)

Lévy-Leboyer, Maurice. *Les Banques européennes et l'industrialisation internationale* (Paris, 1964)

Luthy, Herbert, *La Banque protestante en France de la Révocation de l'Edit de Nantes à la Révolution*, 2 vols (Paris, 1961, 1963)

Margairaz, Dominique, *Foires et marchés dans la France pre-industrielle* (Paris, 1989)

Maza, Sara, *Servants and Masters in Eighteenth-century France: The Uses of Loyalty* (Princeton, 1983)

Perrot, Jean-Claude, 'Voies nouvelles pour l'histoire économique de la Révolution', *Commission d'Histoire Economique et Sociale de la Révolution Française*,

Mémoires et Documents xxxv (Paris, 1978)

Plinval de Guillebon, Régine de, *La Porcelaine à Paris sous le Consulat et l'Empire* (Geneva and Paris, 1985)

Price, Roger, *A Social History of Nineteenth-Century France* (London, 1987)

Pris, Claude, *Une grande entreprise française sous l'ancien régime: la manufacture royale des glaces de Saint-Gobain, 1665–1830* (New York, 1981)

Reddy, William M., *The Rise of Market Culture. The Textile Trade and French Society, 1750–1900* (Cambridge, 1984)

Riley, James C., *The Seven Years War and the Old Regime in France. The Economic and Financial Toll* (Princeton, 1986)

Sabel, Charles and Zeitlin, Jonathan, 'Historical Alternatives to Mass Production: Politics, Markets and Technology in Nineteenth-Century Industrialisation', *Past and Present*, 108 (1985)

Sewell, William H. (Jnr.), *Work and Revolution in France. The Language of Labor from the Old Regime to 1848* (Cambridge, 1980)

Sonenscher, Michael. *Work and Wages, Natural Law, Politics and the Eighteenth Century French Trades* (Cambridge, 1989)

de Vries, Jan, *European Urbanisation (1500–1800)* (London, 1984)

Woronoff, Denis, *L'Industrie sidérurgique en France pendant la Révolution et l'Empire* (Paris, 1984)

Index

Boissy d'Anglas, Comte François Antoine de, 159
Bonaparte, Napoleon (later Emperor), 177
Book of National Charity, 159
Bourdon, Leonard, 141, 142
bourgeoisie: and land ownership, 32, 33; taxation of, 13; use of term, 3–5, 7, 8
Braesch, F., 93, 94, 196
bread: consumption, 39–40; price of, 31, 41, 42, 52; rationing of, 150, 153, 170–1; supplies, 112
Brienne, Loménie de, 27, 28, 29, 42, 48, 201
Brillat-Savarin, Anthelme, 81
Brissot de Warville, Jacques Pierre, 103, 131
Britain, war with, 125
Bruguière, Michel, 194
budget deficit: in 1790, 71, 93–4; in Louis XIV's reign, 18
Buonarroti, Filippo Michele, 171
bureaucracy, revolutionary, 159, 166–7, 194

Cahier de Gerville, 112
Caisse d'Escompte, 25–6, 26, 64–5, 66, 70; compulsory circulation of notes from, 69, 71, 72
Caisse de l'Extraordinaire, see Emergency Treasury
Calonne, C. A. de, 25–7, 201
Cambon, Joseph, 114, 124, 129, 131, 143–4, 145, 157, 165, 167
capital, tax on, 56–7
capitalist organisation, 35
capitalists: nobles as, 7
capitation tax, 13, 20
Carnot, L. N. M., 154, 158, 161
Caron, Pierre, 2, 182, 207
Cazalès, Jacques Antoine Marie de, 50, 74, 75
charity workshops, 56, 94
Chaumette, Pierre Gaspard, 146
churches: looting of, 157; property, nationalisation and sale of, 58, 61–7, 74, 77, 78, 184–5, 188, 192
civil servants, 36; and taxes, 90

Clavière, Etienne, 104, 106, 123, 124
clergy: debts, 26, 64, 75, 85; and the Estates-General, 49, 50; and the fiscal crisis, 20; imposition of civil oath on, 85; and land ownership, 32; and taxation, 13, 14, 90, 103–4, 105; *see also* churches
climatic conditions: and agricultural crises, 36, 39, 42; and famine of Year III, 167–8, 170
Clugny, 23
Cobb, Richard, 168, 169
Cobban, Alfred, 6
Cochin, Augustin, 49
Cochin, J. D. M., 148
coinage, debasement of, 18, 19
coins: and *assignats*, 96–7, 98, 109, 130, 206; and the *mandats territoriaux*, 174; and soldiers' pay, 105
Colbert, Jean Baptiste, 16, 18
Collot d'Herbois, Jean Marie, 141, 147
Commission for the Economic History of the Revolution, 2
Committee of General Safety, 128
Committee of General Security, 154
Committee of Public Safety, 75, 129, 137, 138, 145, 147, 151, 154, 155, 156, 161, 181; and Hébert, 140
commodities: and the Maximum, 134, 149; shortage of, 110; supply of, and *assignats*, 109; tax on, 14–15, 91
common land, rights of, 33, 34
Communes: administration of, 88; Paris, 53, 123, 130, 165
Communist Manifesto, 7
Compagnie Dijon, 176, 177
Compagnie d'Occident (later *Compagnie des Indes*), 18–19, 145
Condorcet, Marie Jean, Marquis de, 49, 79, 105–6, 194
Conspiracy of Equals, 171
Constant, Benjamin, 63
Constituent Assembly, 5, 102–3; and the *assignats*, 44, 68–85, 100–1, 106, 107, 108, 172; finances of, 86–101; and the public debt, 144, 163; reforms, 53–5; seizure of power by, 49–52; *see also* National Assembly